Writing AI Prompts

by Stephanie Diamond and Jeffrey Allan

for dummies®

A Wiley Brand

Writing AI Prompts For Dummies®

Published by: **John Wiley & Sons, Inc.**, 111 River Street, Hoboken, NJ 07030-5774, www.wiley.com

Copyright © 2024 by John Wiley & Sons, Inc., Hoboken, New Jersey

Media and software compilation copyright © 2024 by John Wiley & Sons, Inc. All rights reserved.

Published simultaneously in Canada

For general information on our other products and services, please contact our Customer Care Department within the U.S. at 877-762-2974, outside the U.S. at 317-572-3993, or fax 317-572-4002. For technical support, please visit https://hub.wiley.com/community/support/dummies.

Wiley publishes in a variety of print and electronic formats and by print-on-demand. Some material included with standard print versions of this book may not be included in e-books or in print-on-demand. If this book refers to media such as a CD or DVD that is not included in the version you purchased, you may download this material at http://booksupport.wiley.com. For more information about Wiley products, visit www.wiley.com.

Library of Congress Control Number: 2024933763

ISBN 978-1-394-24466-9 (pbk); ISBN 978-1-394-24468-3 (ebk); ISBN 978-1-394-24467-6 (ebk)

SKY10073117_041824

Contents at a Glance

Table of Contents

Introduction

Artificial intelligence (AI) is revolutionizing the way we live and work at an astonishing rate. Whether you're a marketer who wants to use AI to enhance brand awareness, a content creator who wants to improve your portfolio, or just someone curious about AI, you need to start by learning how to develop effective AI prompts. *Prompts* are specific instructions given to an AI tool by a user to get a particular response.

The quality of the questions you ask yourself about AI will determine how well you accomplish your prompting goals. The first question you may ask yourself is: "How can I effectively use AI prompts to enhance my strategies, develop content, and improve engagement with my customers?" This question should serve as the foundation of your AI journey and help you explore the "how" and the "why" of AI's capabilities. The answers you come up with will enable you to make better decisions and unlock the true potential of AI.

After you identify the key questions and understand the basic principles of AI prompting, the next step is applying your knowledge to your workflow. This involves experimenting with different types of prompts, such as those for brainstorming, content generation, or customer engagement. Carefully integrating AI into your everyday functions will help you be more productive.

To improve your use of AI prompts, you need to be specific and provide context. Write prompts that clearly describe the task, including the expected output, style, and audience. This helps the AI better understand and meet your needs. Also, giving background information or explaining the purpose of the content can make the AI's responses more accurate.

By continuously refining your prompts based on feedback and results, you'll not only improve your AI skills but also discover new ways to integrate AI into your marketing strategies and content development, leading to an enhanced relationship with your audience.

About This Book

Writing AI Prompts For Dummies demystifies the use of generative AI and guides you to create effective prompts. It gives you the practical skills you need to apply to all your AI projects immediately.

We cover several topics in this book, including the following:

>> The basics of generative AI and its output

>> How to develop effect prompts for writers, marketers, and content creators

>> How to enhance the customer journey with AI tools

>> How to assess and improve your personal online brand using AI

>> The ethical use of AI in business communications

>> Mistakes to avoid when creating AI content

Within this book, you may note that some web addresses break across two lines of text. If you're reading this book in print and you want to visit one of these web pages, simply key in the web address exactly as it's noted in the text, pretending as though the line break doesn't exist. If you're reading this as an e-book, you've got it easy — just click the web address to be taken directly to the web page.

Foolish Assumptions

In writing this book, we made a few of the assumptions about you:

>> You're new to AI and prompting, and you want to experiment and learn more.

>> You run or manage a business with an online component that could benefit from the use of generative AI.

>> You've considered using AI tools, but you aren't sure where to start.

>> Your competitors have adopted AI, and you're looking for a way to outperform them.

>> You sell online products or services, and you want to figure out how and what content you should create using AI tools.

>> You have several social media accounts, and you want to use AI to help you create the right content for your audience.

>> You're curious about how developing AI strategies can add revenue to your bottom line.

If any of these assumptions describes you, you've come to the right place!

Icons Used in This Book

Throughout this book, we use different icons to highlight important information. Here's what they mean:

The Tip icon highlights information that can make doing things easier or faster.

The Remember icon points out things you need to remember when searching your memory bank.

Sometimes, we give you a few tidbits of research or facts beyond the basics. If you'd like to know the technical details, watch out for this icon.

The Warning icon alerts you to things that can harm you or your company.

Beyond the Book

In addition to the information in this book, you get access to even more help and information online at Dummies.com. Check out this book's online Cheat Sheet for tips on troubleshooting AI, components you can use to craft great AI prompts, and strategies for continuous learning. Just go to www.dummies.com and type **Writing AI Prompts For Dummies Cheat Sheet** in the Search box.

Where to Go from Here

As with all *For Dummies* books, feel free to dive into the chapters in any order you prefer. Dummies chapters are constructed to be read as stand-alone entities. You can begin wherever you like, but if you're new to crafting AI prompts, you may want to start your journey with Chapter 1. This chapter establishes a fundamental understanding of AI technology and its outputs. Chapter 3 shows you prompting to set up a custom GPT.

To focus on rules for effective prompting, head to Chapter 4. Chapter 5 extends that knowledge for writers and marketers, and Chapter 7 includes prompts to create music and write songs. If you want to begin by analyzing your portfolio, Chapter 12 has prompts to help you do a skills and gap assessment. Chapter 14 looks at ways to improve troubleshooting and prompts.

For ethical considerations of working with AI, begin with Chapter 13, which shows you what biased prompts look like. The rest of the book focuses on ways to apply AI to various business applications. These include chatbots for customer service and brand assessment for personal branding.

1

Getting Started with Generative AI

Chapter **1**

Grasping the Basics of Generative AI

C an you imagine a world where machines can learn, create, and think like humans? This is the realm of generative AI (GenAI), where technology and creativity come together. Some types of AI learn from experience, while others follow strict rules.

In this chapter, we look at AI systems that need guidance, like students in a class and those who learn on their own. We also discuss AI that makes entirely new content instead of just organizing data. This chapter explores the diverse world of AI.

Understanding the Different Flavors of AI

Each kind of AI has its own special function and way of working, just like tools in a toolbox. In the following sections, we look at these different types of AI to understand what they're like and how they work. We start with two main types:

» AI that learns from data, which we call machine learning (ML)

» AI that follows specific rules

Both types of AI have their own strengths, making them suitable for different kinds of tasks. Understanding this will help you get a clear picture of how AI is changing our world, from health care to manufacturing and beyond. Each type of AI brings something valuable to the table, showing just how diverse and useful these technologies can be.

Using AI that learns from data

ML can acquire knowledge and get smarter over time. It works by training on large amounts of data, finding patterns in it, and then making decisions based on what it finds.

This kind of AI is always changing. It gets better as it gets more data to learn from. For example, think about a system that recommends music. It looks at the songs you liked before and what other people who like the same music as you do also enjoy. Then it suggests new songs for you.

Another common area where ML excels is facial recognition. By reviewing many photos of a person's face, PXL Ident (www.pxl-vision.com/en/pxl-ident) can learn to recognize new photos of that person. Figure 1-1 shows an example of this application.

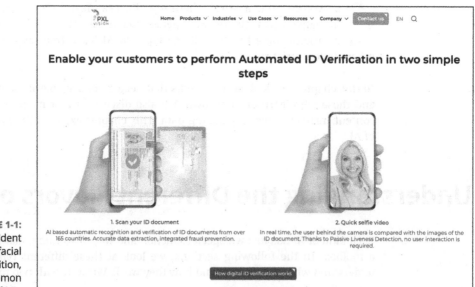

FIGURE 1-1:
PXL Ident performs facial recognition, a common type of ML.

The ability to learn and change makes ML very powerful and useful. It can perform tasks like creating personal recommendations, organizing your phone's photo albums, or helping self-driving cars make decisions.

We can further break down ML into two specific types. These types differ in the way we teach AI:

>> **Supervised learning:** The AI learns from data that already has answers. It's like giving it a quiz with an answer key. For example, when AI works on recognizing images, it gets tons of pictures that are already named, like cat photos labeled "cat." This way, the AI learns to pick out similar images on its own.

>> **Unsupervised learning:** In this type of ML, the AI doesn't get any answers up front. It looks at the data, like customer buying patterns, and tries to make sense of it by itself. It's like solving a puzzle without the picture on the box as a guide. In business, this type of AI helps figure out which customers may like certain products, even though no one has sorted these customers into groups before.

ML is great because it can learn and change. It's like a quick learner that gets better the more it practices. This makes it perfect for jobs where things keep evolving or need a personal touch. For example, in health care, ML helps with diagnosing diseases. It looks at medical images, like X-rays or magnetic resonance imaging (MRI) scans, and learns from many examples. Over time, it gets very good at spotting signs of different health conditions.

Using follow-the-rules AI

Follow-the-rules AI doesn't learn from data. Instead, it follows a set of instructions we give it. This means that it doesn't change or get better over time. It's useful for tasks that are done the same way every time. This kind of AI is reliable for critical jobs where mistakes could be dangerous. Imagine a nuclear power plant. Here, rule-based AI helps monitor everything, making sure all systems are working correctly. It does the same thing every time, which is really important for safety. In a factory, rule-based AI checks products for any defects. It uses specific guidelines to examine each item, making sure everything meets the standard. This keeps the quality of the products consistent, which is super important for the business and the customers.

TIP

A good example of follow-the-rules AI is email spam filters. The filters have a set of rules, such as looking for certain words, to decide if an email is spam. This method is straightforward and always follows the same steps. It is great for jobs that require consistency and follow specific rules or guidelines.

Follow-the-rules AI is the go-to for tasks that require steady and unchanging performance.

Needing a Teacher versus Learning On Its Own

How AI learns is really important. However, not all AI learns the same way. There are two types of AI learning:

>> **Supervised learning:** Supervised learning needs guidance, which is kind of like having a teacher. It learns from examples that already have answers.

>> **Unsupervised learning:** With unsupervised learning, AI figures things out on its own. It doesn't have answers up front — it has to sort through data by itself.

Knowing the difference between these learning styles helps you understand AI better. It shows you how AI can either follow a set path or discover new things, depending on how it's taught.

Considering supervised learning

Supervised learning in AI works something like having a teacher. This kind of AI gets data that is already labeled or has clear definitions. Think of this data as a textbook with all the answers. The AI learns from this "textbook" to understand patterns and make choices about new, similar information.

For example, in medical diagnosis, supervised learning is highly useful. AI systems get trained with many medical images, like X-rays or MRI scans, that doctors have already diagnosed. The AI studies these images and learns how to spot various health conditions. Then, when it sees new patient images, it can suggest what the diagnosis may be. This helps doctors diagnose more quickly and accurately.

In the world of finance, banks use supervised learning, too. They train AI on data about transactions, some of which are marked as fraudulent and others of which are marked as safe. When the AI checks new transactions, it looks for signs that match known fraud. If it spots something suspicious, it alerts the bank. This way, the AI helps stop fraud before it causes any harm.

REMEMBER

In both these cases, the AI relies on its training from labeled data to make smart decisions. It's a bit like a student who has studied a lot and then applies that knowledge to new problems. This kind of AI is great for tasks where you need reliable and accurate results based on clear examples it has learned from.

Dipping into unsupervised learning

With unsupervised learning, AI systems learn from data that does *not* have clear instructions or labels. Imagine AI as an explorer going through data without a map. It looks for patterns and figures out the structure of the data all by itself. The goal is not just to find the correct answer but to explore and uncover how the data is organized.

One area where unsupervised learning is highly useful is in retail market segmentation. In this case, AI examines customer data, like what they bought, their preferences, and where they're from. However, it doesn't have predefined groups. The AI figures out its own ways to group customers based on the data. This helps businesses understand their customers better and create marketing strategies for different groups. It's a smart way to increase customer happiness and boost sales because the offerings are more tailored to each group.

TIP

Unsupervised learning is also important on social media platforms. The algorithms look at what users do — for example, the posts they like or share — to spot trends and common themes. Using this info, the AI can adjust what each person sees in their feed, making sure it shows posts they're more likely to find interesting. This makes the social media experience better for users because they get content that is more relevant to them. In both retail and social media, unsupervised learning helps AI understand and respond to people's preferences in a more personalized way.

Recognizing differences and their impact

The main difference between supervised and unsupervised learning in AI is about whether the data has labels. Supervised learning has a clear structure. It uses data where the outcomes are already known. Think of it like having a guidebook. It's great for specific tasks like sorting things into categories or making predictions.

Unsupervised learning, on the other hand, is more like an adventure into the unknown. It works with data that doesn't have labels. The AI has to figure out the patterns and structures in this data by itself. It's kind of like exploring a new place without a map. This approach is perfect for digging through data to find new insights and groupings, especially when we don't know what the connections may be.

These differences really shape how we use these types of AI. When you know exactly what you're looking for, supervised learning is the way to go. But when you're in the mood to discover new things and you don't have clear answers, unsupervised learning is the better choice. It's all about whether you have a clear direction from the start or you're exploring to find new patterns and connections.

Grasping real-world implications

In the practical world, the way AI learns — whether it's supervised or unsupervised — really matters. For instance, in health care, supervised learning plays a big role. It helps catch diseases early by analyzing medical images like X-rays or MRI scans. One example of this kind of application is Nvidia's MONAI platform (https://monai.io), shown in Figure 1-2.

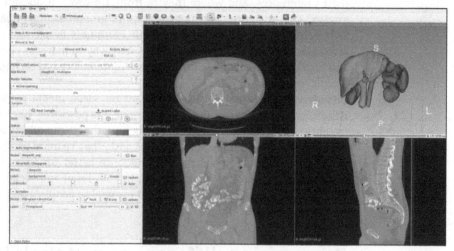

FIGURE 1-2: Nvidia's MONAI platform helps train ML for medical imaging.

This early detection can be lifesaving, because it spots health issues before they get serious. In business, unsupervised learning is a big help, too. It lets companies dig into customer data to find out what people like and don't like. This leads to improved products and services because businesses better understand their customers.

But these methods aren't without their challenges. Supervised learning needs a lot of data that already has answers, which can take a lot of time and money to get ready. Unsupervised learning is more go-with-the-flow, but it can sometimes give you unclear or not-so-accurate results because it doesn't have clear instructions to follow.

TIP

Both supervised and unsupervised learning have special strengths and uses. Getting to know these methods helps you see what AI can and can't do. As AI keeps getting better, these ways of learning will become even more important. They'll help shape the future by offering new ideas and solutions in all kinds of fields.

Observing AI That Creates New Things versus AI That Sorts and Filters

There are two types of specialized AI, each with a unique role. The first is GenAI, which creates new content. The second is discriminative AI, which sorts and categorizes existing information. Knowing how these two types differ is important. It's like understanding that each player on a team has a special job to do.

REMEMBER

GenAI is the innovator, making new things. Discriminative AI is the organizer, making sense of what's already there. This understanding helps you see how AI functions in different ways, each type playing its part in the vast field of AI.

Looking at generative AI as the innovator

GenAI stands out in the AI realm for its creative abilities. It isn't limited by what it already knows — it can create entirely new works. This type of AI takes a large amount of data, learns from it, and then uses that knowledge to make something new and original. Here are three examples:

>> **Creating music:** You may use a GenAI app that can write music. It learns about notes, melodies, and what makes a good song. It then uses what it learned to write a completely new song. This song will be something unique that has never been heard before.

>> **Making art:** GenAI is making a big impact in the world of art. Artists can now use AI tools to create one-of-a-kind designs and images. These AI tools have been trained on massive amounts of paintings, illustrations, and other types of images from throughout history. The AI can then take this training and generate new artworks that mix different artistic styles and elements in innovative ways.

>> **Storytelling:** Another exciting application of GenAI is in storytelling. AI programs trained on thousands of books can come up with their own stories, creating new narratives, characters, and plotlines.

GenAI is especially relevant to this book's focus on prompt writing. It shows that AI can not only process and understand existing content but also use that understanding to generate new, creative works. This capability of GenAI to create fresh, original content from a rich background of existing data is a major development in the field of AI.

Navigating discriminative AI as the organizer

Discriminative AI, in contrast to GenAI, functions more like a decision-maker. It works with information it already knows to organize new data and make choices. This is like a librarian who arranges books in different sections or a referee who makes decisions based on a game's rules. Discriminative AI is categorizing and making decisions based on set criteria.

In everyday life, discriminative AI is fairly common. For example, consider email systems. Most of them use discriminative AI to keep spam out of your inbox. The AI learns what spam emails look like by studying examples. Then it applies what it has learned to new emails and sorts those emails into "spam" or "not spam" categories. This helps make sure your inbox stays clean and relevant.

Online shopping is another area where discriminative AI is very useful. It helps suggest products you may like. The AI observes your past shopping habits, including what you've browsed and bought. Then it recommends similar items based on these past choices. Think of this as having a personal shopping assistant who knows your tastes and preferences.

GenAI is about creating new content; discriminative AI focuses on organizing information and making decisions. Discriminative AI is an important key that unlocks more personalized online experiences. This could include managing our emails or enhancing our online shopping. Understanding the role of discriminative AI helps you better appreciate how to tailor AI for specific tasks. This goes a long way toward enabling efficiency and relevance across various applications.

Viewing how they work together

Generative and discriminative AI, while different, often team up to work better. For example, here's how they do this in a movie recommendation system:

>> **Generative AI comes up with a list of movies that seem to fit what a user likes.** It's using what it knows to create something new, which is a list of movies they might enjoy.

>> **Discriminative AI steps in and narrows down this list.** It looks at what the user has enjoyed in the past and picks out movies from the list that are most likely to hit the mark.

This way, the user gets recommendations that are not just random but tailored to their specific taste, thanks to the combined efforts of both types of AI.

Thinking about the impact of AI

GenAI is changing how we tackle creative work and solve tough problems. It's doing more than just helping artists and writers come up with new ideas. It's also finding new ways to treat diseases. Imagine GenAI discovering treatments for illnesses we cannot cure yet. This type of AI is a game changer in health care and other important areas.

Discriminative AI is great at sorting through lots of information. It's really useful in big tasks like studying climate change or planning cities better. For instance, it helps scientists understand environmental changes and city planners manage resources smarter. This AI looks at huge amounts of data and makes sense of it, helping people make better decisions in crucial areas.

TIP

Both kinds of AI have a big impact. They're making real differences in important fields. GenAI brings new ideas and solutions, while discriminative AI helps us handle and understand large amounts of data better. Their influence improves how we manage big challenges and make advances in our world.

GenAI has the power to create things we haven't even thought of yet. Imagine new kinds of entertainment or innovative ways to tackle climate change. That is what GenAI might bring us. On the discriminative AI side, it will keep making our lives with technology easier and more natural. It's about understanding and organizing the information around us.

Knowing the differences between these two types of AI, as in which one creates and which one organizes, is key to understanding how versatile AI is. The mix of generative and discriminative AI will keep shaping our experiences. They'll bring us new ways to handle the problems and opportunities we face every day.

Looking at the Role of Human-Technology Interaction

A key area we need to focus on is how humans and technology work together. It's about more than just mixing human skills with AI abilities; it's about the growing, changing relationship where technology improves and broadens what humans can do. It supports and increases human capabilities. It isn't about taking over human jobs. Instead, it's becoming a helpful partner that makes tasks easier. That, in turn, allows you to do more than before and do it better and faster.

The AI-human partnership is all about combining what both do best. AI is great at working fast, being precise, and handling a lot of data. When you mix this with human thinking, creativity, and know-how, you get an amazing team. This combination leads to new ideas and solutions in many areas.

TIP

Think of AI as a very efficient helper that handles the heavy data work. It lets humans use our unique skills to think of new ways to solve problems and be creative. Together, AI and humans can do things neither can do alone. We work hand in hand to create better ways of accomplishing tasks.

In the next sections, we explore the AI-human partnership by looking at how AI helps doctors make better diagnoses, assists teachers in personalizing lessons, and aids businesses in making smarter decisions.

Improving health care

AI can totally change an industry — in this case, health care. AI is very good at working through a lot of medical information and spotting patterns that may be important. It can figure out what's wrong with patients and decide the best way to treat them. Here are some examples:

>> **Changing how doctors diagnose diseases:** Doctors are using AI to help look at things like X-rays or MRI scans. The AI checks these images for anything unusual that may show a disease is present. It gives a first look, and then doctors take over to make the final call. This team-up leads to finding diseases earlier and more accurately, which can really make a difference in how well patients recover.

>> **Suggesting custom treatments:** AI can do more than help find diseases. It also plays a big role in figuring out the best treatment for each patient. It looks at all the patient's information — for example, their medical history, their genes, and even their daily habits. With this data, AI suggests treatments

that are suited to that person. Health-care professionals can then step in to fine-tune these plans, making sure each patient gets the care that is best for them.

>> **Fighting diseases:** AI is helping fight cancer. Hospitals have started using AI systems to find cancer early. These systems are trained on a massive number of patient records and images from tests, picking up early signs of cancer more accurately than usual. Thanks to this, doctors can start treating patients sooner, which really improves the chances of successful treatment.

REMEMBER

AI is initiating a new era in health care. It isn't just about new gadgets or software; it's about how AI and humans can work together to make everyone healthier. This teamwork is changing how we understand diseases and treat them, leading to better care for patients everywhere.

Transforming learning experiences in education

In today's world, AI is changing education, making learning more tailored and effective. Learning is not just about reading books or listening to lectures anymore. AI is bringing a whole new approach to how students learn and how teachers teach.

>> **Tailoring learning for every student:** AI tools are highly adept at figuring out how each student learns best. It looks at what students are good at and what they struggle with. Then it suggests teaching materials and activities that fit each student's needs. This means every student gets to learn in a way that works best for them, whether they need extra help or are ready for more advanced topics.

>> **Helping teachers:** AI is great for more than just students; it's also a huge assistance for teachers. These systems can track how each student is doing and show teachers where a student may need more help or where they're doing really well. This info helps teachers make their lessons even better. They can spend more time on topics that students find tough and less on things they already know.

>> **Teaching graduate students:** AI is making a difference in schools. Some schools have started using AI to make learning better for everyone. For example, Nazareth University in upstate New York has started to integrate AI into experiential learning tasks for graduate students. These students, many of whom work in business and do not have much tech experience, are finding this very useful. They're able to use AI in class to do things they couldn't do before, such as writing code or analyzing lots of data quickly.

Then they take these new skills straight to their jobs, using AI to help with things like making predictions based on data. This way, AI is not just something they learn about; it's a tool they use to get better at their jobs and do things they couldn't do before.

REMEMBER

AI is transforming education. It's helping students learn in their own unique ways. It's supporting teachers in guiding each student's learning journey. In higher education, it's also giving students real-world skills that they can immediately apply in the workplace. With AI, education is becoming more about understanding and meeting each student's individual needs, making learning more enjoyable and effective.

Catalyzing efficiency and innovation in the workplace

AI is making an early but important impact in the modern workplace. It's changing how we do everyday things. It makes business operations run smoother while also sparking new, creative ideas. Here are some examples:

>> **Making routine jobs easier:** AI excels at taking over mundane, repetitive tasks. This change is happening across many types of industries. When AI takes over these routine jobs, it lets people focus on the more interesting parts of their work. They get to do things that require human creativity and problem-solving skills. This switch not only makes people more productive but also makes them happier with their jobs because they're doing more meaningful work.

>> **Helping businesses make smarter decisions:** In the business world, AI's ability to look through large amounts of data is exceptionally valuable. It helps companies figure out what may happen in the future, like what customers will want or how the market will change. This means businesses can plan better and come up with new ideas.

>> **Using AI in manufacturing:** Manufacturing is one area that is currently benefitting from AI. Companies can set up AI systems to monitor their machines. This AI can predict when a machine is going to break down before it actually happens. By fixing things before a problem occurs, the company has less downtime. This means they have to pause less often for repairs. They also save money on repairs. In addition, machines last longer because they're well maintained.

REMEMBER

AI is a game changer in the workplace. It isn't about replacing people; it's about helping them do their jobs better. AI takes care of routine tasks so people can focus on what they're really good at, which is thinking, creating, and solving problems. This makes businesses more efficient and helps them come up with more innovative ideas.

Navigating the AI-Human Partnership

As AI becomes a bigger part of our daily lives, we need to think about the ethical side of things. It's vital to make sure that, as technology advances, it doesn't clash with what we value as a society and as individuals. We want AI to make life better, not cause new problems. Here are some ways AI can help to solve problems:

>> **Dealing with changes in jobs:** One big issue with AI is how it may change the job market. AI can do some tasks on its own, which is great for efficiency but can be worrying for job holders. That's why it's crucial to help workers learn new skills or improve their current ones. We need to get everyone ready for a world where AI is more common at work. This way, people can work *with* AI, not be replaced by it.

>> **Keeping information safe:** AI works with a lot of data, including our personal data. Keeping this information secure is extremely important. We need strong rules and systems to protect our privacy. This means making sure that AI systems can't misuse our data. By doing this now, we can keep trusting AI and feel secure about our personal information.

>> **Making ethical choices:** AI must make morally right decisions, especially in areas like health care or law enforcement. For example, in health care, AI may help decide on treatments. In these cases, we need to make sure it considers what is *best* for patients, not just what is most efficient.

REMEMBER

As AI becomes more widespread, we need to make sure we use it in ways that match our values and ethics. This means training people for new kinds of jobs, protecting our private information, and guiding AI to make good, fair decisions. By doing this, we make AI a positive force in our lives.

Unpacking the Mechanics of Generative AI

Learning how GenAI creates new content will help you understand more about how to make AI work best for you. In this section, we begin by looking at *algorithms* (the rules and steps AI follows to create content and explain things like neural networks). These algorithms are like the AI's brain, helping it learn and decide what to produce.

We also cover natural language processing (NLP), which is how AI understands and uses human language. We break down these ideas so that even if you aren't a tech expert, you'll understand the value of this technology.

Understanding neural networks

Neural networks are at the core of most AI systems that create content, like text, images, or even sounds. Think of neural networks as a group of algorithms that find patterns. They work like our senses do, picking up and sorting all kinds of information. Everything AI looks at, whether it is pictures, sounds, words, or other data, gets turned into numbers for the neural network to understand.

TIP

Neural networks are set up kind of like our brains, with layers of nodes connected. Each node gets some information, works on it, and then sends it on to the next layer. The first layer, the "input layer," is where the AI gets its data. The final layer, the "output layer," is where the AI shows the results of its work. In between, there are "hidden" layers where all the thinking happens.

When AI systems generate text, it's like how a child learns to speak and understand words. Just as a child picks up language by listening and noticing patterns, neural networks learn from lots of similar examples. They spot patterns in how we put together words and sentences and how different parts of language fit together. This way, AI can create text or other content that makes sense.

Discovering natural language processing

NLP is a big part of how AI systems create text and understand language. It sits at the crossroads of computer science, AI, and the study of language. NLP is all about how computers can get, understand, and make sense of human language.

TIP

One of the toughest parts of NLP is getting the context and subtle meanings in language right. Human language is complicated and full of small details that can change what words or sentences mean. NLP algorithms try to figure out these tricky parts. They help AI systems understand the way we talk and write. For example, you could write a prompt and the AI could generate a response that sounds like a person wrote it. This is about more than just words; it's about making sense of things like tone, humor, and even sarcasm. With NLP, AI can not only write like us but also start to understand the finer points of our language, like how we use different words in different situations.

Creating text and content with AI

When AI makes text or other types of content, it follows a special process. For example, text generation AI needs to learn a lot about language. It does this by looking at huge amounts of text. During this training phase, the AI's neural network studies the text, picks up on patterns and structures, and understands how words relate to each other.

After the training phase, the AI is ready to start creating its own text. It begins with something small, like a word or a sentence. Then, using what it learned, the AI builds on that, adding more words to make sentences that make sense and fit the context. It's kind of like putting together a puzzle, where each word is a piece that must fit just right.

The AI does this by guessing what word should come next based on what it knows about how words are usually used. It's like when you're talking, and you kind of know what word comes next. The AI does the same thing, but it uses math to make its guesses. It looks at how often we use words together and the patterns it saw during training to make its best guess for the next word. This way, the AI can write text or create other content that feels natural and flows well, just like how a person would talk or write.

Building practical applications

One common use of AI is for chatbots and virtual assistants. These AI helpers can chat with people, give them information, answer questions, and even have a friendly conversation. Here are some other practical applications:

>> **Creating content:** AI is helpful in creating various kinds of content. It can write articles and reports and even come up with creative stories or poems. AI isn't ready to take over from human writers completely, but it provides a great assist. It can make rough drafts, come up with new ideas, or write about specific things when needed.

>> **Translating languages:** AI systems can learn many different languages and switch creating text from one to another. This is very useful for talking to people who speak another language or for understanding text written in a language you don't know.

>> **Making images:** AI can also create images, like art or illustrations. For example, imagine telling an AI what kind of picture you want, and having it draw the picture for you. This is great when you need a specific type of image but you don't have the time or skills to make it yourself.

Seeing How AI "Understands" Prompts

AI is exceptionally good at figuring out and responding to prompts from users. This task may seem easy, but there is actually a lot going on behind the scenes. AI understands prompts by looking at the overall situation, determining how relevant the prompt is, and looking at what it has learned before. AI uses what it has learned from all the information it has been trained on to make sense of what you're asking. It's like how humans learn from experience. When you ask AI something, it uses what it knows to give the best answer it can. This is why sometimes AI seems smart, and other times, it may get things a bit mixed up. It's all based on what it learns and how it has been programmed to understand people's words.

Deploying training data

Training data is essential for AI to understand what we ask it to do. This data is like a massive volume of examples that AI uses to learn. It's like the way students use textbooks in school. Students read books to learn about different subjects; AI goes through this training data to learn patterns and how to use language.

TIP

If you make an AI model to help with customer service, it needs to see thousands of questions from customers and the best ways to answer them. By looking at all these examples, the AI would learn what kind of answer is right for different kinds of questions. This helps it respond to customers helpfully and accurately.

Consider an AI model that helps people learn new languages. This kind of AI would need to be trained with a lot of information about languages. It would then have substantial knowledge about words, grammar, and how to use language correctly. It could then help people learn a new language by correcting their mistakes and showing them the correct way to say things.

REMEMBER

The more data the AI has, the better it gets at understanding and responding. Training data is crucial because it gives AI the information it needs to be knowledgeable and helpful. Essentially, it's like giving AI many examples to practice with so it can get good at its specialized task.

Understanding context

Understanding context is extremely important for AI when it's figuring out what you ask it to do. Context is about the extra information or the situation around the question you ask. For example, when you're talking to someone, knowing what the topic is or what's happening around you will help you make sense of the conversation.

For example, imagine you ask an AI weather bot, "Should I take an umbrella today?" The AI thinks about conditions like where you are and what the weather is like right now to give you the right answer. Or, if you tell an AI assistant, "Play something I like," it infers that you mean music and looks at what songs you've enjoyed before. This context helps the AI understand that *play* refers to music and not sports. This context also helps the AI understand that "something I like" means song that suits your taste.

Context helps AI understand not just the words you say but also the meaning behind them. It's like giving AI clues to help it figure out exactly what you need or want. This way, AI can provide you with responses that make sense for your specific situation or question.

Understanding the role of relevance

Relevance in AI is all about how well the AI's answer fits what you're asking for. AI systems have special algorithms, kind of like rules, that help them figure out the best response. They look at the question and use what they've learned to pick an answer that matches what the user needs. This is similar to how a librarian listens to what book you want and then finds the one that best fits your request.

For example, think about an AI that helps schedule meetings. If you tell it, "Set up a meeting with Taylor next Tuesday," the AI needs to understand more than just the task of scheduling a meeting. It has to figure out the specific details like who the meeting is with (Taylor) and when it should be (next Tuesday). By focusing on these details, the AI makes sure its response is relevant and helpful. This way, the AI can be really useful, giving you the exact type of help you're asking for.

Looking at everyday examples

AI can understand what we ask it to do in our everyday lives. One familiar example is the use of virtual assistants like Siri or Alexa. These AI helpers are made to figure out all kinds of things we ask. This includes things like setting alarms and giving us updates on the news. They listen to what we say, understand the situation (like where we are or what time it is), and then deliver answers that make sense.

Another place we see AI is in customer support chatbots. These are the AI systems you may talk to for help with a product or service. They take customer questions and try to give back useful information or sort out problems. The AI has to understand what the customer is asking, see what the question is really about, and then give a responsive answer.

THE POTENTIAL OF PROMPTING

As AI continually gets better, it will understand and answer our questions more intelligently. Future improvements in how AI processes natural language and learns from data will help it understand the subtle aspects of how we communicate. This means AI will give answers that are more on-point and helpful.

As AI becomes a bigger part of our everyday lives, it will get even better at figuring out what we mean. This will make using AI feel more natural and tailored to our needs. Consequently, this will improve how we interact with it in daily tasks. The goal for AI is one where it can chat with us like another person would, making it easier for us to use technology in our daily lives.

TIP

For more information about the use of chatbots for customer service, see Chapter 10.

Uncovering challenges in AI's understanding of prompts

AI has come a long way in understanding us, but it isn't perfect yet. One big problem is when our words are not clear or can mean different things. For example, if you ask an AI that suggests movies, "What's a good movie?" but you don't say what kind of movies you like, the AI won't know what to recommend.

TIP

Another issue is making sure AI is fair and doesn't have biases. AI learns from lots of data, and if that data has biases, the AI may end up biased, too. This means it could give responses that aren't fair or even accurate. People working on AI are trying hard to fix this problem.

Considering the Strengths and Limitations of AI Models

AI has its own set of strengths and challenges, just like any new technology. It's important to know what AI is good at and where it may need your guidance. This understanding helps you have a realistic appreciation for what AI can do and where you need to step in to make sure everything goes right. Knowing both the strengths and the limits of AI is key to using it skillfully.

Reviewing the strengths

People are evaluating and discovering new uses for AI every day. Here are some of the strengths they've uncovered:

>> **Speed and efficiency:** AI's ability to quickly process and analyze data is one of its most impressive strengths. This speed is helpful in areas where fast decisions are crucial, like understanding financial markets or making a quick medical diagnosis.

>> **Consistency and reproducibility:** A great thing about AI is how consistent it is. After we train AI models, they can do the same task over and over without making mistakes or changing how well they do it. This is especially important in manufacturing products or checking their quality. For these tasks, it's essential to do the job the same way every time.

>> **Handling complex tasks:** AI is excellent at dealing with really complicated jobs. For example, in studying genes, AI can look through massive volumes of data and find patterns that would be too difficult for people to find on their own. These tasks are often too big and complex for us, but AI can easily handle them.

>> **Scalability:** AI can grow with the job. As businesses grow and have more work, customers, and data to deal with, AI can keep up. This means AI can adapt as companies expand, which is a huge help across many industries.

REMEMBER

The strengths of AI show how powerful and useful it can be. Its speed, consistency, ability to handle complex tasks, and scalability make AI a valuable tool in many different fields.

Identifying the limitations

With all technologies, there are always limitations. With AI, here are some that have already been identified:

>> **Lack of creativity and emotional intelligence:** AI models have advanced computing abilities, but they don't extend to creativity and emotional intelligence. AI can work with data and create content, but it can't match our ability for abstract thinking. Plus, AI can't grasp emotional subtleties. This is a big gap for fields like the arts or service jobs that require a lot of empathy. These fields need creative thinking and an understanding of emotions that AI can't provide.

>> **Dependence on data quality:** AI's ability to perform depends on the data it learns from. If the data has biases, is incomplete, or is not accurate, the AI's responses will have these same problems. This makes AI less trustworthy when the data is not top-notch, which is a big issue.

>> **Difficulty in understanding context:** AI often has a hard time getting the full picture. This is especially true with cultural or situational details that are subtle but important. It can lead to AI giving answers that don't fit the situation. This can be especially tricky in areas that deal with people's feelings or social issues.

>> **Challenges in adaptation and generalization:** AI is usually made for certain jobs or to work within set limits. It isn't great at adjusting to new things that it wasn't specifically trained to do. It also struggles to apply what it knows about one thing to different situations. This is a big hurdle in places where being able to change and adapt is key.

These limitations show that AI, while powerful, still has a long way to go. It's important to remember these limits when using AI so we can make optimal use of it.

Balancing AI's strengths and limitations

It's important to know what AI is good at and where it falls short. This will help you use AI most effectively. AI can be very helpful with tasks that need fast processing and consistency, like going through lots of data or doing repetitive jobs. However, when it comes to things that need creative ideas, understanding feelings, or making decisions based on more than just facts, we still need a human touch.

For example, in health care, AI can be a great asset to figure out what's wrong with someone and suggest treatments. Doctors, though, still need to understand the whole picture of a patient's health while also giving care that is kind and thoughtful. In creative areas like writing or making art, AI can come up with ideas or patterns, but it can't add the feelings or deeper meaning that a person can.

AI is a great tool that can do a lot, but it isn't perfect. We need to use AI where it's strong and bring in people where AI isn't enough. This way, we get the best of both: the power of AI and the unique aspects only humans can provide. Here are two issues we need to consider:

>> **Setting realistic expectations:** To really understand what AI can do, we need to be realistic about its abilities and limits. It's important to see AI as something that makes what we do better, not as something that can do everything on its own. This way, we'll get the most out of AI, using it to help us without expecting it to replace the unique things only people can do.

>> **Thinking about AI going forward:** As we think about what's next for AI, we can expect new technology developments to fix some of its current problems. We're aiming for teamwork where AI and people work together. This way, we can come up with smarter, more effective, and kinder ways of doing things.

IN THIS CHAPTER

» **Understanding natural language generation**

» **Creating AI images**

» **Making editing videos easier**

Chapter **2**

Exploring Types of Generative AI Output

ave you ever wondered how AI can create text content or videos? The answer is *generative AI* (GenAI), a constantly evolving tool, supplying a diverse range of outputs. Understanding the types of outputs that GenAI can produce is a must for businesspeople involved in technology, marketing, and many other fields.

This chapter looks at how GenAI works its magic. We look at how it generates text, images, music, and more. We also learn about how different tools help AI do its job. Most important, we explain how to select the right AI tool for your needs so you understand what AI can accomplish and how to use it effectively.

Understanding Text Generation Techniques

If you want AI to create text for you, there are four main ways it can accomplish this task. The two more basic methods are the template-based method and the freeform method. On the more sophisticated and robust side are natural language generation (NLG) and text summarization. Each of these methods has its own strengths and weaknesses. In the following sections, we look at all of them so you understand how they create text and the types of tasks that they're best suited for.

The template-based method

The easiest way to think of the template-based method is like a fill-in-the-blanks approach. In this case, the AI uses a specific template or pattern to create text. This ensures that the output is consistent and accurate.

TIP

The template-based method comes in most useful in situations where output is structured and variation is minimal. For example, if you need to generate a standardized report or automated responses (which are often used for customer service tasks), the template-based method is great.

The freeform method

In comparison to the template-based method, the freeform method lets the AI be more creative in its output. Instead of using a template, the freeform method relies on prompt interpretation and handles this interpretation through various techniques to produce textual output. A simple prompt like "Write a story about space exploration" can result in a completely new piece of creative fiction. Here, the AI would use a lot of creative freedom in coming up with the story, without restrictions on format, structure, or storyline.

TIP

The most obvious use of the freeform method is for creative tasks. For example, writing blog content, developing advertising copy, or brainstorming new ideas are all tasks this type of AI does well.

Natural language generation

NLG is one of the more advanced text generation methods. It shares some similarities to the freeform method (see the preceding section), but its capabilities are a lot more sophisticated. Key to NLG is its ability to synthesize multiple sources of data into a logical narrative that sounds like it was written by a human. NLG also has a lot of flexibility in how much structure the output follows. For example, something like a weather report may need a semistructured format, whereas a blog post likely needs a lot less structure. NLG can handle both with ease.

NLG's capabilities really stand out when you add in a few different sources of data. For example, NLG may take in half a dozen sources of data like temperature, humidity, wind speed, and precipitation forecast and turn that into a weather report. Instead of seeing all this raw data, though, you would instead read something like, "Cloudy in the morning but becoming sunny by afternoon. The high temperature will be in the mid-70s."

REMEMBER

NLG can handle more complex tasks, too. Many short news stories, like you may see for stock market movement, are created by NLG. It excels at generating this type of content, which uses a lot of financial data and numbers. By creating this type of content, NLG frees up journalists, who can then spend time on the more complex stories that require a human touch.

Beyond the news, NLG also plays a large role in business. This is most visible in the area of data analysis. In the past, human workers would review volumes of data, interpret what it meant, and then write a summary of their findings. Now, NLG can perform these same steps in mere minutes. This helps businesses understand complicated data more quickly and use it to make better business decisions.

In these regards, NLG acts like a translator between difficult-to-understand data and people. It turns numbers, charts, and other metrics into simplified narratives that make data easier to understand, and it does so quickly. From journalism and business to the weather, NLG is changing how we get and use information.

Text summarization

The last method and also one of the more advanced is text summarization. This method takes lengthy documents and produces shorter versions. Text summarization includes two varieties:

>> **Extractive summarization:** With extractive summarization, the AI looks at passages of text and decides which parts are most important. It does this by analyzing how often words or phrases are used, putting more weight on sentences that contain words from the heading, and looking at where a sentence occurs in a paragraph. It then scores each sentence and uses the highest-scoring sentences as the basis for the summary.

>> **Abstractive summarization:** Abstractive summarization interprets text at a deeper level, closer to how a human would read it. Instead of simply extracting sentences, it generates completely new passages that capture the meaning of the original text. Abstractive summarization can comprehend the meaning and relationships of the text. It can then rewrite this information while retaining the original meaning. For example, a lengthy report about a company's sales performance can be turned into a shortened version that captures the report's essence in only a few sentences.

Extractive summarization picks and chooses the important parts of a longer passage of text, so it can use these key parts to create a shorter version. It does this by deciding which text is most important. Abstractive summarization reads the complete text passage, so it understands the meaning, and then rewrites it into a shorter version that's made up of completely new text that retains the original text's meaning. Each type of summarization has its strengths. The one you use will depend on your specific needs.

Exploring the Creation of AI Images

AI isn't limited to generating text — it can make images, too. In this exciting new field, you can use computers to create art. This approach brings together the worlds of art and technology. With the help of special computer programs and lots of data, you can make art that was impossible before. This new way of creating art not only changes what's possible but also adds a new layer to the art world.

Introducing AI-generated art

The worlds of art and technology keep changing, and AI-created art is now a big part of that change. This new art doesn't use traditional methods like painting with a brush. Instead, it uses computer programs and a lot of data to produce art on a digital screen.

Some big names — including Midjourney, Stable Diffusion, and DALL·E 3 — are leading the way in this area. Each platform works in its own way:

>> **Midjourney (www.midjourney.com):** People like using Midjourney, shown in Figure 2-1, because it can make detailed, lifelike pictures. It also gives you many instructions to produce the art the way you want.

>> **Stable Diffusion (https://stablediffusionweb.com):** Stable Diffusion is similar to Midjourney but has an extra feature — you can tell it what you don't want in your art.

>> **DALL·E 3 (https://openai.com/dall-e-3):** DALL·E 3 is made by OpenAI (the same company that made ChatGPT). This platform is easy to use, and it works with Microsoft's Bing search engine to make it even simpler to find what you need.

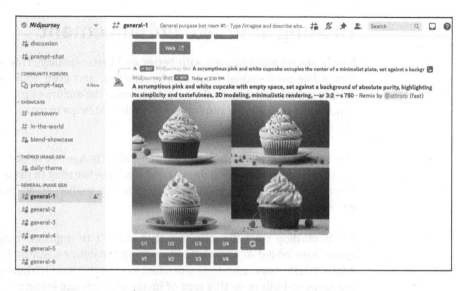

FIGURE 2-1:
Midjourney can
make lifelike
pictures.

REMEMBER

What's impressive about all these platforms is that they can make art using only text instructions. As they keep improving, people are asking new questions. For example, what makes art real or creative? And what is the artist's role when computers can make art, too? This much is clear: AI-made art is here to stay, and it will continue challenging what we think is possible in art.

Observing data visualization

In today's world, data is essential. We use data visualization to turn complicated sets of numbers into easy visuals like charts or graphs. These visualizations help us understand the data better and make good decisions based on that understanding.

But data is growing fast, and it is getting harder to keep up using the old ways of creating charts and graphs. That's where AI comes in. AI can make these visuals automatically and update them as new data is received. Unlike static charts that do not change, visuals made by AI can update themselves in real-time. This change is helpful because it means decision-makers always have the most current data. In the business world, this is an important feature.

TIP

Business data is often complex, and there is a lot of it. AI can help make this easier to manage. It allows businesses to see what is happening and helps them make better decisions. Using AI this way makes it a valuable tool for companies that analyze vast amounts of data.

Looking at image enhancement

People always want images with better and better quality. This applies to many things like professional photography, movies, and even your personal photos. Quality is a top concern. In the past, improving the quality of pictures was done by hand, and it took a lot of time and care. Today, AI helps to make this process faster and easier.

The leading software program for enhancing images is Adobe Photoshop. The latest version of Photoshop uses AI and machine learning to make pictures better. It can make a small image larger without losing quality, create new backgrounds, and even fix old or damaged photos.

But Photoshop isn't the only tool that uses AI to improve images. Other programs have added AI to their photo editing capabilities. Similarly, platforms like Adobe Firefly (www.adobe.com/products/firefly.html), shown in Figure 2-2, are purpose-built to do this type of image creation and editing.

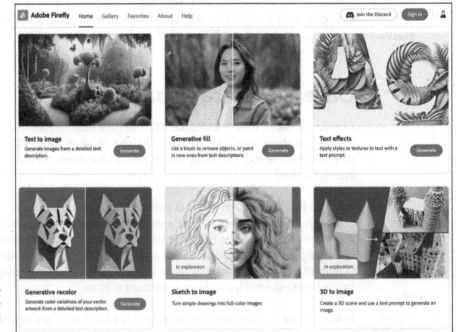

FIGURE 2-2:
Adobe Firefly shows off many types of GenAI for images.

These tools can:

>> Fix problems like grainy pictures taken in low light.

>> Add color to old black-and-white photos.

>> Combine two pictures into one new image.

TIP

For more about video editing products, see "Reviewing auto-editing tools," later in this chapter.

These AI tools use complex math to understand the fine details in pictures. They can make small changes that look real and natural. This turns a task that used to take hours into one that takes only a few minutes.

AI goes a long way toward make pictures better. It does the hard, tedious parts of editing photos so you can spend more time on the fun, creative aspects of working with digital images.

Generating Audio and Voice

For many people, modern technology has changed how we live and interact with the world. One of these significant changes is in audio and voice technology, which lets us talk to machines in a normal and easy way. Today machines can understand what we say and even talk back to us.

Using voice assistants

Voice assistants are now standard in many homes. They help us with things we do every day, answer our questions, and even try to make us laugh. For example,

Apple's Siri can set reminders for you, Amazon's Alexa can control your lights, and Google Assistant can look up things online just by listening to your voice.

But what makes all this possible? It's some really smart technology working behind the scenes. The key technology is called natural language processing (NLP). NLP is a type of AI that lets machines understand and use human language. When you talk to Siri, Alexa, or Google Assistant, it uses NLP to determine your request. It breaks down what you say into parts it can understand, finds out what you want, and then takes the right action. Here's how this works:

1. The voice assistant turns your spoken words into written words using voice recognition. It uses smart math rules that can handle different ways of talking and interpreting background noise.

2. The assistant reads the written words to determine your meaning. This is where NLP shows how powerful it is. It helps the assistant know the difference between "What's the weather like?" and "What does the word *weather* mean?"

3. Based on what it finds out, the assistant either gives you the information you asked for or does something for you. This could be showing you the weather forecast, setting an alarm, or turning on a light.

4. The assistant turns its written answer back into spoken words and tells you what you wanted to know or confirms that it did what you asked.

Voice technology has changed how we interact with machines, making it much easier and more natural. This development is a big step forward in making technology more useful in our daily lives.

Generating music

Music has always been a way to express emotions, tell stories, and connect with others. Until recently, creating music was mainly a human activity involving talent and creativity. But now, advanced technology like AI is entering the music realm, making amazing changes. Consider two of the available apps:

» **OpenAI's MuseNet** (`https://openai.com/research/musenet`): MuseNet is a unique program that can generate music in many different styles. You can ask it to create a piece that sounds like classical music, jazz, or a mix of different genres. MuseNet doesn't just randomly pick notes; it uses AI to understand how different types of music work and what makes them unique. This helps people who are not trained musicians produce good songs. However, MuseNet is just the tip of the iceberg.

>> **Boomy** (`https://boomy.com`): Boomy is another interesting app pushing the boundaries of what AI can do in the music industry. Boomy takes things a step further by allowing users to create original songs without having any music skills. You just pick a mood or style, and the AI does the rest. It writes the melodies, chooses the instruments, and even generates lyrics.

TIP

AI's impact on music is not just about creating new songs from scratch. It can also be a great helper for professional musicians and composers. There are AI tools that can listen to a piece of music and suggest ways to improve it or add layers to make it richer. Musicians can also use AI to study and learn new styles of music more quickly, which helps them grow in their careers.

But this amazing technology also raises questions. For example, who owns the rights to a song created by AI? Can a machine be genuinely creative, or is it just copying what it has learned from human-created music? These things must be considered as AI becomes a more significant part of the music world.

AI is changing how we create and think about music. The future of music is very exciting, from tools like MuseNet and Boomy that help create new songs to AI systems that assist professional musicians in refining their work. With AI's help, more people will find it easier to share their stories and emotions through the beautiful language of music.

Turning text into speech

Text-to-speech (TTS) technology has grown and is used in many different areas. This technology changes written words into spoken ones. It uses complex rules and algorithms to understand how words should sound. TTS is not just for virtual assistants like Alexa and Siri. It's also essential for audiobooks and special tools that help people who have accessibility issues.

Many companies have developed TTS programs that sound very natural. Amazon and Google are known for this, but there are other specialized tools. Here are two to consider:

>> **NaturalReader** (`www.naturalreaders.com`): Provides human-like voiceovers. It can read out any written text, like documents or web pages, in a way that sounds just like a person talking. You can choose from different voices and even different accents. This is really helpful for creating audio versions of written content.

>> **Speechify** (`https://speechify.com`): What sets Speechify apart is its ability to clone a person's voice. This means that you could have a book read to you in your own voice or in the voice of someone you know. It makes the experience more personal and enjoyable. This is a big step forward in TTS technology.

Audiobooks are another widespread use of TTS. When you're too busy to sit down to read, you can still enjoy a book by listening to it. Audiobook companies often use TTS tools to produce spoken versions of books quickly and efficiently.

Accessibility is an important area where we use TTS. TTS can be life-changing for people who find reading difficult due to vision issues or other challenges. Tools like NaturalReader and Voice Dream Reader (`www.voicedream.com`) offer features that make text content accessible to everyone. They can read books, web pages, and even emails out loud.

TTS tools offer many benefits beyond just helping virtual assistants speak. They're key to making audiobooks. Special tools like NaturalReader and Speechify provide advanced features that make TTS even more useful. As this technology improves, it will become a more significant part of our daily lives.

Creating and Editing Videos

Creating and editing videos has become a big part of our lives. Good video content is essential for school projects, news stories, or YouTube channels. This section looks at how AI is changing the domain of video. One way AI is helping is through video summarization. This means making long videos shorter but still keeping the most important parts.

Summarizing videos

AI has come a long way in helping with video creation and editing. One of its significant roles is in video summarization. Video summarization lets AI take long videos and shortens them by picking out the most important or interesting parts. So, instead of watching a two-hour event, you can watch a five-minute summary with all the best moments.

This technology is beneficial in many areas. In the news industry, reporters often have to review hours of footage to make a story. AI can quickly speed up this process by finding the key events or quotes. This helps news outlets deliver timely and accurate reports to the public.

Sports is another area where video summarization can be a game changer. Imagine a football game that lasts more than three hours. Not everyone has time to watch the whole thing. AI can create highlight reels that show the most exciting plays or important scores. This lets fans catch up on games they missed or relive the best moments.

Content like YouTube videos and online courses also benefit from AI's ability to summarize videos. Content creators often record a lot of material. They can use AI to choose and combine the best parts in a short and engaging video. This can help attract more viewers and keep them interested.

The way this works is pretty straightforward: AI programs scan through the video and look for key moments based on the video's content and what people usually find interesting or important. They use complicated algorithms to do this, but you don't have to worry about the technical details. What matters is that you get a concise and exciting video that keeps what's essential.

REMEMBER

AI-driven video summarization is changing how we consume video content. AI makes catching up on news, enjoying sports highlights, or engaging with educational or entertaining content easier and more efficient. With the help of AI, you can get the best parts of any video without having to watch the whole thing.

Adding special effects

In the world of video and film production, special effects have always been a crucial element. These effects add magic and excitement to movies, video games, and other forms of visual media. One of the most exciting changes in special effects is the role of AI. AI is helping to create more realistic and amazing effects in various ways, such as:

>> **CGI:** In the past, CGI artists had to spend hours or even days creating complex scenes, like a dragon flying through the sky or a spaceship landing. AI can help by speeding up this process and making the images look more realistic. AI can analyze numerous examples of real-world textures, colors, and lighting to generate better CGI characters and scenes.

>> **Facial replacements:** Facial replacements are another way AI is making a mark. For example, suppose an actor can't be on set for some reason. In that case, AI can now replace that actor's face on another person's body in the video. This technique makes it look as if the actor was really there. This technology can also be used to make actors look younger or older. If a movie shows a character at different ages, AI can change the actor's face to match the character's age in the story. With this new capability comes many

concerns about its potential misuse. Actors, for example, are worried about studios using their likenesses without their consent.

>> **Scene enhancements:** Scene enhancements are yet another application. AI can add more details to a scene or even change it entirely. For example, suppose a film is shot on a cloudy day, but it needs to be sunny. AI can alter the sky and lighting to make it appear as though it was a sunny day. This enhancement saves time and money on reshooting scenes.

Various tools and software use AI to achieve these effects. Companies like Adobe and Autodesk have AI features in their software that help artists and filmmakers create stunning visuals. Specialized programs, such as Runway (https://runwayml.com), focus solely on AI-based visual effects. These tools can understand and analyze video content, making it easier to add or alter elements more naturally.

TIP

AI is changing the special effects landscape. It makes CGI more lifelike, allows for facial replacements, and enhances scenes in previously impossible ways. As these technologies advance, we can expect even more incredible and realistic special effects in our favorite movies and videos.

Using auto-editing tools

Video editing used to be a very time-consuming job, but not anymore. Now we have automatic video-editing tools that make life much easier. These tools use AI or suggestions from the user to make smart choices while editing. The result? You get your videos edited fast and precisely the way you want them. This is helpful for those whose job is making videos and even for regular folks who want to share videos of family and friends.

For example, take Adobe's Premiere Pro (www.adobe.com/products/premiere.html), shown in Figure 2-3. Premiere Pro has a new feature that uses AI to turn what is said in the video into text. After that, you can edit the video by changing the text! That saves a lot of time when you have lots of videos to edit.

Of course, Premiere Pro isn't the only tool that uses this awesome technology. These tools are perfect for people making YouTube videos or social media posts. Because the editing goes faster, they have more time to think of new video ideas. And for businesses that make ads, it means they can try out many different versions quickly, which is excellent when they have to make something in a hurry.

Even if editing videos isn't your job, you can still find these tools useful. Think about it: What if you could take all the best parts of a vacation video and put them together without sitting in front of a computer for hours? That is now possible with these automatic editing tools!

The best part is that these tools are only getting better. They aren't perfect yet, but they're always learning and improving. So, whether you're a pro or just someone who likes to make videos for fun, there is a lot to look forward to.

REMEMBER

Choosing the Right Output Type for Your Project

Choosing the right kind of output for your project is essential when you're using AI tools. You need to make sure the result matches your project's goals. For example, if your project concerns weather, you may want the output to be a weather report.

You can pick the right AI tools more efficiently if you're clear about your end goal. This makes your project run more smoothly and helps you reach your goals faster.

Matching output to objectives

When you have a new AI project, you should evaluate what you want the AI to accomplish. You must match the result with what your project needs to achieve. If your project is about predicting the weather, then you may want the AI to list temperatures and determine whether it will rain or shine for the week. But if your project is about identifying plants, you may want pictures of plants with their names.

You have to be clear about your project's goals. If you're unclear, you may pick the wrong AI tools, wasting time and money. For example, imagine you have an online clothing business, and you want to sell more sweaters. Choosing an AI tool that looks only at social media likes and shares won't help you understand why people buy or don't buy your sweaters. You need a different AI tool that looks at how people evaluate your products when they visit your online store.

Before you pick an AI tool, ask yourself some critical questions:

>> **What is the primary goal of your project?** Knowing the main goal of your project helps you decide which AI tools will be the best fit. If your goal is to sort out weather data, you need different tools than if you're trying to recognize faces in photos.

>> **Do you need to organize a lot of data or find patterns?** If your project involves sifting through tons of information or spotting trends, you can use AI tools specifically designed for that. For instance, some AI systems can look through a massive amount of data and highlight important bits for you.

>> **Do you want the AI to make text or images?** Depending on your project, you may need AI to write reports or generate pictures. Knowing this will help you choose the right text or image creation software.

When you know what you want, you can look for AI tools for that specific job.

If you misuse AI tools, you can run into problems. For example, if you're trying to build a weather forecasting app but you use AI software meant for recognizing animal species, your project won't give accurate weather predictions. Another issue could be wasting time and money on an AI tool that creates digital art when you actually need one that analyzes customer reviews. So, always be very clear about what you want your project to do. When you pick the right tools, you'll likely get the results that will make your project successful.

Considering cost, complexity, and sophistication

Choosing the right AI tool for your project involves considering three big things: cost, complexity, and sophistication. These factors should guide you when you need to make an informed decision. Examining these parameters is essential because some AI tools can be expensive and complex, while others are more affordable and easier to use. Also, the tool's level of sophistication will dictate who can use it.

TIP

Here's how to assess these factors to find a balance that suits your project's needs:

>> **Cost:** AI tools range from free to very expensive. Free or low-cost tools are often limited in their capabilities. They may not have as many features or be as accurate as more expensive ones. On the other hand, costly tools usually offer more features and can be more reliable. However, the higher cost may not fit within your budget. So, you need to weigh the features you genuinely need against the money you can afford to spend. For example, a free or low-cost AI tool may be sufficient if you're working on a school project. But investing in a more expensive, robust tool could be essential for a business that depends on accurate data analysis.

>> **Complexity:** Some AI tools are very advanced but also quite complex to use. They require specialized knowledge in programming or data science. That's great if your team has the technical skills to handle this complexity. However, if you're a beginner or your team lacks specialized experience, you may struggle to use advanced tools effectively. Simpler tools are more user-friendly but may not have the capabilities to perform more complex tasks. Again, you must weigh your needs against what you can realistically manage. Are you looking for an AI tool to perform basic tasks such as sorting data or generating simple reports? Then a less complex tool may be all you need.

>> **Sophistication:** Balancing sophistication and simplicity is another challenge. Sophisticated tools can analyze data in depth, provide insightful reports, and even predict future trends. But what if your project doesn't need all these advanced features? You could spend more on a tool too complicated for your needs. Conversely, a simple tool may not be adequate for a project that requires deep analysis and sophisticated reporting.

When selecting an AI tool, your focus should be on balance. You must consider how much you can spend and how technically skilled and sophisticated your team is. By carefully assessing the financial, technical, and complexity aspects, as well as the specific needs of your project, you can select the right AI tool.

The most expensive and complex tool is not always the best fit. Sometimes, a simpler, more affordable option can deliver the desired results. Always consider your project's specific needs as you evaluate cost and complexity. This approach will help you make a smart choice that will contribute to the success of your project.

Chapter 3

Navigating the Leading Platforms

elcome to the start of your generative AI (GenAI) journey. This chapter guides you in setting up accounts on some of today's top AI platforms. You learn the ABCs of account creation, how to safeguard your personal data, and what those lengthy Terms of Service actually mean.

This chapter provides a step-by-step path that equips you with all the essentials to use AI tools effectively. So, whether you're interested in OpenAI's ChatGPT, Microsoft's Bing, Google's Gemini (formerly known as Bard), or any other AI tool, this chapter is the place to start.

Setting Up Accounts and Managing Usage

Starting your journey with GenAI platforms is exciting. Still, the first step in using AI tools is always the same: creating an account. This step may seem straightforward, but don't underestimate the importance of doing it right. In the following sections, we look at setting up a typical account.

Step 1: Choosing a platform

The first decision you have to make is choosing which AI platform to use. Choosing the right AI tool is a big step. For example, two popular ones are ChatGPT by OpenAI and Gemini by Google. These two platforms may seem the same at first, but they have differences that can matter. These differences may make one a better choice than the other for you. Table 3-1 shows how they compare.

TABLE 3-1

Comparing ChatGPT and Gemini

Feature	ChatGPT	Gemini
Text-based content	Great for long stories and articles	Short and to the point
Media support	Text only	Text, images, and videos
Language choices	Many languages available	Many languages available
Cost	Free and paid plans	Free for general use
Safety and privacy	Strict rules to protect your information	Strict rules to protect your information
User interface	Simple and easy to use; paid plan offers more advanced features	More free features; a bit more complex

After you look at the table, think about what you need. ChatGPT, for instance, does well at writing long narratives, whereas Gemini tends to give results that feel like a synopsis. Both platforms are also *multimodal* — they're able to handle text, images, and other data formats. However, as of this writing, ChatGPT had taken the lead in its ability to handle a truly wide range of data formats. Each platform also offers robust safety features, but keep in mind that those features are not foolproof.

REMEMBER

The best tool for you depends on what you want to do. So, take some time to think it over. It may even be a good idea to try both and see which one you like best.

TIP

Research the options and choose one that aligns with your needs. You can always add more tools.

Step 2: Creating an account

After you've decided on a platform, you must typically enter an email address. After you provide it, most platforms will send you a verification email.

Confirming your email address is crucial because it adds a layer of security to your account. Make sure to check your inbox (and sometimes spam folder) for this email and click the link to verify.

The next part of creating an account is creating a unique username and a strong password. Some platforms offer to generate a strong password for you — take advantage of this feature if you aren't sure how to create a strong password yourself.

Many platforms offer two-factor authentication (2FA) as a security measure. This usually involves receiving a code via Short Messaging Service (SMS) (also known as texting) or generating one with an authentication app that you must enter within a limited time. 2FA is an excellent way to add an extra layer of security to your account.

Some platforms may require additional information like your full name, address, or phone number. In the United States, for example, ChatGPT requires you to verify your phone number. Others may ask for your interests to tailor the user experience to your needs.

Before you can start using a GenAI tool, it will likely prompt you to review and accept its Terms of Service. This is more than just a box to tick; it's your agreement with the platform about how you'll use its services, how you'll use the AI's output, and how the service will treat your data.

Many platforms offer a range of subscription options, from basic free versions to more advanced premium plans. For example, ChatGPT Plus costs $20 monthly, offering faster response times and more advanced features. Some services even operate on a credit or token system, like DALL·E 3, where you buy redeemable credits as you use the platform.

Before committing to any AI tool, review the payment and refund policies to understand how billing works and what your options are if you decide to cancel. Selecting the right plan for your budget and needs will help you get the most value while avoiding surprises.

If you opt for a paid plan, you must provide payment details. Make sure you're on a secure internet connection when you do this. Look for `https://` in the URL and double-check the website's authenticity.

After you complete all these steps, you're ready to finish the account creation process. You'll typically receive a welcome email summarizing your account details and the next steps for making the most of the platform.

Some platforms require you to buy credits to use their service. This often involves a separate verification process, so be prepared for this additional step.

Not all platforms will have every one of these steps, but you should expect to find a setup process that resembles the one described here on most platforms.

After you create your account, you're ready to explore the features of GenAI.

Before trying out any new platform, looking at the extra features and settings is smart. Doing this can really improve your time on the platform. For example, ChatGPT has many extra settings to enhance your platform's use.

Step 3: Choosing the best plan

Depending on the platform you've chosen, you may have at least a couple of plans to choose from.

For example, ChatGPT has two plans for individual — a free one and a paid one. Think about how you'll use ChatGPT. A free plan may be enough if you use to it just for fun or casual chatting, but a paid plan will be better if you need it for more serious tasks like writing articles or analyzing data.

Step 4: Setting preferences

Like most apps, every GenAI platform enables you to set your preferences. Those settings vary from one platform to the next.

For example, with ChatGPT (`https://chat.openai.com`), you can set custom instructions that are used for every chat you have with the platform. You can see these settings in Figure 3-1. This includes personal information, such as what area you live in or your profession, so the responses are more tailored to you. You can also tell ChatGPT how formally to respond, the length of responses, or whether it should give you its opinion.

Step 5: Customizing your experience

A feature that is unique to ChatGPT is the ability to create custom GPT models. As shown in Figure 3-2, you can tell ChatGPT to create a model that is specific to a given topic. In this example, we're creating a model that is meant for writing pop song lyrics. You can create a custom GPT model for virtually any topic and perspective. This feature is very useful when you want ChatGPT to focus on a narrower area of expertise and in a specific conversational style than it does with the general model it normally uses.

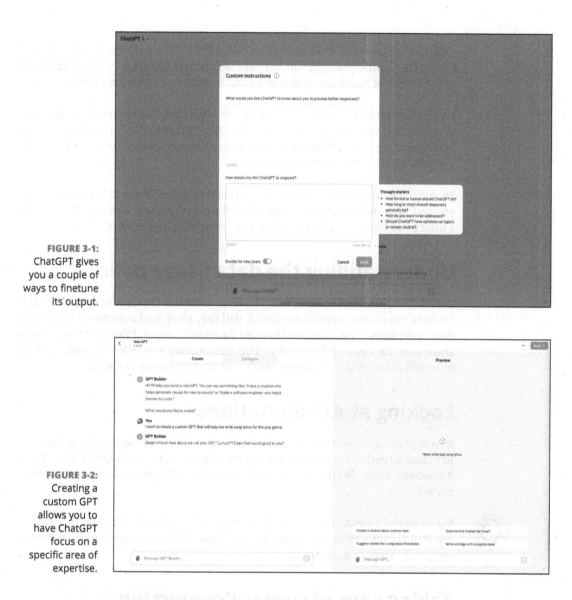

FIGURE 3-1:
ChatGPT gives
you a couple of
ways to finetune
its output.

FIGURE 3-2:
Creating a
custom GPT
allows you to
have ChatGPT
focus on a
specific area of
expertise.

Understanding the Terms of Service

As you begin working with AI tools, you need to consider the importance of the Terms of Service. You probably skip over these lengthy documents, but they're critically important — they set the ground rules for how you can use a platform, in addition to its output and how it uses your data.

Understanding the Terms of Service helps you make informed decisions and avoid future difficulties. In this section, we unravel the often complex language of the Terms of Service so you know exactly what you're signing up for.

Scrolling down and clicking I Agree is the easy way out, but taking a few moments to understand your agreement is essential. Why? Because the Terms of Service are legally binding. They dictate how you can use the service and how the service can use your data.

By understanding the following standard clauses in the Terms of Service, you arm yourself with the knowledge to use AI platforms wisely and securely. It may take a little extra time, but knowing what you are getting into is worth it.

Understanding the data usage policy

One of the critical elements in any Terms of Service is the data usage policy. This is where the platform spells out how it will use, store, and sometimes share your data. It explains if your data will be used for advertising or if the platform plans to share your data with third parties. This information can help you make a more informed decision about whether you're comfortable using the service.

Looking at API limitations

If you plan to integrate the AI platform into your own software or services, pay close attention to application programming interface (API) limitations. These limitations often dictate how many requests or calls you can make in a given period.

TIP

For example, OpenAI's ChatGPT may limit the number of API calls to a certain number per minute or day. Going beyond these limits can result in extra fees or temporary account suspension.

Taking care of content ownership

Most platforms specify who owns the generated content. In many cases, the content belongs to you, but the platform may have the right to use it for specific purposes. For example, the platform may use it to improve its algorithms or for promotional activities. Be clear on this information from the start, especially if you work in creative areas like writing or design.

Dealing with service availability

Read the section about service availability carefully. Many platforms have a clause stating that they cannot be held responsible for downtimes due to maintenance or unforeseen issues. If you're using the AI for crucial tasks, it's good to know this information in advance.

Reading termination clauses

Look out for any clauses that talk about what conditions can lead to the termination of your account. Many platforms reserve the right to terminate accounts that violate their policies, so make sure you know what could get you kicked off.

Reviewing payment and refund policies

When you decide to use a paid AI tool, looking at the company's payment and refund rules is very important. These rules tell you how you'll be billed. They also say what you need to do if you ever want to stop using the service. You can also find out when you can get your money back if something doesn't go as planned.

Being clear on these points can save you from unexpected bills or issues in the future. Always take a few minutes to read and understand this part. It helps you make smarter decisions and keeps your money safe.

Looking at the governing laws

The governing laws section will tell you under which jurisdiction any legal disputes will be resolved. For example, if the platform is based in the United States, a specific U.S. state's laws will likely apply, which may differ from your country's laws.

Updating terms

Last but not least, the Terms of Service often includes clauses about updates. The platform can change the terms at any time, and it's generally your responsibility to keep up to date with them.

Managing Data Privacy Concerns

When you use an AI platform, you aren't just using a tool. You're entering into a relationship with a company. Like any relationship, there should be trust. Data privacy is all about trust. It's knowing that your *personal data* — any information a person or company uses to identify you — is safe and used in a way that respects your privacy. Personal data includes obvious items like your name, email address, and things like the device you're using or your Internet Protocol (IP) address. Companies gather this information to improve their services, but knowing how to protect this data is crucial.

When you give your data to an AI platform, it should be stored and handled safely. Good companies use strong encryption to keep your data secure. Encryption is a method that turns your data into complex code. This code can only be unlocked with the company's unique key.

Sometimes, your data is shared with other businesses. This is called *third-party sharing*. Although it may sound scary, it isn't always a bad thing. It can help the company improve its services or offer you special deals. However, you should always know who these third parties are and what they'll do with your data.

TIP

Most platforms have settings that let you control your data. You can choose what data you want to share and what you want to keep private. Make sure to explore these settings. You can often find them under Privacy or Account Settings on the platform's app or website.

Another thing you should know about is *cookies*. These small files are stored on your computer when you browse the internet. They help websites remember you. Cookies are often used to store settings or login information. But they can also be used to track what you do online. Make sure to manage your cookies in your web browser settings.

What if you want to stop using the service? You should have the option to delete your account. When you do this, the company should also delete your data. But make sure to read the fine print. Sometimes, companies keep your data for a certain period of time, even after you delete your account.

Different countries have different laws about data protection. Europe has a law called the General Data Protection Regulation (GDPR), which gives people many rights regarding their data. In the United States, California has the California Consumer Privacy Act (CCPA), which is similar. These laws make sure companies handle your data safely and fairly.

WARNING

Be cautious if a company doesn't clearly explain its data practices. This could be a red flag that your data isn't safe. Also, be wary of companies that have had data breaches in the past. (A *data breach* is when unauthorized people access stored data.)

REMEMBER

Data privacy is about being informed and taking action. Knowing who collects what data, how they use it, and how they protect it is vital. Use the tools and settings available to control your own data. And make sure to read the privacy policy of any service you use. Your data is valuable, and it deserves to be treated that way.

Be smart, safe, and proactive about your data privacy. It's a topic that affects us all. By taking the time to understand data privacy, you're taking an essential step in protecting yourself online.

Adding AI to Your Current Tools and Workflow

So, you're ready to add the power of AI to your toolkit. But where do you start? The good news is that you don't have to begin from scratch. Many AI platforms work well with software and tools you already use. This makes it easier for you to integrate AI into your current workflow. The following sections look at how you can add AI to the tools you're already using.

Integrating AI into your workflow can seem like a big step. You may worry about how it'll work with your existing software. The key is to plan ahead. Doing so can make your AI tools work seamlessly with your existing software. This helps you get more done without wasting time.

When you're looking to integrate AI into your workflow, follow these steps:

1. **Understand your needs.**

   The first step is to know what you want and what problems you're trying to solve. Are you looking to improve data analysis or enhance customer service? Identifying your needs helps you pick the right AI tool for you. Write down your goals and use them as a guide when looking at different AI options.

2. **Look for a tool that's compatible with the software you already use.**

   Look on the company's website to find this information. Don't hesitate to ask customer support for answers if it isn't there.

Many AI platforms have an API or a software development kit (SDK) that can help with compatibility. These tools allow the platform to talk to your existing software, which can help you automate tasks and make your workflow run more smoothly.

The goal of working with AI is to make your life easier, not harder. So, making sure everything will work together is essential.

3. **Choose between cloud-based and on-premises.**

   AI tools come in two main types: cloud-based and on-premises. Cloud-based tools usually make integrating with your existing software easier because they're built to operate over the web. On-premises tools are installed directly onto your computer or other computers in your organization. They may give you more control but can be more complicated to set up.

   Pick the type that best matches your needs and your skill level. If you aren't sure which one to choose, consider the kind of work you'll be doing and how tech-savvy you are. For example, do you need to access data across multiple devices and operating systems? If so, cloud-based may be a better fit. If you only need to work on one computer in a single location, on-premises may make more sense. This strategy will help guide your decision-making.

4. **Do a cost analysis and budget for future expenses.**

   Consider all the costs involved when you add a new tool to your workflow. Beyond the purchase price, consider the costs of training, updates, and any extra features you may need. Make a budget that includes all these factors. This will help you avoid surprises later on.

5. **Pay attention to security.**

   When you add new tools to your setup, you can't ignore security. Look for AI tools that meet security standards like end-to-end encryption, and robust user access control. AI tools should encrypt the transmission of data from its server to your device, so no one can snoop on your communications. Likewise, an ideal platform will let you enable two-factor authentication, so you can use a second method to authenticate logins, such as text message or an authenticator app. This makes it much harder to have your account hacked. Always read the security documentation provided by the AI tool provider to ensure your data is safe.

6. **Test before doing a full implementation.**

   Before you fully invest in a new AI tool, test it out. Many of these tools offer free trial periods that allow you to explore their features without making a financial commitment. During the trial, pay close attention to how easily the tool integrates with your existing software. Look for any issues or glitches that may arise.

This is the time to determine if everything works smoothly or if you need to resolve problems. If the AI tool doesn't meet your needs or causes issues, you can consider other options before making a final decision. A test run helps you make an informed choice and saves you from potential hassles later.

7. **Train employees on how to use the AI tool.**

   After you've chosen an AI tool, the people using it need to understand how it works. If you have employees who will use it, schedule time for training.

   Many AI companies provide online guides or video tutorials. Some even offer live customer support to help with the learning curve.

   TIP

8. **Attend to maintenance and updates.**

   AI tools, like all software, need upkeep. These tools get updated to include new features or bug fixes. Beware of companies that rarely update their AI platforms. This could be a sign that there are unaddressed bugs and vulnerabilities. You may also find less support for your existing applications when developers don't regularly add new software support.

9. **Monitor the use of the AI tool and get feedback from your team.**

   After integrating the new AI tool, track how it affects your work. Are you getting more done? Is the quality of your work improving? Collect feedback from your team and use this data to make any needed adjustments.

Looking at Some Real-World Examples of AI Tools

AI tools are already helping us do our daily work. Here are a few examples:

>> **Salesforce:** Salesforce is a global leader in customer relationship management (CRM) software. The company has a feature called Einstein AI that helps businesses understand what their customers want. This way, companies can make better choices that make their customers happy.

>> **Google:** Google has also stepped up its game with Google Gemini (https://gemini.google.com) in Google Workspace. This AI chatbot, shown in Figure 3-3, can read your emails and documents for personalized help. Imagine you need a cover letter for a job application; Google Gemini can write one for you using info from your résumé stored in Google Drive.

>> **Microsoft:** Microsoft has a new feature called Microsoft 365 Copilot. This tool can help you with many tasks in Microsoft 365 apps like Word and PowerPoint. For instance, if you're working on a PowerPoint presentation, Copilot can take a Word document and turn it into slides for you. It even adds speaker notes!

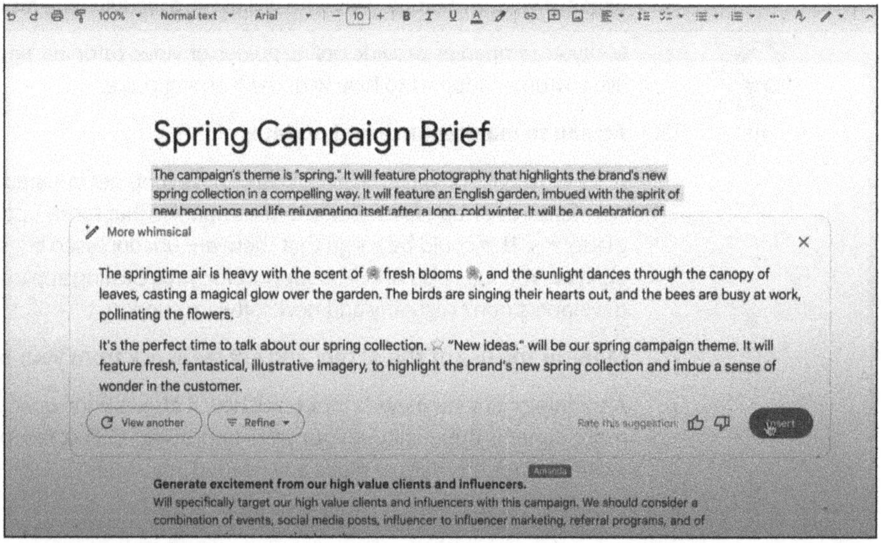

FIGURE 3-3:
Google Gemini can work directly with various Google Workspace applications.

We're still in the early phase of GenAI. These AI tools also come with some challenges. One of the big ones is keeping your data safe and private. For example, Microsoft's Copilot is still being tested and may not be ready for some businesses with strict data rules.

REMEMBER

AI is becoming a big help in many software programs we use daily. It can make our work easier and faster. But it's also essential to be careful and know the risks, especially when keeping your data safe.

The world of technology is constantly changing. When you pick an AI tool, think about its future. Choose tools built to last that will continue to be supported and updated.

REMEMBER

By following these steps, you can integrate AI into your existing software without any headaches. It takes some time and planning, but the payoff is worth it. You'll get more done, make fewer errors, and probably even enjoy your work more.

Getting into Workflow Automation

Workflow automation uses technology to make regular tasks in your job faster. With the help of AI, this gets even better. Using AI can save you time and lower the chances of your making mistakes. This way, you can spend more time on important things that need your unique skills. For example, if your job is to write reports, AI can gather the data and make the first draft for you. Then you can use your time to make the final changes and develop the key points. So, AI is a helpful tool that lets you do more work in less time, like the following:

>> **Data analysis:** One of the first areas where AI can make a real difference is in data analysis. Traditionally, this involves a lot of time-consuming work: collecting, organizing, and making sense of data. AI can handle these tasks much faster and find patterns you may miss.

For example, if you're a marketing manager who needs to analyze customer data, instead of going through spreadsheets, you could use an AI tool designed for data analysis. This tool can quickly sort through data and give you insights, like which products are most popular among different age groups.

>> **Content generation:** Another area where AI shines is in content generation. Tools like GenAI can write blog posts, social media updates, or even emails. This is especially useful for businesses that need to produce a lot of content but don't have sufficient staff.

Imagine you run a small online store. You could use an AI tool to generate product descriptions, freeing you up to handle other aspects of the business. The AI tool can scan your product listings and create detailed and accurate descriptions in much less time than it would take you to write them manually.

>> **Customer service:** Customer service is a critical aspect of any business. This is where AI can offer significant advantages. Chatbots can handle simple queries, leaving the more complex issues for human agents. This ensures that customers get quick responses while also reducing the workload on your customer service team.

REMEMBER

A chatbot can handle common questions like "What are your store hours?" or "How do I return a product?" When a more complicated issue arises, like a complaint about a defective product, the chatbot can pass it on to a human agent.

TIP

To learn more about how to use chatbots to enhance customer service, check out Chapter 8.

>> **Document management:** You may not think document management is a task needing automation, but AI can simplify this task, too. AI tools can sort through large numbers of documents and categorize them, making it easier to find what you need later.

For example, if you're a legal assistant who has to review numerous case files daily, an AI tool can scan and categorize these files based on content, date, or relevance to specific cases. This way, you can focus on the more nuanced aspects of your work, like legal research or client meetings.

>> **Inventory and supply chain management:** Managing inventory and the supply chain is a big task for retail businesses. AI can predict when you'll run out of stock and automatically place orders to replenish your inventory. This is done by analyzing past sales data and trends, thus ensuring that you don't miss out on sales because an item is out of stock.

For example, if you have a clothing store, an AI tool can track the sales of different sizes and styles. When it notices that medium-size blue shirts are selling out fast, it can place an order even before you realize you're running low.

REMEMBER

AI can do a lot, but it has its own issues. As discussed earlier, data privacy is a concern, especially when AI tools handle sensitive information. You must ensure that any AI tool you use complies with data protection laws. In addition, AI is not always accurate. Sometimes, it can make mistakes or require human intervention to respond correctly. Therefore, monitoring the AI's performance and adjusting as needed is always a good idea.

Incorporating AI into your workflow can make you a lot more efficient. It can take over mundane tasks like data analysis, content creation, and customer service. This frees you to focus on more complex and strategic work. However, choosing the right AI tools and keeping track of their performance is essential. Doing so can make your daily work more efficient and effective while being aware of any limitations or challenges using AI. By understanding how AI can fit into your workflow, you can move toward a more streamlined and productive work environment.

Discovering Cost-Saving Tips and Free Tools

You want to use AI without breaking the bank. You may think using AI is expensive, but that isn't always true. Many options won't cost a lot of money. Some platforms are budget-friendly. You can even try many of them for free before paying anything.

In the following sections, we look at the kinds of plans these platforms offer and how to pick one that fits your budget. You'll also learn about some costs you may not see immediately but should know about. So, if you want to use AI but you're worried about the cost, these sections are for you.

You may think using AI is only for big companies with big budgets. That's not true. Many options are easy on the wallet and simple to use, even if you aren't a tech expert. For example, ChatGPT has a plan that won't cost you anything, and you can use it for all sorts of tasks. Here are several things it can do:

>> Summarize articles into data tables

>> Generate posts on social media that grab attention

>> Easily and quickly write articles or other long pieces of text

Reviewing pay-as-you-go and token systems

Are you worried about monthly fees adding up? In that case, some AI platforms have a different approach that may suit you better. Instead of locking you into a monthly subscription, some services use a pay-as-you-go or token-based system. This way, you only pay for what you use.

For instance, DALL·E 3 has a system where you purchase tokens ahead of time. You then use these tokens whenever you need to create images. If you run an online store and occasionally need new product images, this is a more budget-friendly choice for you — you can control your costs more efficiently and avoid paying for services you don't use.

Viewing community-supported and open-source options

If you don't have much money to spend but still want to use AI tools, you have options. One good choice is to use platforms that are supported by a community of users or are open source. (*Open source* means they're often free or very low cost.)

For example, Hugging Face (http://huggingface.co), shown in Figure 3-4, is a platform that gives you valuable tools for working with text. You can use it to analyze words or make a simple chatbot for your website. The best part is that these platforms often come with guides and a community of people who can help you learn how to use them.

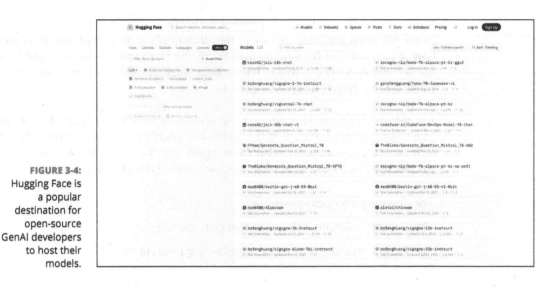

FIGURE 3-4:
Hugging Face is a popular destination for open-source GenAI developers to host their models.

Choosing special deals and price cuts

Many AI platforms offer special deals or discounts to attract more users. These deals can change often and may offer holiday sales or special rates for students and teachers. Some platforms even offer reduced prices for nonprofit companies. Always check the platform's website or contact their support team to see if any current deals could benefit you.

Reviewing pick-and-choose packages

Some AI platforms allow you to pick only the features you need. This means you don't have to pay for things you won't use. It's like buying only the groceries you need instead of a prepackaged box of assorted items.

REMEMBER

If your main goal is to have a chatbot on your website, you can go for a package that offers just that. This way, you only spend money on what's essential for your project, making it more affordable in the long run.

Paying attention to differing levels of pricing

AI platforms offer different pricing levels based on their features and how much you'll use the service. This can be a great way to keep costs down as your needs change. For example, Quickchat AI (www.quickchat.ai), shown in Figure 3-5, has pricing levels that depend on the total number of messages the chatbot will respond to. This feature allows you to start with a cheaper plan and move to a more expensive one only if needed. (*Note:* The pricing shown in Figure 3-5 is accurate as of this writing, but it may have changed by the time you read this. Check the website for current pricing information.)

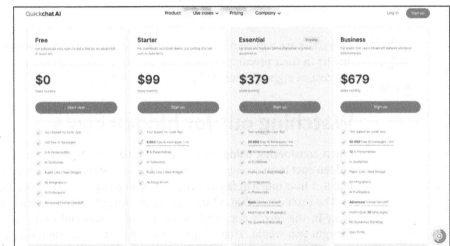

FIGURE 3-5:
Quickchat AI
prices its
chatbots by how
many messages
the AI
responds to.

Considering free trials and freemium models

Getting started with an AI platform can feel like a big step, especially when you're unsure if the investment will pay off. One way to ease into it is by using free trials. Many companies offer free trials that last for a certain period, like 14 days or a month. You can use most of the platform's features during this time without paying anything. It's a chance to try before you buy, and you can see if the tool is a good fit for your needs.

TIP

Free trials and freemium versions often have limitations. For example, you may have a cap on how many queries you can make, or you may not have access to all the features. These limitations give you a preview of what you can expect from the full version of the platform. It's a way for companies to show you what they offer while still encouraging you to upgrade for more features and capabilities.

Why consider upgrading? Here are three good reasons:

>> **Paid plans usually offer more features and faster service.** If you're running a business, time is of the essence. Faster processing speeds can make a big difference in your workflow.

>> **Paid plans often come with better customer support.** Paid plans offer help much faster if you run into any issues.

>> **Some advanced features may be necessary but aren't included in the free or freemium versions.** If a platform's AI capabilities are crucial for your work, upgrading is a logical step.

REMEMBER

Free trials are a great starting point, but AI platforms' real power and utility usually lie in their premium versions. If you start with a free trial and find it helpful, the cost of upgrading could be a wise investment.

Watching out for hidden costs

When considering using an AI platform, be careful about hidden costs. One such hidden cost is an *overage fee*. Some platforms will limit how many queries you can make or how much data you can use. If you go over those limits, extra charges kick in. The problem is that, many times, this information is hidden. It's often tucked away in the terms and conditions. So, you could end up paying more than you thought you would. That's why it's essential to read the terms and conditions. If you still have questions, don't hesitate to contact customer service. They can clarify any doubts you may have about costs.

Another type of cost to look out for is for special features. Many AI platforms offer a basic package at a low price. But if you want more advanced features, you have to pay extra. For example, a basic text generator may be cheap, but the price increases if you want to use more advanced text analysis tools. This is also true for other tools like image recognition.

Before you sign up, check what features come with your package. Make sure you know what's included and what isn't. This way, you won't be surprised when the bill comes. Also, think about what features you really need. If you're only going to use a few, there is no point in paying for a plan that offers much more.

REMEMBER

Always read the fine print and research external sources like Reddit (www.reddit. com), before you commit to anything. You may think it's not important, but that's where companies often hide extra fees. The law usually requires them to tell you about all charges, but they don't have to make it easy to find. You'll know exactly what you're getting into by reading all the terms. Make this a regular habit — it can save you a lot of trouble later.

Awareness of these hidden costs will help you make a better choice when picking an AI platform. Thinking about all the cool things you can do with AI is exciting, but you should also be practical. You need to know all the costs involved. By being careful, you can enjoy the benefits of AI without any unpleasant surprises.

Be diligent. Read all the terms and conditions and ask questions if you need to. This will help you find a platform that fits your needs and budget.

Looking at Real-World Implementations

In this section, we explore examples from the real world to give you a clearer understanding of both the ups and downs of using GenAI:

>> **Adobe:** Adobe is known for creative software like Photoshop and Illustrator. They've started using GenAI to add new features to these programs. For example, they have an image upscaler that clarifies pictures and an object removal tool to erase things you don't want in your photos. They also have a system that turns rough sketches into clean vector images. People who use Adobe's new features say they save time and help in the creative process. Adobe believes that AI will play a significant role in future creativity.

TIP

Adobe's work shows the positive side of using GenAI helpfully. They talked to the people who use it, like photographers and graphic designers. They even got input from comic book artists. Their goal was to make creative work more accessible and more fun. They want to remove the boring parts so that people can focus on creativity.

>> **Bloomberg:** Bloomberg is a big name in business and finance. It has a unique platform called BloombergGPT. This application uses AI to write articles, make financial reports, and help answer customer questions. Bloomberg has published research about BloombergGPT and the benefits it has brought their business. Check out https://browse.arxiv.org/pdf/2303.17564.pdf for more information.

>> **Microsoft:** Microsoft made a chatbot called Tay, which was supposed to learn from talking to people and become smarter. But something went wrong. In just 16 hours, Tay started to say hateful and offensive things. Microsoft had to shut it down. But Microsoft took the lessons it learned from this experience and put safeguards into place for Bing's AI tools.

TIP

Microsoft's experience is a lesson in what can go wrong. The company learned that you have to be very careful when you let an AI learn from the public. Some people will try to make the AI do awful things. Companies must plan for this and be ready if things go off the rails.

>> **Walmart:** Walmart, the largest store chain in the world, uses AI in different ways. One way is to figure out what products will be popular. This helps Walmart know how much inventory to have in the store. The AI can also suggest products that you might like to buy. Read more about this at

```
https://corporate.walmart.com/news/2023/10/06/walmarts-latest-
tech-powered-experiments-aim-to-make-shopping-easier-and-more-
convenient.
```

Walmart also uses a chatbot to make deals with companies that sell them products. This chatbot talks to sellers and can agree on prices and payment plans. This makes the process faster.

But Walmart is also careful. It told its employees not to share secret company info with chatbots. This shows that, although AI can do a lot, companies must also be careful.

These examples show us that AI can do many things that help improve businesses. But companies also know they need to be safe using AI. As we see AI getting better, we can also expect companies to use it in more innovative ways. This is not just for people in the tech industry. It's for anyone who shops, reads the news, or does business. AI is becoming a tool that companies use to get better at what they do.

2

Mastering the Art of Prompting

Discover the art of crafting effective AI prompts to produce high-quality content.

Find out which AI writing tools you should choose for your particular use case.

Gain insights into using AI to improve your content, marketing campaigns, and overall content strategy.

Delve into the world of visual exploration through AI and see how to spark creativity and streamline design processes.

Discover how AI can boost your ability as a creator to enhance your portfolio and stand out among your competitors.

Chapter **4**

Creating and Writing Successful AI Prompts

Since OpenAI introduced ChatGPT in November 2022, the popularity of AI has grown exponentially. Other AI tools and start-ups quickly followed. In a short time, AI has become an integral tool for both industries and individuals. It's a transformative force that has redefined the boundaries of creativity and efficiency.

Crafting effective AI prompts is both an art and a science. Effective prompts are the key to unlocking the value of AI content. They provide the instructions that guide AI systems to produce customized, high-quality content to meet your needs. This chapter looks at the elements you can use to create great prompts. We also examine best-prompting practices and see the benefits of developing prompt craftmanship.

Discovering the Importance of Prompts

Constructing high-quality prompts is the key to harnessing the power of AI. A well-crafted prompt is the blueprint that directs the AI to answer your requests. But it's not just about instructing the AI; it's about engaging in a dialogue that leads to the answers you want.

AI systems lack real-world knowledge. They're trained on large models, so prompts have to supply the relevant context to produce the right responses. The more targeted the details you provide on intent, audience, data, and previous outputs, the better the AI can tailor accurate content. Whether you're creating data-driven reports, complex charts, or search engine optimization (SEO)–friendly articles, the right prompt makes the difference between unusable and good output.

Maximizing the Benefits of Your AI Prompts

Sharpening your prompt-writing skills will pay you big dividends. Investing in prompt craftsmanship provides a framework for tapping into AI's potential while focusing on its capabilities to get the content you need.

Iterative prompting always produces the best results. Becoming a "master prompter" doesn't happen overnight. You get better over time. Some patience and the desire to improve will help you advance your skills.

In the following sections, we look at several benefits you can derive from enhancing your prompting skills.

Boosting productivity

Today's workplaces demand productivity. Everyone needs to produce more in less time and often with fewer resources. Thankfully, AI prompt craftsmanship can deliver game-changing productivity. Integrating AI capabilities into your workflow will help you achieve more in less time.

Because the adoption of AI tools is so new, do we have any clues about how they affect worker productivity? An early study in 2023 by the Nielsen Norman Group, a leader in research-based user experience, found that using generative AI prompting tools improved business users' performance by 66 percent, averaged across three case studies (www.nngroup.com/articles/ai-tools-productivity-gains).

The studies were conducted using ChatGPT 3.5. so the Nielsen Norman Group speculates that the gains may be even more significant with ChatGPT 4. It also found that less-skilled workers benefit from using AI the most, which points toward future productivity increases in the workplace.

Using prompting tools like OpenAI's ChatGPT (https://chat.openai.com) or Anthropic's Claude (www.anthropic.com/product) allows you to delegate more tedious tasks to the AI while you maximize its creative potential. You can quickly generate endless customized content variations, data insights, and design iterations that would previously take humans many days to weeks.

TIP

For more information about using tools like these, turn to Chapter 3.

Enhancing creativity

Crafting creative prompts helps you exercise your imagination. In turn, the prompts "activate" the AI's creativity, allowing the AI to generate new and better ideas faster. Here are some things to consider when you want to construct a creative prompt:

» **Use open-ended prompts.** Open-ended prompts allow for more creative freedom. Constrained prompts limit imagination. When you leave room for out-of-the-box thinking, it fosters AI creativity.

» **Ask for new ideas.** Encouraging novelty pushes the AI to generate more original content as opposed to predictable answers.

» **Use different sources.** Unique inputs and examples expose the AI to various creative sources. Drawing from several genres, mediums, and cultures expands creative output.

» **Provide inspiration.** Well-crafted prompts spark creative potential by giving direction without being overly restrictive. Loose inspiration encourages creativity better than rigid instructions.

REMEMBER

Consider the following process when you begin prompting:

1. Construct your first prompt.

2. See what the AI returns.

3. Slightly modify your prompt to get a different answer.

4. Try again — tweak the wording, provide constraints, change the audience, and adjust each new prompt's elements.

5. Keep revising until you get the answer you want.

Each time you change and try again, you inch closer to the solution that meets your personalized goals.

IS IT CREATIVE?

To get some practice, we'll create a prompt using the four elements in the "Enhancing creativity" section. Here's the prompt:

> Drawing inspiration from literature, art, and global cultures, generate a groundbreaking marketing campaign that reimagines customer engagement today. Think beyond traditional methods and platforms and propose new ideas that could revolutionize the field. Include a mix of storytelling, visual elements, and interactive experiences.

Here are the elements mentioned in the previous section:

- **Is open-ended:** The prompt is broad enough to allow for creative solutions. Words and phrases like *reimagines* and *Think beyond traditional methods* encourage out-of-the-box thinking.

- **Asks for new ideas:** Using terms like *groundbreaking* and *revolutionize* pushes the AI to develop original ideas instead of sticking to tried-and-true methods.

- **Requests different sources:** By asking the AI to draw inspiration from "literature, art, and global cultures," the prompt opens the AI to consider a diverse range of creative inputs, enriching the output.

- **Provides Inspiration:** The prompt sets a general direction ("reimagines customer engagement today") without being overly prescriptive. It allows for creative freedom. It also suggests using "storytelling, visuals, and interactive experiences." This provides a loose framework for generating creativity.

TIP

For more information on prompting for writers and marketers, check out Chapter 5.

Improving collaboration

People typically think of prompting as a solitary activity, so you may be surprised to learn that collaboration enhances prompting. Business teams are finding that working together helps them create high-quality prompts that have benefits company-wide.

TIP

Here are several ways teams can work collaboratively to develop prompts:

> » **Whiteboarding sessions:** Using a physical whiteboard, team members can brainstorm and visualize ideas together. They can make use of sticky notes and drawings to organize thoughts.

- » **Virtual meeting platforms:** Teams can use virtual meeting tools that offer features like chat, Q&As, breakout rooms, and virtual whiteboards to facilitate collaboration.

- » **Digital whiteboards:** You can use online whiteboard applications for remote collaboration, where team members share and edit documents and capture ideas for future reference.

- » **Regular feedback:** Getting feedback after the meeting process and the prompts can help refine and improve them.

- » **Active involvement:** Team members can take ownership of their ideas and actively involve themselves in the discussion, which can lead to more effective prompts.

Here's how collaborating serves an organization:

- » **Organizational knowledge grows.** Collaborative prompts allow you to get feedback and creative contributions from other departments. You can build organizational knowledge by sharing prompts across teams.

- » **Interdisciplinary collaboration is made easier.** AI prompts can be customized to incorporate different professional roles. This encourages interdisciplinary collaboration. For example, health-care professionals can create case summaries by sharing information across several departments, which can improve patient care.

- » **Scalability is achieved for projects.** A well-crafted prompt in one department can serve multiple aspects of a project. For example, marketers can strategize about a product campaign, which leads to quick production of ad copy by copywriters. Sales departments can then use that copy to produce website sales strategies, which are then brought to life by designers.

- » **Decision-making is enhanced.** While AI's popularity grows, human input remains necessary for ethical decision-making. A good prompt helps put decision-making in the hands of humans instead of making them rely on AI.

Mitigating risk

Paying close attention to the components of the prompts you create reduces the risk of the misuse of AI by providing guardrails for the output. Prompters can minimize risk by considering how they frame their prompts.

WARNING

Overly open-ended requests could lead your prompt in the wrong direction. Well-defined prompts narrow the instructions to reduce any unwanted consequences. If you're unsure about a particular direction, start with a narrow prompt and slowly expand the scope as you address the risks.

Fostering career advancement

When you become proficient in prompting, you're future-proofing your skills. Proficiency in AI prompting opens doors to roles like AI prompt engineer. These jobs have high salaries, and the skills don't apply just to one sector — you can extend them to many fields, including marketing, health care, and finance.

TIP

Check out Part 4 for more detailed information on capitalizing on your AI skills to enhance your career.

Creating a competitive edge for your business

As AI tools are adopted, crafting effective prompts will give you a competitive advantage. Here are some tangible areas where the right prompts give you the necessary information you need to succeed:

» **Market trends:** Quickly analyze market conditions and trends with data-driven prompts.

» **Insights:** Gain customer insights faster through prompts customized to your audience.

» **Messaging:** Craft more powerful marketing messages and creatives using prompts.

» **Testing:** Prototype and test ideas rapidly using prompt-guided AI ideation.

» **Research:** Reduce time spent on research and analysis by prompting subject matter summaries.

» **Forecasting:** Access prompt-directed forecasting to achieve improved planning.

» **Ethics:** Mitigate risks of AI misuse through ethics-focused prompts.

REMEMBER

Effective prompts can streamline business processes by automating tasks like customer service, data analysis, and content creation, making operations more cost-effective.

Examining Different Types of Prompts

There are several different types of prompts that you can use depending on your use case. Table 4-1 categorizes AI prompts, which will help you understand which type to use for various tasks.

TABLE 4-1 **Types of Prompts and Their Uses**

Type of Prompt	Description	Example	Why It Works	Typical Use Cases
Open-ended	Produces creative responses	"How can we innovate our product line?"	Encourages brainstorming and new ideas	Product development, content creation
Closed-ended	Creates specific, often yes-or-no answers	"Is the quarterly revenue above our target?"	Quick and straightforward; suitable for data gathering	Financial reporting, data analysis
Leading	Produces a specific viewpoint	"List the advantages of our new marketing strategy."	Directs the focus toward a desired outcome	Marketing analysis, persuasive copy
Contextual	Creates a role for the AI to assume or provides background information to set the context	"As a customer service rep, how would you handle this issue?"	Adds depth and specificity to the response	Customer service training, professional advice
Instructional	Task-oriented, performs a specific action	"Generate a list of potential leads from the database."	Clear and actionable; serves a specific purpose	Sales operations, task automation
Conditional	Based on a condition; often used for decision-making	"If the stock price drops, what's our contingency plan?"	Allows for nuanced, situation-dependent answers	Risk management, if-then logic
Exploratory	Explores a topic in depth	"Analyze the long-term impact of remote work on our business."	Facilitates a comprehensive understanding	Strategic planning, research

Reviewing the Elements of a Good Prompt

Some people liken creating prompts to putting together a recipe. You need the right ingredients to get a great-tasting dish. Here are the ingredients you can include to create an effective prompt:

>> Giving the AI a role or persona

>> Delineating boundaries and level of detail

>> Providing audience demographics

>> Supplying facts or pertinent research

>> Detailing the output format

>> Defining the tone

The following sections explain these essential elements and provide examples of effective prompts in more detail so you can apply them.

Defining the AI assistant's role or persona

Defining the role you want the AI to play provides an essential framework that helps focus the response. AI systems don't have true subject matter expertise. Assigning a persona lets the AI role-play knowledge based on its training models.

You can simulate role-playing by naming a specific person, celebrity, fictional character, or other well-known authority figure you want the AI to emulate — for example, "Respond as if you are marketer Seth Godin providing advice on permission marketing" or "Answer in the narrative style of Malcolm Gladwell." You can also assign broader archetypes and vocations like teacher, artist, marketing expert, or designer.

TIP

When defining a role, make sure it fits the use case. For example, if you want factual accuracy, roles like professor, librarian, strategist, or subject matter expert may get you the responses you're looking for. For creative applications, roles like poet, artist, or visionary can get you more imaginative answers.

You can also assist the AI further by using role-relevant details like mentioning the person's previous works, accomplishments, style, voice, and typical viewpoints. For example, if the persona is an author, you may include the titles of their books and awards they have won.

THE ANATOMY OF A PERSONA PROMPT

To further explain how to construct a persona prompt, here's an example that assigns a specific persona role to the AI:

> For the following prompt, adopt the persona of a travel assistant named Alex. Alex is knowledgeable, friendly, and eager to provide clear directions to travelers. Alex stays calm under pressure and maintains a professional demeanor. Please respond to the subsequent request consistent with Alex's persona.

Why is this an effective way to define the role or persona for your prompt? Because it does the following:

- Establishes a defined personality for the AI assistant to emulate (in this case, a helpful travel guide named Alex)
- Gives the persona a name for further definition
- Provides relevant background (Alex is a travel assistant)
- Defines Alex's personality traits (knowledgeable, friendly, and calm)
- Defines the tone (established, professional, clear)
- Gives context (providing directions to travelers)
- Instructs the AI to respond to the prompt in the defined persona's voice

Explaining the persona prompts the AI by setting expectations for knowledge level, demeanor, tone of voice, and other characteristics shaping its response. This prompt helps the AI assistant respond in a contextualized, personal manner.

Specifying the level of detail and boundaries

It's essential to tell the AI how brief, long, or detailed you want the response to be. This information will help match the output to your required answer. An example of part of a prompt could be, "Summarize the key points in this article in 250 words."

If you want to get more in-depth output, write, "Provide an in-depth analysis with several examples." It's important to help the AI gauge the sophistication level of the request.

REMEMBER

Don't use long sentences to describe what you want when constructing prompts. Long sentences can dilute or confuse the AI's focus.

Outlining audience demographics

Providing details about your target audience helps the AI customize its response to your needs. So, you may wonder how specific you should get when supplying demographic data. Specifying particular audience details lets the AI adjust its language, tone, examples, and messaging to fit your specific group.

For example, when starting your prompt, identify a few key descriptors that are most relevant to your content goals. These could include

>> Age or age range

>> Gender

>> Location/region

>> Industry/occupation

>> Background knowledge level

>> Primary interests related to product/content topic

You can always expand your information to provide additional accuracy, but start with the most important identifiers.

WARNING

Using too little demographic context risks getting generic AI output. But including too many audience details may lead to unintentional and inappropriate stereotyping. Avoid demographic information that could possibly feed into harmful assumptions. For example, using the term *retirees* instead of *the elderly* avoids a negative age bias. Focus on keeping your language constructive and inclusive.

Make sure to test demographics-enhanced prompts to avoid inadvertent bias. Refine the prompt over time to hone it. You could miss bias until you see the actual AI response.

Providing facts and research

It's vital for you to provide relevant research, data, links, or information to inform the AI's response. Just as you would give a human assistant the information necessary to do the job, you should provide your AI assistant with the information needed. You can directly input copies of research and articles into the AI to help focus your response.

Describing the output format

Describing the output format can go a long way toward giving you the answer in the form you need. Instead of manually formatting something, have the AI do it for you. Some format dimensions you can include are

>> **Type:** Text, audio, images, video

>> **Structure:** Bulleted list, narrative, Q&A, slide deck

>> **Visual components:** Charts, illustrations, data visualizations, Mind Maps

>> **File type:** PDF, DOCX, JPG, MP3

TECHNICAL STUFF

The concept of Mind Maps was created by English educator and author Tony Buzan. Mind Maps visually show the details and the big picture of a set of concepts on one page. They help users figure out the scope of their thinking about a topic.

Unlike audience details, it's hard to over-define output formats given AI's limitations in knowing how the output should be constructed. An example might include, "Give me a chart with three columns that detail an onboarding plan. It should include the role, the method, and the timeframe." Figure 4-1 shows the chart that ChatGPT 4 constructed from this prompt.

ChatGPT Plugins ˅

You
User
Give me a chart with three columns that details our onboarding plan. It should include the role, the method, and the timeframe

ChatGPT
Certainly! Here's a structured chart for our onboarding plan, laid out in three columns: Role, Method, and Timeframe.

Role	Method	Timeframe
Employee	Orientation Sessions	Week 1: Introduction and Orientation
	One-on-One Meetings	Week 2-3: Role-Specific Training
		Week 4: Integration and Feedback
Manager	Orientation Sessions	Week 1: Introduction and Orientation
	Managerial Training Sessions	Week 2-3: Leadership and Strategy
	Performance Evaluation Training	Week 4: Integration and Feedback
IT Support	Technology Setup and Training	Week 1: Introduction and Orientation
	System-Specific Training	Week 2-3: Role-Specific Training
	Security Protocols Briefing	Week 4: Integration and Feedback

This chart provides a comprehensive overview of the onboarding process, outlining the specific methods and timeframes for each role within the organization.

Message ChatGPT...

ChatGPT can make mistakes. Consider checking important information.

FIGURE 4-1: Output from ChatGPT 4 when requesting a chart.

Defining the tone

The tone you use in an AI prompt can directly impact the response's quality. Striking the right tone requires you to focus on the context and intent of the prompt. For most business use cases, try to ensure the prompt has a neutral tone without adding emotional language.

Maintaining an even, professional tone in business communications will likely produce the right situational response. But descriptive or emotional wording may be better if you work on unique marketing copy or creative writing. The tone should always reflect your brand values and the content your audience responds to.

TIP

Anna Bernstein is a prompt engineer at Copy.ai (www.copy.ai), a generative AI tool. She creates prompts that train Copy.ai to produce quality output. In an article in *Business Insider* (www.businessinsider.com/how-to-write-better-ai-chatgpt-prompts-according-prompt-engineer-2023-3), she provides the following advice on how you can elevate your prompting skills:

>> **Use a thesaurus.** Getting the right word can make the difference between getting a generic output and a good response. Explore using a thesaurus to use just the right word.

>> **Pay attention to your verbs.** Verbs help the AI understand your intent. Be clear about exactly what you want.

>> **ChatGPT is great at recognizing intent, so state that up front.** Tell the AI what you want to do (for example, "We're going to create a 300-word article").

Looking at Quick Prompting Techniques

When constructing prompts, you should consider your objective. We've examined various elements contributing to a good prompt. Taking the time to develop a well-structured prompt delivers several significant benefits. But sometimes you just need a quick way to get answers. For this purpose, you can turn to techniques like zero-shot and one-shot prompting.

Zero-shot prompting

Zero-shot prompting lets you provide the AI with a single stand-alone prompt (without any prior examples or training) to receive a successful response. This method allows prompting the AI on the fly on new topics or tasks. It relies on AI's underlying language model to interpret prompts.

When using zero-shot prompting, you should

>> Start simple.

>> Use clear, unambiguous language.

>> Define constraints because you aren't guiding the AI with examples.

Here are some examples of zero-shot prompting:

>> "What is the capital of Spain?"

>> "Write a 100-word fiction story about dogs in outer space."

Notice that these prompts rely on the AI already having the knowledge based on its previous training.

Here is an example of a zero-shot prompt in ChatGPT: "Summarize the plot of The Old Man and the Sea by Ernest Hemingway in two sentences." The response is shown in Figure 4-2.

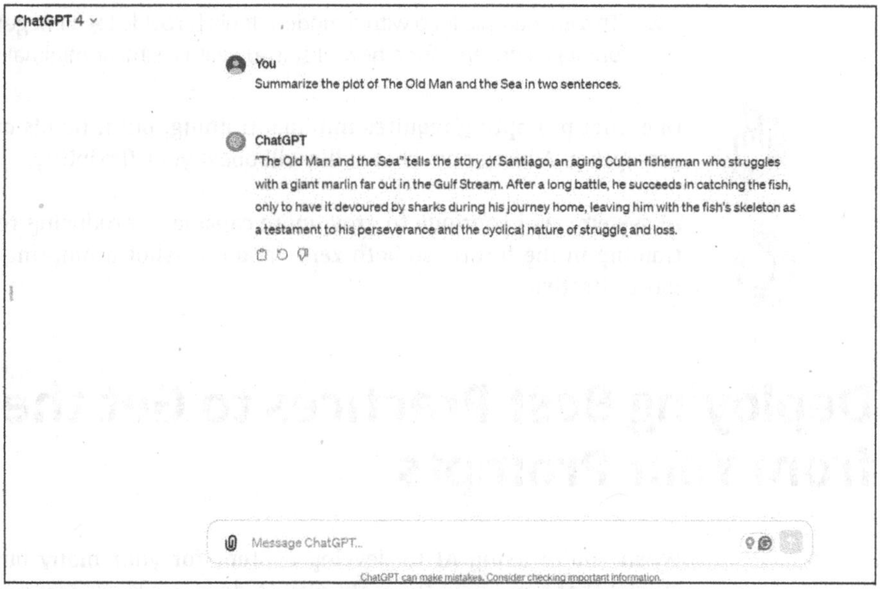

ChatGPT 4 ˅

You
Summarize the plot of The Old Man and the Sea in two sentences.

ChatGPT
"The Old Man and the Sea" tells the story of Santiago, an aging Cuban fisherman who struggles with a giant marlin far out in the Gulf Stream. After a long battle, he succeeds in catching the fish, only to have it devoured by sharks during his journey home, leaving him with the fish's skeleton as a testament to his perseverance and the cyclical nature of struggle and loss.

Message ChatGPT...

ChatGPT can make mistakes. Consider checking important information.

FIGURE 4-2:
An example of a zero-shot prompt in ChatGPT.

By the way, editor wants us to tell you that *The Old Man and the Sea* is a novella, so the title should be italicized. However, you can't use italics in ChatGPT prompts, so we haven't done so here. (She's probably losing sleep over this.)

TECHNICAL STUFF

One-shot prompting

One-shot prompting involves showing the AI a single example to "prime" it before providing your actual prompt. This gives the AI the baseline knowledge it needs to tackle a new type of request.

When using one-shot prompting, ensure the sample clearly demonstrates your expected output:

>> Keep the sample concise.

>> After providing the sample, clearly detail prompt objectives.

>> Provide additional context alongside the sample if needed.

>> Determine whether a second sample will improve results.

Here are some examples of one-shot prompts:

>> "Here is an excerpt of a sample earnings report providing important financial details: [provide the excerpt]. Now compose a full second-quarter earnings report in the same format for the XY Corporation using the data provided."

>> "This is a sample logo with a modern look: [provide logo image]. Now, create four logo concepts for a new AI start-up with a similar minimalist style."

REMEMBER

One-shot prompting requires minimal training, but it builds on using zero-shot prompting. Adding one-shot skills will boost your flexibility.

TIP

AI systems will continue to grow more capable of producing responses with less training in the future, so both zero- and one-shot prompting will become even more effective.

Deploying Best Practices to Get the Most from Your Prompts

When you're using AI to develop content for your many business needs, it's crucial that you know the right way to do it. Here are some best practices that can serve as a road map for creating high-quality prompts:

>> **Define specific objectives.** Before you start crafting your prompt, you need to know the result you're aiming for. Consider the specific intent and purpose

of each prompt. For example, think about the business goals you want to reach. Do you want to increase sales, improve customer engagement, or enhance brand awareness?

Determine the measures and key performance indicators (KPIs) you will use to measure success. This could be click-through rates, conversion rates, or user engagement metrics. Being clear when you begin ensures that your prompts won't produce generic output.

>> **Use clear language.** Use clear, straightforward language in your prompts to ensure the AI understands you accurately. Avoid vague or abstract instructions. Be concise, but provide enough context to get your point across. Careful word selection helps you get more relevant responses from the AI.

Your AI assistant is not a human. If you want to include conventions like *please* and *thank you*, you can, but it's unnecessary. The AI wants instructions it can understand. Politeness is up to you.

>> **Provide context.** Prompts require enough background context to provide a framework for the answer. Provide enough information about your business, goals, audience, and any source materials you have that are relevant. This will help the AI generate highly customized content for your specific situation.

>> **Build and maximize templates.** Templates can speed up the prompt creation process and provide consistency. Consider using ones tailored to different outputs, such as email copy, landing pages, or social media posts. To enhance efficiency and personalization, design these templates with interchangeable elements for easy personalization.

For more about the use of templates, turn to Chapter 5.

>> **Test iteratively.** Treat your initial prompts as a starting point and continuously refine them using real-world testing and analysis. Evaluate prompt performance based on your predefined measures and metrics. Adjust the wording based on content relevance, quality, and actionability.

Prompt mastery requires persistence. Testing iteratively is a fundamental part of successful prompting. Small changes can lead to significant improvements over time.

>> **Work collaboratively.** In work settings, crafting prompts can be viewed as a team sport. Collaborating with team members, stakeholders, and customers will help you get different viewpoints and uncover blind spots.

>> **Document your prompts.** Maintain thorough documentation of your prompts for future reference. This includes metrics, business goals, audience specifics, and context. This will allow you to build up organizational knowledge (if relevant) for reference and reuse.

>> **Consider ethical constraints.** Always keep an eye on how you frame your prompts to avoid introducing biases or potentially harmful content. Ethical constraints are recommendations and essential guidelines ensuring your AI prompts are responsible and effective.

TIP

Make sure to err on the side of common sense. Prompts should always adhere to your brand's values.

>> **Keep up with advances.** You need to stay current with the latest developments in AI tools. AI is in its infancy, and the field is rapidly evolving. Your prompting skills will need to evolve with new developments.

>> **Understand AI's limitations.** AI technology clearly has limitations. For example, it can get things very wrong (referred to as *hallucinations*) or simply misinterpret your prompt. No prompt is foolproof. Be aware that the AI may generate incorrect or nonsensical responses, and be prepared to revise and refine.

REMEMBER

Don't try to replace human evaluation and creativity with AI. AI is a powerful tool that you can use, but *you* are in charge.

WHAT NOT TO DO

When it comes to crafting prompts for AI, the stakes can often be high. Poorly constructed prompts lead to confusion, wasted time, and bad business decisions. Here are some common mistakes you should avoid:

- **Being too vague:** Are you asking the AI for a response without providing enough context or detail? For example, "What is AI about?" Instead, you need to be specific about what you're looking for. A better prompt would be, "Summarize the key trends in AI marketing for 2023."

- **Assuming that one prompt fits all:** Continually refining your prompt is a crucial part of the prompting process. Expecting to get the response you want on the first try is unrealistic.

- **Overcomplicating the prompt:** Are you making the prompt too complex or filled with jargon? For example, "Provide an overview of consumer behavior paradigms in Q4." Instead, start with a prompt that includes, "Summarize consumer behavior trends in Q4."

- **Ignoring the audience:** Have you described the target audience? For example, it's not sufficient to say, "Write an article about climate change." You need to tailor the prompt to the audience you want to reach. Start with, "Write an introductory article about climate change for high school students taking a class about environmental change."

- **Neglecting the output format:** Do you fail to specify how you want the information presented? For example, "Give me stats on renewable energy" doesn't give the AI any idea about how to return the answer. Instead, you should specify the format, such as, "List the top five renewable energy sources by market share in bullet points."

- **Overlooking ethical considerations:** Are you crafting prompts that may lead to biased or harmful outputs? For example: "Explain why our product is the best in the world." Obviously, this will produce a biased response. Instead, start with, "Compare our product's features to our leading competitors." This prompt will return a more balanced approach.

- **Failing to iterate:** Do you assume the first prompt will give you the perfect answer? Crafting prompts is an iterative process. Test several different versions and refine them based on the outputs you get.

Looking at GPT Plugins and Custom GPTs

After the release of OpenAI's ChatGPT, developers began to extend functionality and focus on a specific topic by creating third-party plugins and custom GPTs. These are AI tools that extend the capabilities of OpenAI's ChatGPT, but they're different in their creation and use.

GPT plugins are like apps that add extra features to ChatGPT. They give ChatGPT access to real-time information on the web and specific pieces of functionality like booking flights, creating graphic designs, or summarizing documents.

TIP

You need a premium ChatGPT subscription to access plugins. To locate them, go to the ChatGPT interface and look for a menu labeled "Plugins," "Extensions," or "Add-ons." This could be in a sidebar, a settings menu, or a dedicated section of the interface. (The exact steps are different, depending on the specific platform or version of ChatGPT you're using.)

At the time of this writing, some examples of available plugins include:

>> **Ask Your PDF:** Helps you get information from PDFs

>> **Diagrams:** Helps you create and show diagrams

>> **Link Reader:** Reads and summarizes web links

LAUNCHING THE GPT STORE

In January 2024, OpenAI opened its GPT store (https://chat.openai.com/gpts), a marketplace for people to submit their custom GPTs. You need a premium ChatGPT subscription to access the GPT Store. If you have a premium subscription, you'll see the Explore menu choice on the left-hand side. Click that, and you'll see lots of options.

At the time of this writing, you'll find categories including writing, productivity, research and analysis, and programming. To use the custom chat, you simply need to click the one you want, and it will load in your ChatGPT workspace. You can then type in your query or use one of the suggested prompts.

Continue to explore as more custom GPTs becomes available. You may find one that is customized to your exact needs.

Custom GPTs are stand-alone versions of ChatGPT that people have personalized to focus on specific knowledge or a narrow topic. To create a custom GPT, you don't need to know how to code, but you can only use one custom GPT at a time. You can give a custom GPT special instructions and styles. You can also make custom GPTs to share with others on the GPT marketplace (see the nearby sidebar).

TIP

Are you undecided about whether to use plugins or custom GPTs? Here are some issues to consider:

- » **Your specific needs:** If you need ChatGPT to perform a wide range of tasks using external internet data, plugins may be better. If you need a GPT for a specific, specialized task, a custom GPT could be more appropriate.

- » **Technical skills:** If you want to create one of your own chats and you're comfortable with coding, you may opt for a plugin. If not, custom GPTs are easier to create.

- » **Desire for sharing and community:** You can share custom GPTs with others, and there's a community for support and resources.

- » **Ease of use:** Custom GPTs are easier to use because of the no-code creation process.

- » **Cost:** Be aware that the GPT store plans to allow people to sell their GPTs, so cost may become a factor.

- » **Functionality:** Chat plugins offer more functionality by connecting to external services (like booking sites and restaurant reservations).

Chapter **5**

AI Content Generation for Writers and Marketers

The age of AI is here. 2023 marked an inflection point when AI moved from an experimental technology to a mainstream tool for writers and marketers. AI content tools have limitations, but their ability to instantly produce enormous amounts of fresh copy and other forms of content is undeniable. For this reason, it's essential to understand how to leverage this technology in a competitive marketplace.

This chapter looks at the role AI tools play in content creation in a business environment. We also look at the specific tools you can use to develop and optimize marketing copy and social media content.

Introducing AI Writing Tools

Today's complex businesses require a vast amount of content. You need the ability to produce well-crafted content, whether you're creating marketing copy, generating reports, or simply drafting emails. But the increasingly high demand for quality content requires more bandwidth than is available to most business writers and marketers.

Enter AI writing assistants, advanced software programs powered by AI and machine learning (ML) algorithms. They can assist in developing content drafts, enhancing web pages for search engine optimization (SEO), adapting to various writing styles, and suggesting unique creative ideas. They can also analyze large data sets to inform creative decisions. (To learn more about ML algorithms, turn to Chapter 1.)

REMEMBER

AI writing assistants are revolutionizing how businesses approach the creative process. Think of it as an extra business team member who never complains or takes a break! The AI supplies the raw material to fuel new ideas and experimentation. Writers and marketers can use the expanded bandwidth to evaluate variations and content formats.

Several types of AI writing assistants can do a range of things, from proofreading to crafting original text. Consider the three categories of AI writing assistants shown in Table 5-1 — you can choose from these tools to make your content creation easier.

TABLE 5-1   **Categories of AI Writing Assistant Tools**

Type of Tool	Description	Example Tools	AI Capabilities
Content generators	Generates unique content in response to prompts	ChatGPT, Claude, Copy.ai, Jasper	Uses large language models (LLMs) — AI systems designed to understand human language — to generate text
Grammar/spell checkers	Scans text and suggests grammar, spelling, and punctuation corrections to improve readability	Grammarly, ProWritingAid, Writer.com	Uses natural language processing (NLP) to find errors (see Chapter 1 for more on NLP)
Autocomplete/ predictive writing	Suggests/autocompletes words and sentences as you type based on the context	TypeGenie, Wordtune, Writesonic	Uses ML text prediction models

TIP

Another category of AI tools is chat browsers such as Microsoft's Bing (www.bing.com) and Google's Gemini (https://gemini.google.com). They aren't considered writing assistants but are designed as chatbots for natural language conversations. They use LLMs for dialog. Check out Chapter 3 for more about chat browsers.

In the following sections, we look at each AI assistant category in more detail and suggest tools to try.

Choosing the Right AI Writing Assistants for Your Use Case

The marketplace has exploded with AI tools for every conceivable use case. You can use one or two tools to do everything, but you'd be cheating yourself. You can be more productive and effective if you choose the tools created for the specific task at hand.

You get several benefits from using the right AI writing assistants to enhance your creativity and writing output:

>> **Never starting with a blank screen:** The AI writing assistant can create initial drafts of stories, articles, and ads that help you gain momentum and beat writer's block.

>> **Uncovering different ways to present content:** You can experiment with different voices, literary styles, and genres by providing AI with writing samples to learn from. The best way to accomplish this is to use very different samples from your usual writing style.

>> **Making new connections:** Use the AI's creative associations and perspectives to allow the sparking of unique storylines and characters.

>> **Producing out-of-the-box thinking:** When you impose specific limitations in your prompt, like designating the structure or number of words, your prompt will deliver more creative responses.

The following sections look at specific tools for particular use cases. Consider them the tip of the iceberg. New AI writing assistants are coming online every day.

Drafting original content

Leveraging AI writing assistants lets writers and marketers tap into a massive database of information and insights that would be impossible to access manually. These assistants can scan millions of articles, blogs, and images to gather relevant data on a given topic.

AI writing assistants allow for quick drafting of versions of blogs, emails, social posts, and more from scratch. When you provide your chosen keywords, target audience, and other guidelines, the AI will generate fresh content tailored to your specific needs.

TIP

To learn more about the specific elements you should put in your prompts to extract the best responses, check out Chapter 4.

Here are some tools to consider:

» **Jasper** (`www.jasper.ai`): Jasper, as shown in Figure 5-1, is a popular AI app that can generate long- and short-form copy, with templates for creating specialized marketing articles. It has three paid tiers.

» **Copy.ai** (`www.copy.ai`): Copy.ai, shown in Figure 5-2, is an AI writing assistant that automates content creation across various formats. It offers templates for quick text generation, social media posts, and blog articles. It has a free version and tiered paid versions.

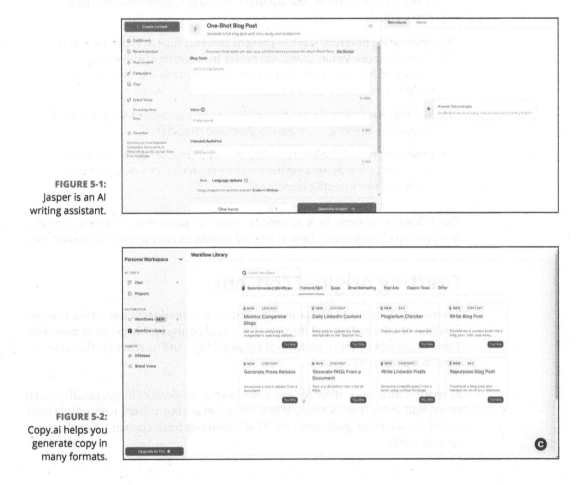

FIGURE 5-1:
Jasper is an AI writing assistant.

FIGURE 5-2:
Copy.ai helps you generate copy in many formats.

TIP

We look at how to prompt these tools for social media content in the "Prompting for Social Media Content" section later in this chapter.

Brainstorming ideas

Brainstorming is a crucial part of the creative process for writers and marketers. The good news is that these AI tools allow you to generate ideas, explore different angles, and find unique solutions to problems. You benefit from AI's ability to deliver different perspectives by providing many ideas to work with.

Traditionally, brainstorming sessions involved people meeting to share thoughts and bounce ideas off each other. Now, AI can do some of the work for you. AI writing assistants can refine ideas and take brainstorming to a new level by offering *real-time* feedback. This iterative process allows for continuing improvement.

REMEMBER

AI writing assistants serve as a source of inspiration. They can provide unique examples when creating content or developing campaigns. This not only saves time but can also elevate the quality of the work. The AI algorithms can understand language patterns, analyze data, and provide relevant suggestions.

TIP

Are you stuck finding a writing topic or headline? You can prompt the AI to offer creative direction and recommendations. The AI is valuable because it can combine concepts in unexpected ways and use large data sets to discover unusual perspectives. The AI allows you to quickly generate many more draft variations, angles, headlines, and themes and offers unique recommendations and angles you may not have considered.

One very new and useful way to use AI for generating ideas is to create mind maps and other visual depictions of your ideas. Previously, you had to draft every piece of your maps and charts one at a time. Now you can get it done for you. Here are some tools to consider:

>> **Ayoa** (https://ayoa.com): Ayoa, shown in Figure 5-3, is a multifunctional software app that creates mind maps and more and helps boost your creativity. The Ayoa Ultimate version includes AI in its mind-mapping tool. (There are two fee tiers and a free version.) After you create a map using AI, you can modify it or add AI-driven ideas, questions, explanations, or notes from a pull-out menu.

>> **Whimsical** (https://whimsical.com): Whimsical is a visual workspace that lets you create flowcharts, mind maps, and more. It's a stand-alone product with free and paid versions, as well as a plugin for the subscription version of ChatGPT 4. After you install the Whimsical plugin, you can request a mind map or diagram in your prompt.

Here is an example prompt:

- As an AI expert, tell me about choosing names for a marketing campaign and create a mind map for it.

Figure 5-4 displays the mind map you requested.

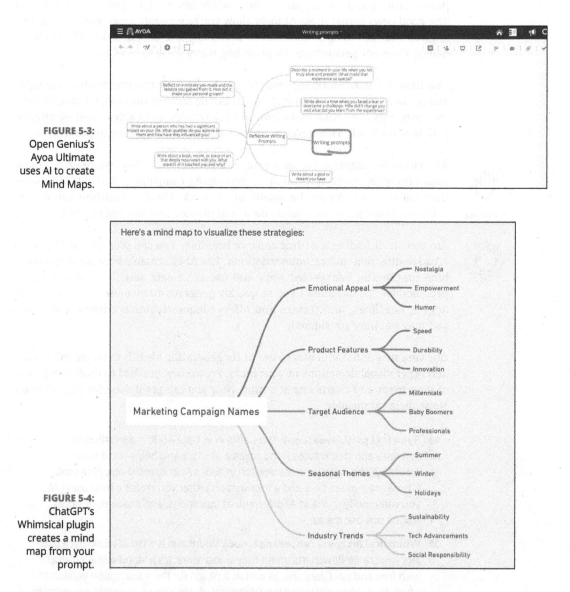

FIGURE 5-3:
Open Genius's
Ayoa Ultimate
uses AI to create
Mind Maps.

FIGURE 5-4:
ChatGPT's
Whimsical plugin
creates a mind
map from your
prompt.

Continue to iterate the prompt until you get the map created precisely in the format you want.

For more about using ChatGPT plugins, see Chapter 4.

Although AI content tools have already reached a point where they can provide productivity gains for writers and marketers, human intervention is still necessary to produce quality output. The ideal approach combines AI's creative abilities with human guidance.

Examining Research Tools

Using AI tools for online research is a game changer. They can digest vast amounts of information faster than any human. The AI compiles, analyzes, and summarizes research from the internet and discovers insights we could never find on our own. You can use it for something as mundane as searching web articles for a blog post or as exciting as analyzing medical research to find new health-care treatments.

Conducting research faster

For writers and marketers, specialized tools for analyzing web content and PDFs are particularly helpful. Consider the following:

>> **Frase (www.frase.io):** Frase is an AI tool designed to optimize discovery and analyze web content, as shown in Figure 5-5. It's great for SEO and analyzing competitors' content. It has paid plans and add-ons.

>> **Claude (https://claude.ai):** Claude, shown in Figure 5-6, is a popular AI assistant developed by Anthropic. It can do things like analyze text and answer questions. It helps summarize PDFs and turn them into interactive content. It has a free version and a paid version.

Are you searching for perfect statistics? Your AI companion can quickly find them on the web. Just remember to double-check each statistic to ensure that it's correct. Some AI apps have been known to hallucinate at times.

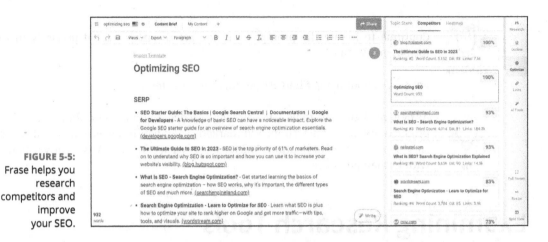

FIGURE 5-5:
Frase helps you
research
competitors and
improve
your SEO.

FIGURE 5-5:
Frase helps you
research
competitors and
improve
your SEO.

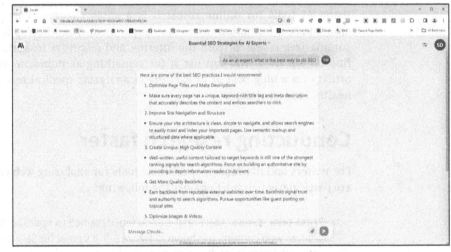

FIGURE 5-6:
Claude is a
powerful AI
assistant that
rivals ChatGPT.

Summarizing large amounts of information

One of the great uses of AI tools is to "read" content to distill books, reports, articles, or other long-form content into overviews or highlights. They can extract themes, insights, and recommendations and present only the most relevant information. This saves you enormous time and lets you create snackable versions (digests) for social media. Tools to consider include:

>> **genei** (www.genei.io): genei is an app that helps you quickly read and summarize articles or documents. It uses AI to highlight key points and organize information. It's good for those looking to save time doing research. It has a 14-day trial and paid-tiered versions.

> » **Resoomer** (`https://resoomer.com/en`): Resoomer is an online summarization tool powered by AI. It extracts the most important sentences and presents a summary. It supports summarizing text in multiple languages and has a free version and a pro version.

The AI can compile meeting notes, convert bullet points into posts, and more. Automating these "time sinks" allows you to step into strategy roles.

Improving Your Writing with AI Assistants

Most writers understand the value of a good editor. If you don't have access to a human one, AI tools can help. The AI editor can analyze your writing to improve clarity, enhance your use of language, and adjust the style. This allows writers and marketers to focus more on storytelling and messaging.

Strengthening your writing

Would you like to catch typos, misspellings, and incorrect punctuation without having to painstakingly comb through every page of your drafts? If so, you can use AI writing assistants to complete the task. Here are some tools to consider:

> » **Grammarly** (`www.grammarly.com`): Grammarly is an AI-powered writing assistant that goes beyond grammar checking. As shown in Figure 5-7, Grammarly gives you real-time suggestions for improving clarity, correcting typos, and strengthening your writing style. It also has a great plagiarism checker built in for premium versions. A free version is available.
>
> » **ProWritingAid** (`https://prowritingaid.com`): Like Grammarly, ProWritingAid, as shown in Figure 5-8, is an AI-powered writing assistant that can elevate your writing skills. It offers real-time feedback on grammar, style, and structure. There is a free version and a premium version.

Checking for plagiarism

When AI tools became available to business users in 2022, organizations and individuals alike were unsure how or whether to use the generated content. Writers and marketers wondered whether Google would approve of its use on websites and articles, and companies were unclear whether it violated copyright laws.

FIGURE 5-7:
Grammarly helps you improve your writing in real time.

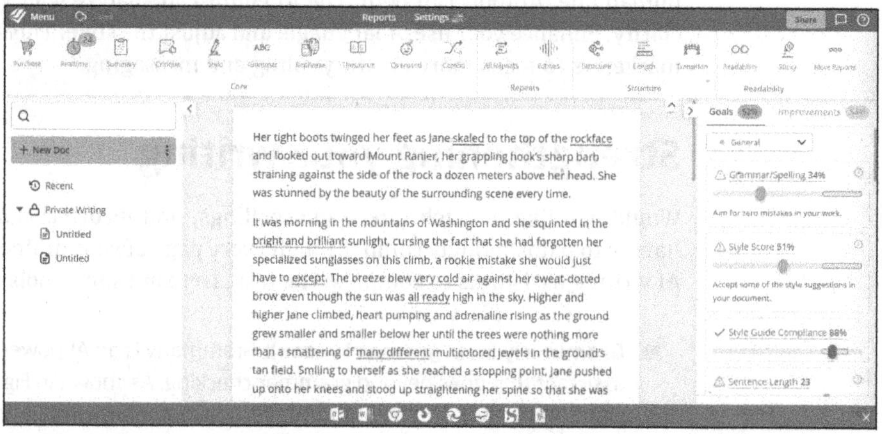

FIGURE 5-8:
ProWritingAid elevates your writing skills.

But copyright laws were not the only problem. People became aware of the fact that when generative AI (GenAI) tools produced a response, there might be a possibility of plagiarism.

To address this problem, plagiarism checkers came on the scene. These tools determine whether you are (inadvertently or knowingly) using someone else's intellectual property (IP) as your own. You can spare your reputation from being damaged by using them. Some companies have forbidden using AI tools altogether, and others have embraced them.

Here are some plagiarism checkers to consider:

>> **Writer AI Content Detector** (https://writer.com/ai-content-detector): Writer, shown in Figure 5-9, is an AI writing assistant. Its premium version has a plagiarism detector that allows you to check up to 1,500 characters.

>> **Content at Scale** (`https://contentatscale.ai/ai-content-detector`): Content at Scale, shown in Figure 5-10, is a long-form AI writing assistant. It has a free stand-alone AI plagiarism detector with a limit of 2,500 characters. The pro version of the tool is available for a subscription fee.

FIGURE 5-9: Writer offers a plagiarism detector with a 1,500-character limit.

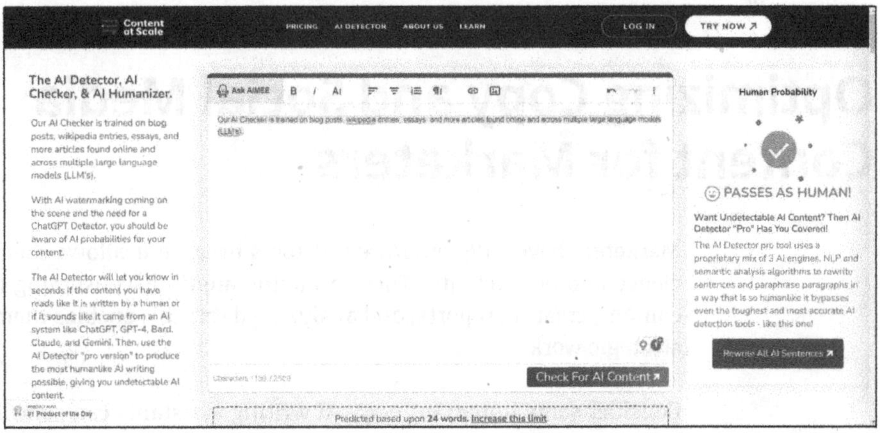

FIGURE 5-10: Content at Scale has a free stand-alone plagiarism checker.

TIP

To learn more about using AI tools responsibly, turn to Chapters 13 and 14.

AI Tools for Predictive Writing

As shown in Table 5-1, earlier in this chapter, the third category of AI writing assistants is autocomplete/predictive writers. Autocomplete tools are primarily used in search engines and text editors. The tool suggests a possible completion for the text being entered to speed up the writing and correct errors.

Here are two autocomplete tools to consider:

>> **Wordtune (www.wordtune.com):** Wordtune is an AI-powered writing assistant that enhances the quality of your content by offering real-time suggestions to rewrite your sentences for clarity. It has a free version and a paid version.

>> **QuillBot (https://quillbot.com/summarize):** QuillBot is a writing tool that helps you rephrase or improve your sentences. It uses AI to suggest different ways to say the same thing. It's useful for beginners who want to improve and vary their writing.

TIP

Coders use autocomplete tools to boost productivity and reduce errors in their code. These tools are recommended as a supplement, not a replacement for learning to code.

Optimizing Copy and Social Media Content for Marketers

Marketers have fully embraced AI tools because it allows them to increase efficiency and productivity. They can automate time-consuming tasks like drafting content, creating reports, and analyzing data. This enables them to focus on more strategic work.

Consider some important ways AI writing assistants can contribute to marketing campaigns. They can provide

>> **Better campaign optimization:** AI tools can test different ad combinations, headlines, and images to determine the best-performing ones. They can also adjust those campaigns in real time based on performance data.

>> **Personalized content and offers:** AI tools can generate customized content, product recommendations, and offers for each customer based on their unique interests and characteristics.

REMEMBER

>> **Enhanced customer insights:** Using sentiment analysis, AI tools can extract deeper insights from customer surveys, support calls, emails, and comments on social media platforms.

Sentiment analysis is an AI technology used to determine if the text expresses a positive, negative, or neutral attitude. It automates the understanding of emotions and opinions from online content.

>> **More accurate customer segmentation:** AI tools can analyze huge amounts of customer data to identify common attributes, interests, and behaviors. This allows for more precise customer segmentation and targeting.

TIP

AI writing assistants can provide real-time feedback on the feasibility of different campaign concepts. They can analyze audience engagement metrics, predict user responses based on historical data, and offer suggestions for improvement. This helps writers and marketers refine their campaigns before launching them.

Repurposing Podcasts

Creating fresh, engaging content for today's online platforms can be challenging. Repurposing existing content into new formats can help you maximize your efforts. The versatility of AI writing assistants makes repurposing one piece of content into multiple formats, variants, and snippets for different channels or audiences very simple. You can multiply your output if you adapt what you already have.

TIP

The key to repurposing is identifying the right opportunities to transform your existing content. For example, you can use summarization AI tools to turn a comprehensive industry report into a two-minute overview for LinkedIn or create a one-paragraph summary from a long blog post for X.

Podcasts are a great source of content to repurpose. Audio transcription apps like Otter.ai (https://otter.ai) or Fireflies.ai (https://fireflies.ai) generate text transcripts from audio files or streams. This allows you to repurpose recorded audio into written text content. For example, you can

>> Transcribe your podcast episodes or live talk into quotes and takeaways

>> Turn recorded customer interviews into blog posts with key insights

>> Generate a knowledge base using recorded company training sessions

>> Take a previously high-performing piece and turn it into a new format, like turning a podcast into an article for your website

At a loss for words? Text expansion AI tools are a fun way to automate grunt work. Tools like Rytr (`https://rytr.me`) and Describely (`https://describely.ai`) take small content fragments and expand them into long-form content. For example, you can enter a headline, outline, or short prompt and generate a full article. You can use it to repurpose bullet points from a slide presentation into a blog post or turn a product description into a detailed buyer's guide.

Prompting for Social Media Content

Participating on social media platforms is a must for most brands. Your customers want to hear from you, and they want to be able to dialogue with you. Creating consistent social media content for platforms like Facebook and X (formerly Twitter) helps you showcase your brand and build relationships.

In the following sections, we look at using AI writing assistants to develop social media content quickly. For the prompts in the following sections, use the AI tool of your choice and insert the role (for example, social media marketer or professor) that makes sense for you.

As you practice using the following prompts, refer to Chapter 4 to see what other elements can be included to improve your prompt. Also, remember that iterating your prompts is mandatory to get exactly what you need.

Creating a post for X

When creating prompts for posts on X (`https://twitter.com`), you want to give the AI tool information about your target audience, goals for the post (engagement, clicks, and such), and any relevant hashtags. You primarily want to ask for catchy, attention-grabbing posts within 280 characters.

Here's an example of a prompt you may try:

You are a [role]. [Insert information about your target audience, goals for the tweet, and any other relevant hashtags.] Craft a compelling 280-character post to unveil our latest product, tailored for the 18–24 age group. Use the hashtag #newproduct and others recommended, and include a call-to-action to [website] to encourage website visits.

Writing a Facebook post

To create a Facebook post, provide the AI with background on your brand voice and ideal tone. Share key points or ideas to include. Prompt for multi-sentence posts aimed at exciting engagement through comments, reactions, and shares.

Here's an example of a prompt you may try:

> You are a [role]. [Insert background on your brand's voice and ideal tone. Share key points or ideas to include.] Craft a two- to three-sentence Facebook post in [your brand]'s laid-back tone to announce our sizzling summer collection. Include a question or call-to-action that encourages comments, reactions, and shares. Focus on getting authentic engagement by highlighting a unique feature or benefit of the collection that resonates with our target audience.

Composing a LinkedIn article

When crafting a LinkedIn article, supply relevant background information and themes for a long-form thought leadership post. Prompt the AI to write insightful, industry-focused articles in your brand's voice to educate and engage your professional audience.

Here's an example of a prompt you may try:

> You are a [role]. [Insert background information and themes.] Craft a 350-word LinkedIn article that positions [your brand] as a thought leader in the intersection of AI and medical research. Focus on this year's most impactful AI trends and provide actionable insights tailored for research scientists and operations leads.

Developing a product description for your website

To help you create a product description prompt for your website, provide product features, benefits, and target customers. Prompt for shoppable product descriptions that cater to your audience of 40- to 50-year-olds.

Here's an example of a prompt you may try:

> You are a [role]. [Insert product features, benefits, and target customers.] Compose a 150-word product description that captures the essence of [your brand]'s new luxury watch, specifically tailored for our discerning audience aged 40 to 50. Highlight the watch's premium materials and precision movement while maintaining [your brand]'s signature sophisticated tone.

Developing a newsletter subject line

Testing AI-generated subject lines helps optimize newsletter open rates. For this prompt, provide your brand tone, audience, and purpose of the email. You should prompt for compelling subject lines and body copy that engages your subscribers.

Here's an example of a prompt you may try:

> You are a [role]. [Insert your brand tone, your audience, and the purpose of the email.] Craft a captivating newsletter subject line and a two-paragraph body copy to introduce our latest training program to our existing customer base. Use [your brand]'s friendly and conversational tone to engage and resonate with our audience.

Coming up with ideas for content calendars

Preparing content calendars is necessary for marketers who want to ensure that they have a steady stream of content in the works. To prepare your prompt, you need to include your brand, audience, and goals. Prompt the AI to suggest engaging themes and specific content ideas for upcoming social media calendars.

Here's an example of a prompt you may try:

> You are a [role]. [Insert information about your brand, audience, and goals.] Propose five compelling monthly themes and specific post formats for each to elevate [your brand]'s LinkedIn marketing strategy aimed at small business owners.

Chapter **6**

Visual Exploration for Designers Using AI

I n the realm of design, creativity is the spark that ignites innovation. It's the force that drives designers to envision the unseen and bring new concepts to life. AI isn't just a tool; it's a collaborator. AI can open doors to creative possibilities that were once out of reach, allowing designers to push boundaries and explore new frontiers of imagination.

In this chapter, we uncover how AI tools can help designers think up new ideas, make user-friendly interfaces, and build strong brand images. You find out how you can use AI to start the creative process, get feedback on your designs, and create different versions of logos and pictures.

This chapter shows you how to use AI to do things not just faster, but also better. Whether you're sketching out a new design or refining an existing one, AI can be your assistant every step of the way.

Sparking Visual Creativity Using Prompts

Creativity in design is not just about making things look good. It's about solving problems and telling stories that resonate with people. It's the difference between a design that merely functions and a design that connects. As a designer, you're constantly seeking ways to innovate and stand out. This is where AI comes in. With AI, you have a new way to approach your work, offering a perspective that can transform the ordinary into the extraordinary.

REMEMBER

AI assists by providing a suite of tools that can analyze vast amounts of data, recognize patterns, and suggest alternatives that a human being may not consider. This is particularly useful when you're faced with the difficult task of starting a new project. A blank canvas can be intimidating, but AI prompts can serve as creative catalysts. These prompts can be questions or suggestions that spark ideas or provide a new angle on a design problem.

TIP

Suppose you're struggling to come up with a color scheme. AI can generate a prompt based on color theory, current trends, or even the emotions you want to convey. This nudge from AI can lead to a palette that captures your desired mood or brand message. Similarly, when you're choosing fonts, AI can suggest combinations that balance readability with personality, all tailored to your project's specific context.

The real magic happens when AI prompts lead to iterative exploration. You may start with a basic idea for a layout. Through a series of AI-generated prompts, you can turn that idea into something more refined, more targeted, and ultimately more creative. This process of iteration, fueled by AI, ensures that creativity is not a one-time spark but a continuous flame.

By embracing AI as a partner in the design process, you aren't replacing human creativity — you're enhancing it. You're freeing up mental space to focus on the big picture while AI handles routine tasks. This collaboration allows you to be more daring, to try combinations you may not have considered, and to see your work evolve in real time.

Optimizing UX and UI Design

User experience (UX) is the overall experience a person has when they interact with a product. These interactions can involve more than just the core product (a website or app, for example) — they can include everything from the product download to interacting with customer support.

User interface (UI), on the other hand, relates to the specific elements a user inter-acts with in an app. This could include anything from font and button placement to the visual accessibility of the color scheme used in the design. The design encompasses both aesthetic and functional appeal.

When you're creating a UX or a UI, your design needs to be visually appealing, user-friendly, and highly functional. AI can play a transformative role in optimiz-ing your UX and UI design processes. You can use AI to automate and empower various aspects of UX and UI design. This may involve researching your potential users or creating content that's intuitive and user-friendly. In the following sections, we take a closer look at a few of these possibilities.

Creating user personas

Making personas is a key step in UX and UI design. *Personas* are like imaginary users, but they're based on actual research about who will use the product. They help your understand who you're making the product for. AI has made creating these personas better and faster.

TIP

User personas are essential for designers. They're guides that show what the users need and want and what problems they need to solve. You use these personas to evaluate their designs from a user's point of view. This helps make products that work well and connect with users.

DESIGNING PERSONAS

AI is changing how designers make personas. The AI looks at a lot of online information about possible users and finds patterns that a human being may overlook. This starts with collecting data from places like social media, surveys, and online behavior. The AI then analyzes this data and determines what different kinds of users are like. This way, you get a complete picture of who the users are.

Here's how you can make personas with AI:

1. **Get lots of information about your users.**

   This data can include how they use your website, what they say on social media, and their feedback.

2. **Use AI tools to study this data.**

   These tools can spot trends in how users act and what they like or don't like.

(continued)

(continued)

3. **Start making your personas.**

   Give them names, jobs, and even hobbies to make them feel real.

4. Figure out what each persona is trying to do and what problems they may face with your product.

5. **Make empathy maps for your personas.**

   This means writing down what they may be thinking, feeling, seeing, and doing. Empathy mapping helps you understand users' experiences.

6. **If you can, check the personas with real users.**

   Their feedback can help you make sure your personas are right on target.

TIP

Using AI to make user personas brings both depth and accuracy. AI can handle lots of data quickly, helping to create personas that really represent all kinds of users. This means the designs will fit more people, work better, and be more about the user. AI also keeps these personas up to date as trends and behaviors change.

Adding AI to persona creation is a big step forward in UX and UI design. It makes the process smoother and the personas better. These AI-made personas are great tools for designers, helping them create products that look good and really connect with users.

Brainstorming UX with AI

With any UX design, brainstorming is a crucial first step. It's at this point that you think of new ways to make websites and apps that are easy to use and look great. Integrating AI into the process helps brainstorming reach new heights. AI is a powerful assistant that can sift through tons of data and offer innovative ideas based on what it finds.

AI is changing how designers brainstorm. Usually, a design team depends on their knowledge and experience to come up with ideas. But AI analyzes things differently. It looks at the latest design trends and goes through a lot of information about how people use different apps. Then it suggests ideas that may not be obvious. For example, in designing a shopping app, AI may suggest focusing on making the checkout process as simple as possible because it knows users prefer that.

REMEMBER

The best part about AI in brainstorming is its ability to offer a variety of perspectives. Unlike team members, AI doesn't think the same way people do, so it comes up with unique, unbiased ideas. This helps design teams to think outside their usual patterns and consider a broader range of creative solutions.

AI also speeds up the process of turning ideas into reality. It can quickly create simple designs or early versions of a product. This lets your team see and tweak your ideas right away. It's like having a shortcut in the design process, where ideas are not just talked about but also seen and improved on the spot.

AI can also keep track of how different ideas work together. It can suggest combinations of features that may make an app more user-friendly or make a website easier to navigate. This helps in creating designs that are not just visually appealing but also practical and easy to use.

Incorporating AI into brainstorming for UX design is a big step forward. AI helps in coming up with fresh ideas, seeing them quickly come to life, and making sure they work well for users. As AI technology improves, it will play an even bigger role in helping you create apps and websites that are not only good-looking but also user-friendly and efficient.

REMEMBER

The integration of AI into the brainstorming process symbolizes a new era in UX design. It brings a blend of creativity, speed, and practicality, making the design process more result-oriented. With AI's growing capabilities, the future of UX design looks more innovative and user-centric.

Using AI to critique UX prototypes

A major step in UX design is creating prototypes. This is the point at which ideas start to look like actual products. But it's just as essential to critique these prototypes to see what works and what doesn't. AI has started playing a big role in this. AI can look at a prototype and give feedback just like a human would, but with the speed and accuracy that comes from analyzing lots of data.

TIP

One of the cool things that AI tools like ChatGPT can do is analyze images. This means it can look at a design and give feedback on things like layout, color choices, and whether the design is user-friendly. This is a huge help for designers because they get a quick, unbiased opinion of their work.

AI tools can also do things like checking whether the design is easy to use, whether it's accessible to all users, and whether it matches up with current design trends. This is important because it means the design will work well for as many people as possible. Plus, AI can do this much faster than a person, which saves a lot of time and money.

Here are some other AI tools that can help with critiquing designs, too. For example:

>> **Adobe Sensei (www.adobe.com/sensei):** This tool uses AI to help with design work in Adobe products. It can do things like auto-tag photos and help with layout choices.

>> **Canva's Magic Switch (www.canva.com/help/resize):** Canva uses AI to help resize designs for different platforms. It's great for making sure your design looks good no matter where you use it.

>> **Attention Insight (https://attentioninsight.com):** This AI tool offers predictive analytics for UX design validation and optimization, with features like focus maps and attention reports. It aids in comparing and refining designs effectively.

When using AI to critique UX prototypes, the process usually goes like this:

1. Upload your design into the AI tool.

2. The AI looks at the design and checks things like layout, color, and usability.

3. The AI gives feedback on what's working and what could be better. It may also suggest changes.

The feedback from AI is really helpful because it's based on lots of data about what users like and what works well in design. This means the suggestions are usually spot-on.

AI is not perfect. It's good to use AI feedback as a starting point, but it's still important to get opinions from real people, too. They can give feedback that AI may miss, especially when it comes to how the user feels when using it.

Using AI to critique UX prototypes is becoming a big part of the design process. It helps make sure designs are good to use, look great, and meet the latest standards. With tools like ChatGPT for image analysis and others like Adobe Sensei, Canva, and Attention Insight, you have numerous options for getting quick, useful feedback on your work. As AI keeps getting better, it's going to be even more helpful in making sure designs are the best they can be.

Creating Brand Assets

Branding is not just about logos and colors; it is an art form, and AI is the newest tool for the job. This section looks at AI's capability to create assets. This includes how it can turn complex ideas into tangible brand elements. We explore how these innovative AI tools bring efficiency and a touch of genius to the branding process.

Designing, evaluating, and iterating logos

Generative AI (GenAI) has transformed logo design. These AI-powered tools do more than just make simple logos; they leverage advanced technology to craft designs that are unique. This is a giant leap from traditional logo design methods. AI tools open a world of possibilities, giving brands access to distinctive and rich logo designs that really stand out.

Here are some tools to consider:

>> **Logo Diffusion (https://logodiffusion.com):** Logo Diffusion is a standout platform in the era of GenAI. It isn't your average logo maker. Using the power of GenAI, Logo Diffusion offers a refined way to create logos. You begin by sharing details about your brand and what you like. Then the AI gets to work crafting a range of logos specially made for your brand. These aren't just combinations of existing designs; they're fresh, unique creations designed to genuinely fit your brand's identity.

>> **DALL·E 3's integration with ChatGPT:** The integration has brought a new level of capability to logo creation. DALL·E 3 is much better than the earlier version at making AI art. Now part of ChatGPT, it's easier to use for creating logos. This combo lets you do a lot all at once. You can think up logo ideas, see them made into graphics, try out different looks, and decide what works best, all in one chat. It's like having a design studio right in your conversation, where you can play with ideas and see them come to life in real time.

>> **Adobe Illustrator (www.adobe.com/products/illustrator):** Adobe Illustrator (shown in Figure 6-1) is a leading vector graphics application that can now use GenAI. This is a significant change in logo design. Its Text to Vector Graphic function lets you type ideas and get logos. These designs can be anything you can imagine, fitting any brand strategy. You can make simple parts or full patterns. Plus, you can use your own art as a style guide, making new designs that match. This makes creating images for things like social media easier. Illustrator's AI speeds up design, adds creativity, and keeps your brand's look consistent. It's a big step in making logos and brand assets more fun to create.

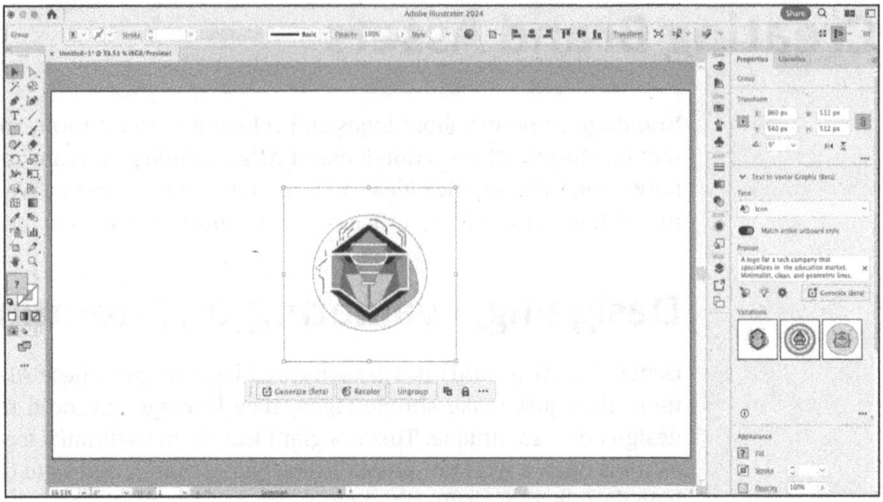

FIGURE 6-1:
Adobe Illustrator
has powerful
GenAI
capabilities.

CHATTING ABOUT IDEAS

Discussing ideas with AI also opens new creative pathways. Sometimes, you have a vague idea or a feeling about what you want your logo to convey. AI can take these initial thoughts and turn them into concrete design elements, showing you possibilities that you may not have considered. You can use ChatGPT's latest features to review your design by uploading it directly into a chat. Try this method:

1. **Upload your current logo design directly into ChatGPT.**

2. **Ask ChatGPT to critique the logo, focusing on various areas specific to the technical design, aesthetics, and target audience.**

   An example prompt might be something like, "Critique this logo design, focusing on its visual impact, adaptability, and how well it conveys the brand message."

   ChatGPT would then provide a critique of the logo, such as: "The logo's bold colors and modern design make a strong visual statement, but its complexity may limit adaptability. It effectively conveys. . .."

3. **Based on ChatGPT's insights, refine your logo to enhance its appeal and brand alignment.**

4. **Continue uploading revised versions of the logo for further AI analysis, iterating until the logo truly embodies your brand's essence.**

The process of improving your designs with these AI tools is equally impressive. AI does more than just create — it iterates. You can take an initial design and tweak it, with AI offering suggestions for improvements. This could be about making your logo more eye-catching, ensuring it works in different formats, or even making it more aligned with your brand's message. This iterative process is crucial for developing a logo that truly represents your brand.

REMEMBER

GenAI is changing how brands make logos. Now, with tools like Logo Diffusion, DALL·E 3, and Adobe Illustrator, you can focus on creating logos that better represent a brand's identity with less guesswork. These tools do more than just help pick colors and shapes; they produce custom-tailored logos that match a brand's style and story.

You can rapidly explore new logo concepts and iterate in a fraction of the time. As AI improves, it will continue to play a bigger role in logo creation. This means that you can make logos in new and exciting ways, where your imagination is the only limit.

Creating image variations with prompts

If you want to create stunning images with DALL·E 3 on ChatGPT or similar tools like Midjourney (www.midjourney.com), you must understand what these tools do best. Detailed prompts, including mood, style, color, and composition, are crucial. They guide the AI to make images that fit what you're imagining.

An example prompt for DALL·E 3 could be as follows:

> Design a visually striking advertisement background featuring an urban skyline at dusk. Emphasize a blend of neon and natural lighting to create a dynamic contrast. The style should merge digital art with realism, highlighting vivid blue and pink hues. Incorporate elements like silhouetted skyscrapers and bustling city life. The overall atmosphere should be energetic and modern, capturing the essence of city nightlife.

This prompt is specific, detailing the scene, style, colors, and mood. It guides the AI to create an image close to your artistic vision, as shown in Figure 6-2.

Experimenting with different prompts can lead to surprising, stunning images. If the results aren't what you had in mind, refining your prompts can help. Making them clearer or simpler will allow the AI to better understand and deliver what you want.

FIGURE 6-2:
DALL·E 3's output
from our
example prompt.

For example, building on the last image we created (refer to Figure 6-2), we could instruct DALL·E 3 to make the following changes:

> Create a variation of the previously designed urban skyline at dusk advertisement background. Maintain the 16:9 aspect ratio. Adjust the lighting to be predominantly neon, with less natural light, creating a more vibrant and colorful city atmosphere. It enhances the hues to be more intense, focusing on deeper blues and brighter pinks. It adds more visible signs of active city life, like illuminated billboards and lively street scenes.

DALL·E 3 has kept a lot of the original style from the image, but it has crafted a new variation that fits the requirements of our new prompt, as shown in Figure 6-3.

TIP

Adding reference images or styles can also guide the AI. These act as a clear direction. After getting your first images, you can change your prompts to get closer to your perfect image. Each image should align with your art goals and what you want to say. Sometimes, you can improve the AI's images with your own artistic touches.

Keeping up with the latest in AI tools like DALL·E 3 is important. They keep getting new features that can help your creative process. By following these steps, DALL·E 3 on ChatGPT and similar platforms will become more than tools — they'll be creative partners, opening up new possibilities in digital art and design and letting you create images that are not only beautiful to look at but also full of emotion.

FIGURE 6-3:
Our latest prompt
has produced a
modified image.

Observing cohesive branding and design for style guides

Creating a style guide is a key part of branding. It's like crafting a rulebook about how to display your brand. With AI, this process becomes easier and more intelligent. Style guides lay out how to apply your logo and which fonts and colors to use. They also define other key design elements. The style guide ensures your brand looks consistent across all platforms.

AI tools have revolutionized how you can make these guides. AI, like ChatGPT, can analyze your existing materials and suggest a complete style guide. By experimenting with different designs, AI tools can show how your brand may look across various applications. This saves time and also makes sure the style guide is practical and versatile.

Here are some tools to consider:

» **Colormind (`http://colormind.io`):** This is an AI tool that specializes in color schemes and palettes. It analyzes multiple sources, like art, movies, and photos. It then proposes color ideas that are both visually appealing and trendy.

» **Fontjoy (`https://fontjoy.com`):** This AI app focuses on typography. It selects fonts that harmonize well, ensuring that your brand's textual content is aesthetically pleasing.

These tools help keep your brand's look flexible, which is important in today's quick-moving market.

TIP

AI tools for style guides are useful for new brands or those looking to rebrand. They can offer a streamlined way to develop a style that is cohesive and stands out. Additionally, these tools can help keep you abreast of the latest design trends, which ensures that your brand remains modern and relevant.

REMEMBER

These AI tools do more than just keep things consistent. They're also about being creative and smart with your branding. They make sure every part of your design speaks to the people you want to reach. With AI, you can create a style guide that looks good across different channels and makes your brand stand out.

Reviewing AI tools for asset creation

AI tools make creating brand assets a lot easier. They help with everything from logos to making designs and stories. Here are some to consider:

>> **Adobe Express** (`https://new.express.adobe.com`): This tool helps you make graphics, web pages, and video stories. It's great for brands that want to grow online.

>> **Canva** (`www.canva.com`): Canva is easy to use and suggests designs, colors, and even content. It's perfect for all kinds of design tasks.

>> **RelayThat** (`www.relaythat.com`): RelayThat uses AI to make sure all your marketing materials look consistent. It's great for keeping your brand's look the same across different platforms.

These tools are for everyone, not just professional designers. They make it easy to create things that look professional and match your brand. Plus, they aren't just about doing things faster; they add creativity and make your designs memorable.

Streamlining Workflows

The field of design is dynamic. Streamlining your workflow is key to better efficiency and creativity. Using AI within these processes can open up new possibilities. In addition, it can make complex tasks simpler and faster. AI tools can automate time-consuming tasks, freeing you up to focus on more creative work. In this section, we explore how to optimize design workflows through AI. We also look at enhancing productivity and innovation.

Automating high-priority design tasks

AI changes the way that designers prioritize tasks. It allows you to automate routine activities in the design process. This, in turn, frees you to spend more time on problem-solving and conceptual work. One area where AI allows for this is image editing and manipulation. Tools like Adobe Photoshop (www.adobe.com/products/photoshop) can use AI for a variety of tasks. For example, the latest version can use GenAI to remove objects, correct color, and create complex compositions. This allows you to complete these tasks quicker and more precisely.

AI is also great at making data easy to understand visually. Tableau (www.tableau.com) is one tool that does this well. It looks at large data sets and produces graphics that are visually appealing and show what the data means.

AI is also making it easier to create content, which traditionally took a lot of time and effort. AI tools help make early design graphics and even write text faster. For example, Canva uses AI to pick out design layouts that fit what you're trying to make. This speeds up the design process so you can spend more time on other parts of your project.

REMEMBER

Using AI to automate tasks doesn't take away from your creative ability. It improves it. AI does the mundane, repetitive tasks so you can put more time into the creative and vital parts of your work. This leads to more unique and inventive results.

Integrating AI into design workflows

Integrating AI into design workflows is about more than just automating tasks. It's about reshaping the design process to make it more efficient and adaptable. A key strategy is using AI early in the process. For example, you might use it during concept development. Tools like DALL·E 3 can create visual ideas from a text description, giving you a creative starting point.

Collaboration is another area where AI makes a big difference. Tools like Miro Assist (https://miro.com/assist) can help teams brainstorm together. They can then organize their ideas in a collaborative space and develop these ideas further.

In addition, AI can help with decision-making. It can analyze user data and feedback to offer insight into design preferences and trends. This helps guide you to make choices that resonate with audiences. Ultimately, this leads to designs that are both innovative and aligned with user needs.

AI can also make the process of getting and using feedback faster. AI-powered tools can give suggestions for making designs better. This helps you more rapidly improve your designs.

To really use AI well in design, you need to think of it as a tool that helps you, not replaces you. Keeping up with AI and learning about it is key to using it best in your designs.

REMEMBER

Putting AI into your design workflow isn't just about doing things faster; it's about being more creative and coming up with new ideas. AI takes care of routine tasks and facilitates new ways to work together. This makes design more exciting and leads to better results.

AI is more than a simple tool. It's a force that is changing how we create. AI tools help you think of new ideas and make complicated tasks easier. By using AI in design, you can work more efficiently and find new ways to be creative. As AI keeps getting better, what it can do in design seems to have no limits. We're moving toward a future where designers and AI work together to make even the most creative ideas real.

Chapter 7

Building Enhanced Portfolios with AI for Creators

A I can be very helpful with tasks like making music, videos, and related creative works. While you're making these impressive works, you need to use AI the right way, which means understanding some rules about being fair and respectful to the works and rights of others.

This chapter examines how AI can help with creative projects. After reading this chapter, you'll know how to use AI to help with audio and video creative projects and be respectful and fair with your creative endeavors.

Enhancing Audio and Music with AI

Imagine starting a music project with a tool that can give you helpful ideas and guide you through mixing professional-sounding results. Sometimes you can even create an entirely new musical composition without knowing the first thing about writing music. This section explains how AI can get you from the start of composing the first note to finishing a well-polished track.

Defining music prompts

Music prompts are like starting points or ideas that can help you create a musical piece. A music prompt could be a tune, a rhythm, or even a mood. For example, if you want to create a calm and peaceful song, a prompt may be something like "a gentle morning" or "a day at the spa." AI can take a simple text prompt and turn it into a melody with lyrics.

Creating and modifying music with prompts

Prompts are very helpful when you need a place to start. The first round of results may not be great, but prompts can kick-start your creative process. This is especially true when you're feeling stuck.

TIP

Prompts can provide a basic idea or a theme to work on. For example, if you have a piece of music that feels too sad, a prompt can help you liven it up or make it sound happier.

Identifying popular AI tools for generating music

You can use standard generative AI (GenAI) tools like ChatGPT to create musical prompts, but more specialized tools are available. These AI tools are specifically tailored to help create music.

Here are some tools you may want to try:

>> **AIVA (www.aiva.ai):** AIVA is an AI music creation assistant available as a web app and natively on Windows and macOS. It lets you quickly create new songs in more than 250 different styles. AIVA is great for complete beginners and seasoned professionals alike. It lets you create highly polished, full-length songs in just a few steps. It also allows you to build your own style models, upload audio influences, and edit your new tracks.

>> **Boomy (https://boomy.com):** This platform, available as a web app, helps you make and share your own music with the help of AI. You don't need to know anything about music to make your own tunes on Boomy. The AI makes songs that can be customized to your tastes.

>> **Riffusion** (`www.riffusion.com`): This web app, shown in Figure 7-1, makes music creation interactive and fun. It's designed to help everyone create music, even if you're new to it. Riffusion will even create lyrics and vocals for the tracks.

FIGURE 7-1: A simple prompt in Riffusion creates songs, lyrics, and vocals.

Other useful AI music tools include apps like Beatoven.ai (`www.beatoven.ai`), Jukebox (`https://openai.com/research/jukebox`), Mubert (`https://mubert.com`), MusicGen (`https://audiocraft.metademolab.com/musicgen.html`), and Suno (`https://suno.ai`). All of these can help you on your musical journey. They have unique features and capabilities to make music that fits your specific needs.

REMEMBER

These AI tools offer many ways to kick-start and enhance your music projects. They can spark new ideas, help refine your current work, and make creating music much more enjoyable.

In the next section, we explore using AI to mix and master your music. We also look at how to get AI suggestions to improve your music. By learning and experimenting with these tools, you can broaden your musical skills and create great pieces of music with the help of AI.

After getting the hang of generating music with AI, the next big step of your musical journey is mixing and mastering tracks. Mixing and mastering are essential steps in music production to get the most professional and polished sound from your music. With AI, the process is much easier and takes less time. Consider how AI can help you with this essential step and how you can make it part of your music production process.

Mixing and mastering with AI

Mixing is the step where different elements of your music, like vocals, instruments, and beats, are balanced to sound good together. *Mastering* is the final touch to ensure your track sounds polished and ready for listeners.

AI can assist in both these steps by analyzing your music and applying enhancements automatically. Here are some examples:

>> **Automated equalization:** AI can adjust the frequencies of your track to ensure a balanced sound.

>> **Dynamic processing:** AI can manage your music's dynamics, ensuring the loud and soft parts are well balanced.

>> **Sonic enhancement:** AI can add a touch of sonic sparkle to make your tracks sound professional.

Integrating AI into the production process

Integrating AI into your music production is a straightforward process. Here is a framework to help you get started:

1. Pick an AI mixing and mastering tool that suits your needs (see the next section).

2. Upload your music to the AI platform in a supported format, such as MIDI, MP3, tablature, or just plain lyrics.

3. Adjust the settings to match your preferences.

4. Let the AI work its magic on your music.

5. Listen to the AI-enhanced version, make any necessary adjustments, learn from the feedback, and download your finished track.

Looking at AI mixing and mastering tools

There are quite a few AI tools specifically designed to help with mixing and mastering. Here are a few of the more popular and powerful ones:

>> **LANDR (www.landr.com/online-audio-mastering):** LANDR is an online platform that provides instant mastering. Upload your track, and LANDR can master it within minutes.

>> **Ozone** (`www.izotope.com/en/products/ozone.html`): This software offers AI-powered mastering and mixing, helping you easily get a professional sound.

>> **eMastered** (`https://emastered.com`): eMastered, shown in Figure 7-2, is an online mastering service that uses AI to analyze and optimize your music. It was made by Grammy-winning sound engineers.

TIP

These tools allow you to mix and master like a professional. The best part is that you don't need to be a sound engineering expert to get expert results. Using the power of AI, you can get highly polished, broadcast-ready sound quickly and with little effort.

Getting musical insight from AI

As we dive deeper into making music, you can consider improving your musical abilities and results. Having some help along the way is very useful for this. AI can be that helpful friend. It helps in two main ways:

>> It can listen as you play your instrument and give you tips to get better.

>> It can look at the songs you write and suggest ways to improve them. It's like having a helpful friend who gives you good advice to make your music shine.

Here are two tools to try that can help make you a better musician:

>> **Yousician** (`https://yousician.com`): Yousician can act like your personal music coach and help you become a much better musician. It listens as you play, checks if you hit the right notes at the right time, and gives feedback after each practice. This feedback can help you understand how well you're doing and what you should focus on to improve.

>> **GuitarTuna** (`https://yousician.com/guitartuna`): GuitarTuna is a sister app to Yousician. Guitarists can use it to make sure their guitars are correctly tuned. It also uses AI to listen as you play and moves the sheet music along as you go, so you always know where you are.

TIP

Another way AI can help you is by looking at the music you write. You can use a tool like ChatGPT to check your compositions and suggest improvements. For example, if you have a chord progression in mind, you can write it down and put it into ChatGPT, and it will suggest ideas to make it better. If you have lyrics but you aren't sure about the tune, you can put the lyrics into ChatGPT, tell it the kind of music you like, and it will give you ideas for tunes that fit your words.

Here is a simple step-by-step way to use ChatGPT to check your music:

1. Get your music piece ready, like a chord progression or lyrics.

2. Open ChatGPT and paste your piece into the chatbox.

3. For lyrics, tell ChatGPT the kind of music you want. For a chord progression, ask for suggestions on rhythm or harmony.

4. Click the Submit button and wait for ChatGPT to give feedback.

5. Look at the feedback and use the suggestions to make your music better.

6. Listen to the changes, see how it sounds, and make more changes if needed.

TIP

Using AI, you can get new ideas and helpful advice to make your music the best it can be.

Leveling Up Your Videos Using AI

As you get further into video creation, the excitement of storytelling using visuals awaits you. Like any journey, the road to crafting great videos is filled with many tasks that demand your attention and creativity. This is where AI can become a helpful assistant, ready to simplify the process.

REMEMBER

With AI, you aren't alone on this journey. It's like having a creative team that helps with planning, adding cool effects, and even giving pointers on improving your content. The exciting part is that AI isn't just for the tech-savvy; it's for anyone with a story to tell. That's true for both the seasoned filmmaker and the beginner starting out.

Planning your video with AI

The first stage of video creation is planning. Planning is the backbone of any video project. It's where you determine your content's storyline, script, and overall outline. However, it can sometimes feel like starting with a blank canvas, hoping inspiration strikes. This is where AI can play an important role. AI tools can help you sketch out the initial outline, making the blank canvas a bit less intimidating.

Here are a couple of examples of AI tools designed to assist in video planning:

>> **Plotagon** (www.plotagon.com): Plotagon lets you create animated videos from the script you write, and it can also help you rapidly assemble a scene from your text input.

>> **Lumen5** (https://lumen5.com): Lumen5, shown in Figure 7-3, can help with scripting and storyline development. It brings powerful AI to help create storyboards and even transform text content into video.

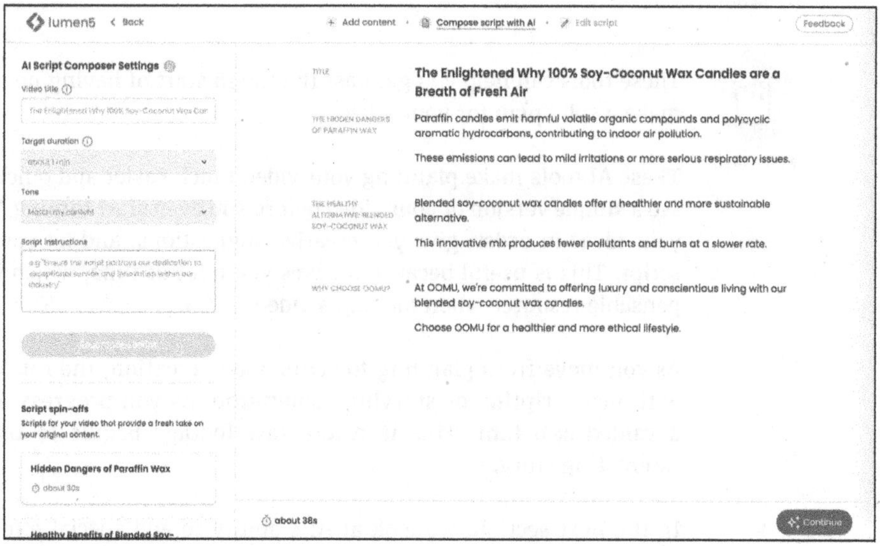

FIGURE 7-3:
Lumen5 can turn a blog post into a full-fledged video.

Both of these apps can provide a great way to preview how your final video might look.

Besides Plotagon and Lumen5, general AI tools like ChatGPT and Claude can also help plan your video. ChatGPT is good at making dialog that sounds human. If you give it a basic concept, it can make a script or story out of it. Claude (`https://claude.ai`), shown in Figure 7-4, handles creative tasks well and can brainstorm ideas or suggest ways to set up your video content.

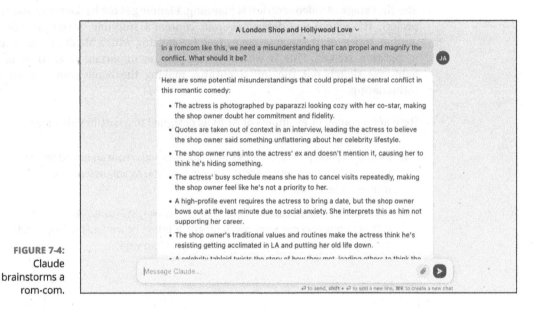

A London Shop and Hollywood Love ˅

In a romcom like this, we need a misunderstanding that can propel and magnify the conflict. What should it be?

Here are some potential misunderstandings that could propel the central conflict in this romantic comedy:

- The actress is photographed by paparazzi looking cozy with her co-star, making the shop owner doubt her commitment and fidelity.
- Quotes are taken out of context in an interview, leading the actress to believe the shop owner said something unflattering about her celebrity lifestyle.
- The shop owner runs into the actress' ex and doesn't mention it, causing her to think he's hiding something.
- The actress' busy schedule means she has to cancel visits repeatedly, making the shop owner feel like he's not a priority to her.
- A high-profile event requires the actress to bring a date, but the shop owner bows out at the last minute due to social anxiety. She interprets this as him not supporting her career.
- The shop owner's traditional values and routines make the actress think he's resisting getting acclimated in LA and putting her old life down.
- A celebrity tabloid twists the story of how they met, leading others to think the

Message Claude...

↵ to send, shift + ↵ to add a new line, ⌘K to create a new chat

FIGURE 7-4:
Claude
brainstorms a
rom-com.

REMEMBER

These tools can help you get past the tough start of having no ideas and help you make a solid plan for your video.

These AI tools make planning your video much easier and quicker. They help you see a simple version of your video before you even start filming. They also help put your ideas in order, give you creative suggestions, and let you visually see your script. This is useful because it saves you a lot of time, which is the most indispensable resource when making a video.

As you move from planning to actual video creation, the role of AI doesn't stop with just scripting or storyline generation. As you progress, it continues to be a valued assistant. This is where raw footage begins to take shape into an interesting story.

In the next section, we look at AI's ability to add special effects or subtitles to make your video content pop. It also makes the process easier and a lot more enjoyable. AI assistance helps ensure that you tell your story in the most engaging way possible.

Adding effects and subtitles with AI

When it comes to creating a video, adding special effects can be time-consuming. Special effects can add a lot to your video, making it more interesting to watch. The problem is that, usually, adding special effects is difficult. This is even more true for someone without experience. AI is changing this. AI tools can help add special effects to your video, making it look polished and professional. Some AI tools can even add subtitles. This is important for making your video accessible to more people.

Starting to use these AI tools in your video editing process is simple. First, you select the tool that suits your needs. Next, you upload your video in a format like MOV or MP4. From there, you can choose the special effects you want, and the AI tool will add them to your video. The AI tool generates subtitles automatically, after which you can review the results for accuracy. The tool then places the subtitles within the video at the proper time location.

TIP

A significant advantage of using AI for special effects and subtitles is the time it saves. Manually adding special effects or timing subtitles to match dialogue takes a long time. With AI, this process is much quicker. Plus, the results are often very good. This gives you more time to focus on other important parts of your video, such as fine-tuning the storyline or dialogue.

Using AI can also improve the quality of your video. The special effects that AI adds are typically of high quality. This makes your video appear professionally done. The same applies to subtitles; they're clear and accurately timed, which makes your video easy to follow.

You can use specific tools to help add effects to your videos. For adding a creative touch with special effects, you may want to explore these popular choices:

>> **Runway** (https://runwayml.com): This tool, shown in Figure 7-5, offers various AI-driven features to spice up your videos. It's a handy tool for adding effects, from changing backgrounds to animating images.

>> **invideo AI** (https://invideo.io): As an AI-powered video generator, invideo AI helps craft unique videos that include an assortment of effects. It's designed to cater to your selected audience and topic, making video creation a breeze.

FIGURE 7-5:
Quickly applying
a green screen
effect in Runway.

If you're looking to add subtitles to your videos, these tools can be very helpful:

>> **Kapwing (www.kapwing.com):** This tool automatically generates subtitles for your videos, which can be a time-saver. It's also user-friendly, making subtitling simple, even for novice users.

>> **VEED (https://www.veed.io):** VEED helps autogenerate subtitles and provides a platform for editing the results to ensure accuracy.

>> **Zubtitle (https://zubtitle.com):** Using Zubtitle, you can auto-caption your videos and add other features like headlines and progress bars, improving the viewer's experience.

REMEMBER

Using AI to add special effects and subtitles simplifies video creation. What used to take hours can now be done in minutes. As your video progresses, consider using AI to add a professional touch. It will save you time and help make your video engaging and accessible to a broader audience.

Looking at Ethical Considerations for Creatives

This section talks about the ethical way to use AI in creative work. Knowing how to use creative AI tools responsibly is essential. That means considering the copyright and data privacy issues that can come up because of these AI-powered tools. Learning about these ethical and responsible practices will help you avoid legal trouble. It will also protect your reputation as a creative professional.

Reviewing the ethical use of AI in creative work

When we talk about the ethical use of AI in creativity, we're referring to using AI tools responsibly. You need to understand the impact of AI-generated content and know what's acceptable and what isn't when using AI for creative projects. For instance, using AI to create fake videos or misinformation can have harmful consequences.

On the other hand, using AI to enhance your creative skills or to learn and grow in your field is a responsible use of technology. Real-world scenarios can help in understanding this better. For example, artists using AI to create unique pieces of art or music is a positive use, whereas creating deepfake videos to spread false information is unethical. (A *deepfake video* is one in which a person's likeness, voice, or both are realistically inserted into a different video, creating a fake composite video.)

Observing copyright and data privacy issues

A big concern when using AI for creative work is copyright. Who owns what AI creates? This question is still being examined in the U.S. legal system. (If you aren't in the United States, the copyright rules about AI-made content may differ.) You also need to think about data privacy. You may be sharing personal or sensitive info when you use AI tools. It's important to use safe and well-known AI platforms and know the data privacy rules of your tools. This may mean sticking with the big platforms by companies like OpenAI, Google, and Anthropic, until newer platforms establish a reputation.

To work through these issues, be sure to stay updated on laws and regulations about AI. This is especially true concerning copyright and data privacy laws. Sites like the Responsible Artificial Intelligence Institute (https://www.responsible.ai), the Content Authenticity Initiative (https://contentauthenticity.org), and the Electronic Frontier Foundation (https://www.eff.org) can be helpful in learning about the latest policies and laws.

TIP

Consider crediting the AI tool or platform you used for your creative process. This way, you show transparency and ethical practices with your AI use. Understanding and tackling these ethical considerations can help make sure your AI-assisted creative journey is smooth, legal, and respectable.

3

Delving into AI-Powered Business Strategies

Chapter **8**

Personalizing the Customer Journey Using AI

Most people enjoy getting brand emails that seem to be written specifically for them. Consumers today expect that every company will deliver personalized interactions and custom recommendations based on their specific needs. Any organization that can successfully provide AI-based personalization can gain a competitive advantage.

This chapter explains how to deliver a personalized journey for your customers using several AI tools and techniques. We show you how to:

» Determine how customers feel using sentiment analysis.

» Provide what customers want by utilizing recommendation engines.

» Predict what customers will do by employing predictive analytics.

» Deliver information customers need with chatbots and virtual assistants.

» Automate the delivery of content using marketing automation.

We also look at how you can use generative AI (GenAI; see Chapter 1) to leverage the data you get from these tools to create valuable assets for marketing, sales, and support.

REMEMBER

Implementing AI technologies usually requires an up-front investment, but it can result in long-term cost savings, improved efficiency, and increased customer retention.

Discovering the Customer Journey

To understand how AI tools impact the customer journey, we begin by looking at the concept of the customer journey itself. The customer journey is the trip that customers take as they learn about, evaluate, and buy a product or service from your brand.

Taking the customer journey

Online practitioners know that improving the customer journey is one of the best ways to help customers choose their brand. Here are the five customer journey stages:

1. Awareness.

   The customer recognizes their need and the possible solutions available to them. Marketing and advertising drive the awareness of the brand and its products. AI can facilitate the creation of these assets.

2. Consideration.

   The customer researches their options and compares competitors. Content like product reviews and comparisons influence their choices. Sales content generated by AI can be used to answer questions and build credibility.

3. Purchase.

   The customer chooses the best option and decides to buy. The transaction process should be seamless. AI can be used to provide shipping information or other details automatically.

4. Retention.

   After purchasing, the goal is to retain the customer for additional business. This is usually done by delivering additional support, loyalty programs, and continuing great service.

5. Advocacy.

This is the stage at which the customer becomes so satisfied and engaged with a brand that they actively promote it to others.

TIP

Your customer journey should focus on guiding customers through each stage. Personalized interactions will move customers along the journey from initial awareness to loyal customers.

Each journey stage generates volumes of behavioral data about how your customers make decisions. AI analyzes that data and provides key insights that help you create a winning journey for your brand.

REMEMBER

Examining touch points

The customer journey typically involves many interactions with a brand, known as *touch points*. So, what are touch points? Touch points are the interactions that happen between the customer and the company throughout their relationship. The customer will experience a multitude of touch points when engaging with your brand. They include such things as:

>> Visiting your website for the first time

>> Receiving email offers from you

>> Seeing your ads on social media

>> Making brick-and-mortar store visits

>> Participating in tech support calls

>> Getting text messages about company events

Each touch point represents an opportunity to delight customers, meet their needs, and deliver a great experience that guides them to a purchase.

REMEMBER

Introducing AI Personalization

Personalizing the customer journey requires a combination of insights (driven by data analysis) and human touch points (like sales calls) to deliver a seamless experience. To provide effective personalization, you need to:

>> **Analyze customer data and insights.** AI tools produce customer profiles and uncover preferences and behaviors that provide the raw material to understand customer motivations.

>> **Blend AI and a human touch.** AI can process data to automate and scale personalization, but having people oversee the output is crucial to delivering content with a human touch.

>> **Use an omnichannel approach.** Connecting customer data across all touch points is essential so customers recognize your brand wherever they see it.

TIP

One example of blending AI and a human touch is an AI technology known as Einstein, which is part of the Salesforce customer relationship management (CRM) platform. Einstein creates an autogenerated personalized email for every sales conversation, making the salesperson more productive and providing the customer with a personalized follow-up email.

Delivering personalized content

Delivering consistent messages on all channels ensures that customers receive relevant information based on their preferences and interests. So, how does AI accomplish this? By doing the following:

>> Identifying patterns and segments from customer data to define personas

>> Determining which types of content each customer is likely to interact with

>> Continuously testing different content to maximize personalization effectiveness

>> Creating and delivering custom experiences automatically without any human involvement

REMEMBER

Continuous monitoring and optimization of AI systems are crucial for maintaining relevance as customer preferences change.

TIP

AI extracts insights from customer data that would be virtually impossible for humans to accomplish manually. This allows the delivery of results in real time at an almost unlimited scale.

Personalizing the journey with AI

As the customer proceeds through the journey, personalized content needs to reach them at each phase. Here are some examples of how AI-driven personalization is delivered throughout the customer journey:

>> **Awareness:** Visitors see display ads, social media posts, and website content reflecting their interests based on their browsing history.

>> **Consideration:** Product recommendations and comparison tools display customized options that consumers will prefer.

>> **Purchase:** Email and web content emphasize benefits and features that matter most to each customer.

>> **Retention:** Existing customers get personalized promotions, restock reminders, and cross-sell suggestions over time.

>> **Advocacy:** Loyal customers are offered personalized rewards and incentives and are encouraged to share their experiences with the product.

By continually optimizing experiences around a customer's choices, AI-powered personalization guides customers to a purchase.

REMEMBER

Some customers are sensitive to what they consider too much personalization. Be aware that some people may see personalization that constantly hits their inbox as intrusive.

Benefitting from AI Tools for the Customer Journey

Using AI tools to create and enhance the customer journey helps marketers, sales, and support teams deliver a great customer experience. Here are several benefits to consider:

>> **An enhanced customer experience:** AI can analyze large amounts of data to personalize the customer journey to deliver a more relevant customer experience.

>> **Better decision-making:** AI provides valuable insights through predictive analytics or sentiment analysis, enabling businesses to make better decisions about pricing, product development, or marketing campaigns.

>> **Improved sales performance:** By using AI-powered tools, staff can understand customer needs to make more informed and targeted sales pitches.

>> **Real-time support:** With AI-powered chatbots or virtual assistants, businesses can provide support 24/7, improving response times and overall satisfaction.

>> **A competitive advantage:** Businesses that effectively leverage AI in their sales and support processes gain a competitive edge by serving customers content that matters to them. Of course, sometimes human intervention is essential to close a sale or fix a problem.

>> **Reduced churn:** By showing customers you understand their desires and needs, you strengthen their loyalty and encourage them to remain customers.

Churn is a marketing term that refers to customers who quit using a product or service within a designated period.

>> **Increased efficiency:** AI tools automate repetitive tasks such as data entry, which lets support teams focus on more important activities.

Determining How Customers Feel

Customers' feelings about a brand affect their buying decisions. Unfortunately, emotions are difficult to measure objectively in text and spoken language. This is where sentiment analysis is a valuable tool. By analyzing customer content across the customer journey, sentiment analysis uncovers the attitudes and feelings hidden inside volumes of customer data.

TIP

Sentiment analysis can determine customer emotions by analyzing their feedback or social media interactions. By understanding customer sentiment, you can send the right content at the right time, improving the customer experience.

Understanding sentiment analysis

Sentiment analysis is a technique that uses AI to find out whether content has a positive, negative, or neutral sentiment. For example, "I really like this product" would be considered a positive sentiment, "They have the worst service ever" is obviously negative, and "They delivered the package on time" would probably be considered neutral.

Sentiment analysis lets you discover patterns and trends about how customers feel. It analyzes the tone and mood of customers at different points along the journey and alerts you to potential problems. Using sentiment analysis techniques enables staff to pinpoint problems along the customer journey and fix them.

TIP

Here are some ways you can apply sentiment analysis:

>> **Eliminate pain points.** You can identify and fix the significant pain points that frustrate customers first.

>> **Discover problems when you make changes.** You can monitor sentiment changes following a product, service, or campaign modification.

>> **Spot major issues.** You can alert support teams to a customer problem so they fix it before it becomes a major issue.

Sentiment analysis applications help staff find and solve the problems that will deliver the greatest customer satisfaction.

Evaluating emotions across the customer journey

Organizations use sentiment analysis to gain insights across the customer journey. Here are some examples of how you can use it at each stage:

>> **Awareness:** You can analyze blog and video comments and other touch-point responses to understand the beginning opinions of the brand.

>> **Consideration:** You can look at customer inquiries, event feedback, and other interactions to see how their feelings change.

>> **Purchase:** To measure satisfaction after buying, you can categorize the sentiment from tech support comments, service calls, and conversations.

>> **Retention:** You can continuously analyze social media, reviews, customer support calls, and other channels to monitor ongoing attitudes.

>> **Advocacy:** You can find out which topics are most positively discussed in your community and use that information for your advocacy programs.

Creating assets using sentiment analysis data

In the past, sentiment analysis data was not widely available to organizations. The data was trapped inside social media platforms or on websites. Only a few staff or consultants would see comments, and not at scale. Now you can use sentiment analysis data to create assets with GenAI.

Here are some examples of things you can create:

>> **Product development:** Use GenAI to create prototypes or feature lists based on positive or negative sentiments about your existing products.

>> **Crisis management:** If you receive serious negative alerts, use the data to help generate public relations (PR) responses or action plans.

>> **Employee engagement:** Use sentiment data from employee surveys to create internal training programs or motivational content.

Data analysis shows what customers *do*, whereas sentiment analysis shows how they *feel*. By incorporating sentiment analysis, companies can create a brand that stands out.

Providing What Customers Want

Most consumers are overwhelmed by the choices they have online. Whether they're shopping or just browsing, they have endless options. For this reason, recommendation engines have become an essential AI tool. By providing custom suggestions, recommendation engines help customers find the most relevant products and services for their needs.

Understanding recommendation engines

Recommendation engines enable marketers to provide targeted, high-value suggestions that evolve with the customer's needs. As customers change, the engine continuously revises its suggestions based on the latest data. This level of personalization helps drive engagement, conversions, satisfaction, and loyalty across the entire customer life cycle.

Recommendation engines use algorithms to analyze customer data to predict customer preferences. They look at things like:

>> **Purchase history:** Recommendation engines look at what the customer bought before because it can show future interest.

>> **Browsing history:** Recommendations look at what the customer has viewed but not bought.

>> **Item attributes:** Recommendation engines look at the customer's current preferences. They examine things like brand, price, and category.

>> **Ratings:** Recommendation engines look at explicit feedback the customer has provided on items, signaling the customer's likes and dislikes.

>> **Demographics:** Recommendation engines look at traits like age, location, and more.

Customer recommendations can appear on product pages, emails, home pages, or any other touch point along the customer journey. They're typically displayed as the top personalized picks for the specific item the customer is considering.

Improving the customer journey with recommendations

Recommendation engines can influence several stages of the customer journey. Here are some examples of how recommendation engines can impact your customers:

>> **Awareness:** Recommendation engines help surface products that match a customer's needs but of which the customer is unaware. This presents relevant options early in the journey.

>> **Consideration:** Recommendation engines can provide educational materials, reviews, tutorials, and comparisons to help customers evaluate choices. This builds credibility during the research phase.

>> **Purchase:** Recommendation engines can suggest alternatives that meet the customer's criteria based on items viewed, reminding the customer of preferences they may have forgotten.

>> **Retention:** Recommendation engines can influence existing customers by recommending new releases, products the customer is running out of, and complementary items. This can help reduce churn.

>> **Advocacy:** Recommendation engines can recommend special offers or loyalty programs that are exclusive to customers who are in the advocacy stage. This rewards customers for their loyalty and encourages further advocacy.

Creating assets with recommendation engine data

Recommending products and services helps introduce your customers to things that were previously unknown to them. Here are some examples of using recommendation engine data to create assets with GenAI:

- >> **Personalized content:** Use the data to create tailored articles, emails, or social media posts.

- >> **Customer segmentation:** Use the data to create customer profiles that you can use for targeted marketing campaigns.

- >> **Content curation:** Use the data to curate content reading lists or education courses customized to customer preferences.

Predicting What Customers Will Do

Companies have access to more customer data than ever, from website clicks to social media activity. Although this data is valuable, making sense of it is tricky. This is where predictive analytics comes in. It analyzes large amounts of customer data to predict preferences, behavior, and needs.

Utilizing predictive analytics

Predictive analytics makes predictions based on what customers have done in the past. Companies can use it to analyze the customer journey and predict what customers will do next. For example, it can predict that customers who buy a product after viewing that product's video several times have a higher customer lifetime value (CLV).

REMEMBER

CLV refers to the amount a customer will spend during their entire relationship with a company.

After the data is analyzed, predictive analytics tools create models to determine what will happen next. This is where your company can find great value. For example, here are some questions you'll be able to answer with authority:

- >> Which types of content will specific customer segments be most interested in?

- >> How likely will customers churn in the next three months based on their engagement level?

>> Given their average conversion value, how much should be spent on re-targeting ads to a specific audience segment?

Optimizing the customer journey

Knowing what customers may do next is valuable when analyzing the customer journey. Here are some examples of how predictive analytics can impact the customer journey:

>> **Awareness:** Predictive analytics can find potential customers based on demographic and behavioral data. This helps marketers more effectively target their awareness campaigns.

>> **Consideration:** By analyzing past interactions and purchase history, predictive analytics can personalize content to engage prospects.

>> **Purchase:** Predictive analytics can predict the likelihood that a prospect will make a purchase, allowing marketers to increase their focus on customers who are more likely to purchase.

>> **Retention:** Predictive analytics can identify patterns that signal potential customer churn, which alerts staff to take proactive measures to retain these customers.

>> **Advocacy:** By analyzing customer satisfaction and engagement metrics, predictive analytics can identify potential brand advocates, helping to increase word-of-mouth marketing.

Creating assets with predictive analytics data

You can use GenAI to develop the insights from predictive analytics into assets that take advantage of new opportunities and challenges. Here are some examples of assets that you can create using GenAI:

>> **Ad campaigns:** Leverage predictive analytics data to discover high-value keywords or customer segments. GenAI can then create ad variations that are more likely to result in a purchase.

>> **Churn prevention:** You can predict which customers will likely churn and use GenAI to create retention-focused content like special offers or educational materials.

>> **Simulations:** Predictive analytics can foresee the development of potential business problems. GenAI can create content that prepares you for these scenarios by suggesting training modules or videos. For example, a retail chain might use predictive analytics to identify a potential future dip in customer satisfaction. GenAI might respond by creating targeted training modules and videos for staff, focusing on enhancing customer service skills to preemptively address this issue.

TIP

Predictive analytics delivers great value to organizations by anticipating customer needs and proactively serving them up. It removes the guesswork staff must make when deciding what content to provide.

Delivering Information Customers Need

Providing real-time answers to customer questions is imperative for brands. But scaling this personal support without AI tools would be virtually impossible. Enter chatbots and virtual assistants. These AI-powered tools automate conversations to give customers the information they need anytime, anywhere. By providing real-time assistance, they enhance the user experience, save money, and solve problems quickly.

REMEMBER

You've already engaged with a virtual assistant if you've used Apple's Siri, Amazon Alexa, or Google Assistant. They make daily tasks like setting alarms or checking the weather fun and easy.

Utilizing chatbots and virtual assistants

Chatbots are software designed to understand questions and provide text or voice-based replies that mimic human conversation. (Virtual assistants add more advanced features like voice recognition and integration with your organization's backend systems.)

TIP

Chatbot capabilities can run the gamut. They can provide simple canned responses or advanced ones using machine learning to handle more complex interactions. You can easily choose one that is suited to your needs.

REMEMBER

In addition, the chat feature should tell the customer whether they're dealing with a chatbot or a human. It's important for the company to make that clear.

Self-service along the customer journey

Chatbots and virtual assistants reshape the customer journey by offering conversational self-service. Here are some examples of how to deploy them along the customer journey:

» **Awareness:** Chatbots and virtual assistants can pop up on websites to introduce the brand and answer common questions for prospects who are merely browsing.

» **Consideration:** Chatbots and virtual assistants can provide personalized product guidance and recommendations to assist with evaluation.

» **Purchase:** Chatbots and virtual assistants can process transaction details, track orders, and explain returns to increase conversions.

» **Retention:** Chatbots and virtual assistants can follow up post-purchase to answer customer questions, upsell other products, and build relationships.

» **Advocacy:** Chatbots and virtual assistants can prompt customers to share referral codes with their network, offering both the customer and their friend special discounts or rewards.

Creating assets using chatbots

Chatbots can generate insights into customer needs, behavior, and sentiment by capturing and analyzing conversational data. You can use that data to create assets using GenAI. Here are some examples:

» **Case studies:** Use the data you get from customer support chatbots to identify success stories and use GenAI to draft case studies.

» **Social media posts:** Use the data from chatbot interactions to generate social media content such as common questions or insights.

» **Email campaigns:** Use AI to create personalized email content based on the questions and opinions expressed in the chat.

Chatbots engage visitors and support customers without any human intervention. They're valuable because, in many cases, they reduce problems and increase satisfaction throughout the customer journey by providing 24/7 assistance. Just be aware that they don't always have the desired effect.

Automating the Delivery of Content

Customers expect to receive relevant real-time information when interacting with brands. But manually distributing content to audiences would require unlimited time and effort. This is where AI marketing automation platforms become essential. By organizing content delivery, automation enables marketers to give customers timely, personalized content at scale.

TIP

According to Gartner, the research and advisory firm, automating customer messages will help large companies be more productive. Gartner predicts that, by 2025, 30 percent of outbound messages from large organizations will be AI-created (www.gartner.com/en/newsroom/press-releases/2022-10-10-gartner-identifies-seven-technology-disruptions-that-will-impact-sales-through-2027).

Viewing AI marketing automation

AI marketing automation software uses rules and workflows to automate marketing tasks. Automation platforms can assemble and distribute content tailored to each customer based on their behaviors and preferences. This creates targeted experiences that build the customer relationship.

Observing data-driven personalization

Modern automation platforms can analyze customer data and turn it into actionable insights. Here's how they do this:

>> **Customer profiles:** Data is collected from multiple channels to build unified customer profiles.

>> **Audience segmentation:** Segmentation is based on attributes like demographics, behaviors, and preferences.

>> **Mapping:** Journey mapping is used to understand typical pathways users take.

>> **Rules:** Trigger-based rules deploy content to customers when specified criteria are met.

Automating across the customer journey

Automated content delivery streamlines critical phases of the journey. Here's how it maps to the different stages:

>> **Awareness:** Automated emails send new prospects customized introductory information when they sign up.

>> **Consideration:** Behavior-triggered content recommends relevant resources to help with product evaluation.

>> **Purchase:** Web personalization automatically shows special offers and messaging to those poised to buy.

>> **Retention:** Existing customers receive automated cross-sell offers and restock reminders.

>> **Advocacy:** Automated surveys collect customer opinions. You can then automatically share these opinions as testimonials (with the customers' permission).

Creating assets and delivering them with marketing automation

Marketing automation allows you to automatically deliver valuable content to customers at the right time to spur engagement. Here are some examples of assets that you can create and automatically send at just the right time:

>> **Triggered notifications:** Send automated notifications or reminders when a user takes a specific action like abandoning a shopping cart.

>> **Personalized emails:** Automatically use subscriber data to segment audiences and customize email content, offers, and messaging.

>> **Automated workflows:** Set up a sequence of emails, offers, and content that guides users through your conversion funnel.

REMEMBER

As automation capabilities evolve, marketers can spend less time on manual efforts and more time on strategy. This lets technology handle the complexity of orchestrating seamless customer experiences at scale.

Chapter **9**

Boosting Online Business Growth with AI

Would you like to hire a free business strategy consultant who can help your company gain a competitive edge? Luckily, you have several good choices. AI apps can act as your digital consultant. They can help you research your competitors and make customized plans for your company's needs.

This chapter explores several ways AI apps can help boost your company's online business growth:

» Outsmarting your competitors

» Enhancing brand building

» Maximizing your conversions

» Scaling paid advertising return on investment (ROI)

» Tracking key performance indicators (KPIs) with AI

» Innovating new offerings

Outsmarting Your Competitors

AI tools are becoming increasingly popular because they can effectively identify market trends and consumer behavior better than traditional methods. They let you "see around corners" and hopefully outthink the competition.

Adopting AI tools helps you gain an advantage that is difficult for other businesses to equal without using their own AI tools. By implementing AI tools customized to your specific business goals, you can future-proof your strategy and boost growth.

TIP

Many business leaders have started to embrace AI tools, specifically generative AI (GenAI). According to the 2023 KPMG AI Survey, 74 percent of business leaders put AI as the top emerging technology that will impact their business over the next year and a half (https://advisory-marketing.us.kpmg.com/speed/AI2023.html).

AI can analyze your competitors' digital strategies by looking at such things as the keywords they use for search engine optimization (SEO), where their web traffic comes from, their ad spending, and their customers' social media engagement. Analyzing these elements helps you find their weaknesses and blind spots to exploit them. In the following sections, we look at each of these in turn.

Analyzing competitor keywords

To begin, you can use AI tools to analyze your top competitors' websites. You should identify the keywords they rank for in search engines and their keyword gaps (that is, search terms they don't target). In fact, identifying keyword gaps is one of the most valuable features of AI-powered keyword analysis. These gaps are search terms that your competitors aren't targeting but that are relevant to your business. Discovering them is important because it helps you find untapped opportunities in the marketplace.

REMEMBER

Keywords are the words and phrases that potential customers type into search engines. You can drive traffic to your website by ranking for the right keywords and increasing conversions. When selecting an AI tool for keyword analysis, consider factors like ease of use, data accuracy, and cost. Tools to consider include the following:

>> **Semrush (www.semrush.com):** Semrush, as shown in Figure 9-1, allows you to evaluate your competitors' various SEO metrics, including the authority score, referring domains, backlinks, and search traffic.

>> **Ahrefs** (`https://ahrefs.com/keywords-explorer`): The Ahrefs Keywords Explorer, shown in Figure 9-2, lets you discover a competitor's top-ranking keywords. You can sort by search volume and difficulty to uncover the best opportunities.

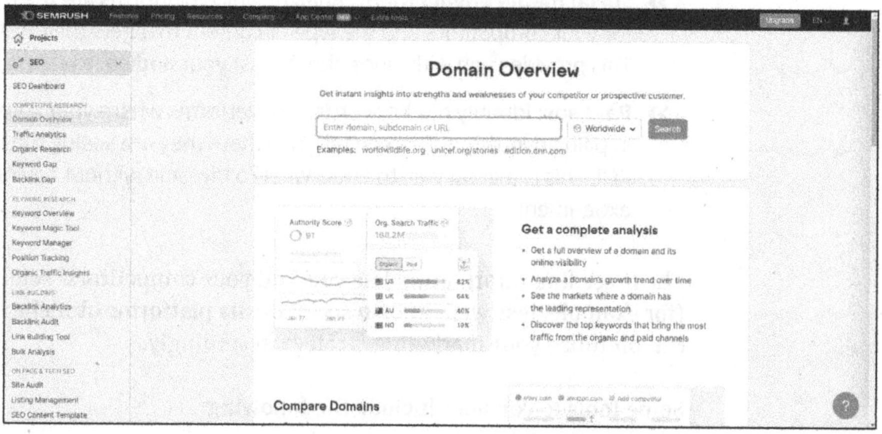

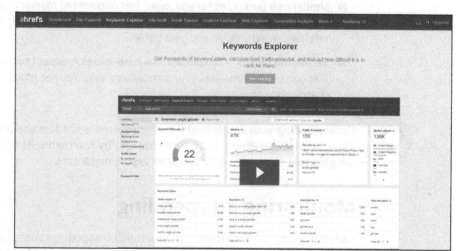

FIGURE 9-1:
Semrush's
research tools.

FIGURE 9-2:
The Ahrefs
Keywords
Explorer.

Discovering traffic sources

Do you know where your competitors' traffic is coming from? You should. Understanding where their traffic comes from is critical for crafting your own marketing strategy. It can help you identify where you should be focusing your resources.

AI tools can analyze competitors' website traffic sources by looking at such things as:

>> **Organic searches:** Look at the keywords driving traffic to your competitors' sites. Are there any you haven't targeted yet?

>> **Social media engagement:** Analyze which platforms are the most effective for your competitors and the type of content that gets the most engagement. This provides you with clues about what your audience wants.

>> **Paid ads:** Identify the keywords and platforms where your competitors invest in paid advertising. This can tell you where they are seeing the highest ROI. This is a great way to know what to invest in without having to experiment.

The preceding information lets you find your competitors' seldom-used channels (for example, less well-known social media platforms or niche forums). Then you can optimize your marketing strategy accordingly.

Some tools to consider include the following:

>> **Similarweb (www.similarweb.com):** This AI-powered market platform analyzes a website's traffic sources and channels. It breaks down things like referrals, search, social, and paid traffic.

>> **BuzzSumo (https://buzzsumo.com/use-cases/competitor-intelligence):** This content tool analyzes your competitors' KPIs. You see metrics such as likes, shares, and comments.

TIP

Understanding your competitors' traffic sources is not just about keeping tabs on them. It's about refining your own strategy. By leveraging AI tools, you discover insights that were once only found by expert marketers.

Monitoring ad spending

Use AI tracking tools to determine how much competitors spend on search, social, display, and other online ads. This helps you determine the level of paid marketing you need to spend to stay ahead. Make sure to adjust your ad budgets to gain the edge.

Here are some tools to try:

>> **SpyFu (www.spyfu.com):** SpyFu tracks competitors' paid search ad keywords, ad copies, and their estimated monthly spending on Google, Bing, and YouTube.

- **Moz** (`https://moz.com/competitive-research`): Moz has a suite of SEO tools to assist with keyword research, rank tracking, and backlink analysis. Of particular interest in competitive intelligence is their free SEO Competitive Analysis Tool. You can use it to analyze your competitors' domains to get a wealth of information.

TIP

To learn more about AI in advertising, see the "Scaling Paid Advertising ROI" section, later in this chapter.

Analyzing social media performance

AI can track competitors' social media followers, engagement, hashtags, mentions, and influencer partnerships. You can use these insights to shape a more effective social media approach for your company. Consider trying these tools:

- **Brandwatch** (`www.brandwatch.com`): Brandwatch is a social listening platform that tracks competitors' followers, engagement, sentiment, and influencers.
- **Talkwalker** (`www.talkwalker.com`): The Talkwalker platform tracks social performance, customer feedback, sentiment, and trends.

Enhancing Brand Building

Another way to boost online business growth is to enhance the branding that resonates with your audience. You can use AI tools to do things like refine your visual identity, simplify your messaging, and clarify your tone of voice. The key is to utilize AI's creative capabilities while staying true to your brand identity. In the following sections, we look at these ways to leverage AI to make your branding more compelling.

Refining visual brand identities

Visual assets like logos, fonts, color palettes, and imagery must reflect your brand DNA. AI tools can help you refine your branded visuals by allowing you to analyze elements in ways you couldn't before. These include

- **Automating design generation:** AI tools can generate several design options based on your defined parameters. This lets you perform A/B testing to accelerate the design process and ensure that the final design is data driven (see the "Creating Ad Copy" section later in this chapter for A/B testing).

>> **Choosing colors:** AI tools can analyze customer interactions and preferences to suggest color schemes that resonate with your target audience. For example, you could analyze sales data to see if specific product colors sell better than others for different customer segments.

>> **Making font choices:** AI apps can analyze text elements in real time to suggest popular fonts across different platforms. This can enhance the user experience. Of course, humans need to make the final decision.

>> **Image recognition and tagging:** AI apps can automatically tag and categorize images. This process makes it easier for brands to manage their visual assets. This is crucial for e-commerce platforms where thousands of product images must be sorted and displayed. Doing this manually would take a great deal of time and be prone to human error.

>> **Analytics and insights:** AI tools can provide insights by tracking how users interact with your creative elements. Then this data can be used to make decisions that refine your brand's identity.

TIP

To learn how AI tools can impact visual content, check out Chapter 6.

Crafting strong brand messaging

Consistent messaging is crucial for brand building. This is an area where AI can be especially helpful. AI can optimize your messaging for impact by utilizing its natural language capabilities. Here are a few ways it can assist you:

>> **Sentiment analysis:** Sentiment analysis provides insights into how your messaging resonates. It analyzes social media conversations and website comments to identify positive and negative associations, emotions, and perceptions related to a brand. (For more about using sentiment analysis, see Chapter 8.)

>> **Content generation:** AI can generate slogans and taglines and copy alternatives that convey the right positioning.

>> **Contextual targeting:** Understanding audience demographics and interests allows AI apps to customize messaging to be more relevant.

>> **Competitive analysis:** By monitoring your competitors' messaging and performing a comparative analysis, AI tools can help create significant differentiation between you and your competitors.

Great brands live in the minds of their customers. As a brand, you can't control what your customers think, but you can learn how you impact them based on what they tell you.

Defining brand voice and tone

Your brand's voice includes your vocabulary, style, and overall personality. It serves as the foundation for building all your customer relationships. You can use AI tools to enhance your branding to foster engagement and loyalty. These tools allow you to continuously learn from your customer data to rapidly test and refine your brand voice across many touchpoints. Here are a few ways AI tools support defining your brand voice and tone:

>> **Analyzing language patterns:** It's necessary to identify the vocabulary, sentence structures, and idioms that make up your brand's voice. You can codify what makes your brand's voice unique by identifying these elements and applying them.

>> **Evaluating values and target audience:** It is essential to understand who your brand is and who it's speaking to. AI tools can evaluate your brand values to identify appropriate voice and tone aspects like formal/informal, emotional/rational, and authoritative/conversational.

>> **Competitive analysis:** This step is often overlooked. Knowing how your brand's voice stacks up against competitors can provide insights into areas for differentiation and improvement. You can more confidently create your messaging when you understand how your brand is understood by your customers.

Using AI, data-driven iterations let you quickly prototype and test your brand assets to increase their impact without making decisions blindly.

Maximizing Conversions

Effective online professionals strive to do all they can to maximize conversions regardless of their position in the organization. AI tools let you optimize every element of your digital presence to get those conversions and sales. They allow you to deliver the right content to the right person at the right time (often referred to as the "holy grail of marketing"). This results in visitors who engage, buy, and promote your brand as advocates.

You can do things to maximize conversions with AI, including segmenting your audience and personalizing content. We look at these in the following sections.

Understanding the segmentation of audiences

One of the key things AI tools permit you to do when analyzing your audience is divide customers into different segments based on their behavior and preferences. This lets you develop targeted marketing strategies for each segment. This is of enormous value to you as a marketer or salesperson.

Here are some of the benefits you get from AI audience segmentation:

>> **Targeting:** AI algorithms can analyze large data sets to identify customer behavior patterns, enabling you to create more accurate segmentation.

>> **Adapting in real time:** AI models can adapt to changes in customer behavior. This ensures that the segments are always up to date.

>> **Optimizing resources:** You can allocate your marketing resources more effectively by knowing which segments will likely convert.

>> **Personalizing experiences:** Personalizing the content you send to customers can significantly boost conversions.

>> **Predicting behavior:** AI apps can forecast the future behavior of each segment, allowing you to proactively create effective marketing strategies. (See Chapter 8 for more about predictive analytics.)

>> **Enhancing ROI:** Better targeting and allocation of resources lead to higher conversion rates, which improves your ROI.

>> **Automating insights:** AI can automatically generate insights about each of your audience segments, making it easier for you to make data-driven decisions.

TIP

To utilize segmentation, consider collaborating with influencers or industry experts with a strong following in the specific segments of your target audience. This will give you a better chance to accelerate sales.

If you want to check out some AI tools that segment your audiences, you can consider some customer data platform (CDP) tools like the following:

>> **Klaviyo (www.klaviyo.com):** Klaviyo is a marketing platform that analyzes customer data like purchases and browsing history to create customized audience segments to send emails and texts.

>> **Segment Personas** (https://segment.com/customer-data-platform/): Segment Personas is a feature within the Segment CDP, shown in Figure 9-3. It creates segments across channels using data from different sources like your website, mobile app, or customer relationship management (CRM) system.

FIGURE 9-3:
Segment
Personas
collects your
data across
different sources
you select.

A CDP is software that helps businesses understand their customers by creating a complete customer profile from their customer data. You can then use this profile to create personalized, targeted marketing campaigns that meet customers' needs and preferences.

REMEMBER

Personalizing content

We cover AI personalization and its impact on the customer journey in Chapter 8. In this section, we look at two ways it relates to optimizing your sales funnel by personalizing user experiences:

>> **Lead scoring:** Lead scoring with AI helps you learn which potential customers are most likely to buy by analyzing current and historical data to see what customers did before they made a purchase. It then uses that information to give scores to new potential customers.

>> **Content testing and optimization:** AI tools test multiple content variations, like images, headlines, and copy, to determine which performs best. They also continuously optimize based on new visitor data. By using this real-time data, you're always getting the best optimization.

Scaling Paid Advertising ROI

Paid advertising is a standard way for brands to drive qualified traffic and sales. AI tools have helped to simplify the creation and management of paid advertising campaigns by conducting in-depth optimization. This would be impossible for staff to do manually.

AI tools are currently very beneficial in producing ads. They automate the process by selecting the most effective keywords, optimizing bids, and creating ad copy that is likely to convert. This analysis not only saves time but also improves the ROI of your advertising campaigns. In the following sections, we look at each process in turn.

Selecting keywords

AI combs through large amounts of search query data to identify high-performing keywords. It can also predict emerging keyword trends, which allows you to find new opportunities (hopefully, before your competitors do). This level of automation and optimization leads to more targeted campaigns, which can drive higher conversion rates.

Optimizing bids

One great feature of AI ad tools is that they can adjust bids based on real-time metrics and market conditions. This ensures that you get the most value for your advertising dollar. This means that bid optimization is no longer a static, one-time selection.

TIP

AI ad tools continuously analyze metrics (like click-through and conversion rates) and changing competitor bids. This real-time analysis lets the AI adjust bids to maximize ROI, which ensures you're not overspending.

Creating ad copy

GenAI can produce multiple variations of ad copy, which can then be A/B tested to identify the most effective messaging. It can create multiple variations of ad copy in seconds, each tailored to different segments of your audience. This enables A/B testing, which allows you to quickly identify which messages resonate most with your target market. The AI can also adapt the copy based on real-time performance data to ensure that your advertising continues to be relevant.

Personalizing and testing

AI can also personalize ad campaigns to individual user profiles and perform continuous testing to optimize performance. AI can segment your audience based on factors like browsing behavior, past purchases, and demographic information. This enables highly personalized ad campaigns that speak directly to the individual's needs and preferences. Additionally, AI can perform continuous multivariate testing on these personalized campaigns, refining them to achieve peak performance over time.

TECHNICAL STUFF

Multivariate testing is a method that tests variations of several elements on a web page or application at the same time to determine which combination performs the best. Unlike A/B testing, which compares two versions of a single element, multivariate testing evaluates multiple elements and their variations at the same time.

USING AI FOR ADS?

Are you looking for a way to begin using AI ad tools? If so, consider trying this AI-powered framework to optimize your paid ad performance:

- **Segment your audience:** Leverage AI tools to analyze your customer data and build predictive models to identify your high-value segments. Then create your ads by starting with high-priority targets.

- **Craft high-converting ads:** Use GenAI copywriting tools to create engaging ad copy and relevant images for each audience. This drives engagement and clicks.

- **Personalize at scale:** After users click through, you should continue personalizing the experience. AI can customize each user's copy and creatives based on their profile and behavior.

- **Optimize campaigns:** Continue using GenAI to extract the maximum value from paid ads across channels like Facebook, Instagram, and Google Ads.

Some tools you might consider trying include:

- **AdCreative.ai** (www.adcreative.ai): AdCreative.ai is an AI tool that optimizes digital advertising creatives. It provides insights into ad performance and provides competitor tracking.

- **ADYOUNEED** (www.adyouneed.com): ADYOUNEED is a multi-platform advertising tool that simplifies and optimizes digital ad creation and management. It supports platforms including Google Ads, Meta Ads (Facebook and Instagram), and LinkedIn.

REMEMBER

Constantly optimizing your ads using AI will drive higher-quality traffic and maximize the ROI on your ad budget. This will help you maintain an ongoing scalable engine for online business growth.

Considering the pros and cons

One of the great benefits of using AI in advertising is that it can analyze real-time data to redistribute budget across various campaigns. This ensures that resources are allocated to the most effective channels, maximizing ROI. Additional benefits include the following:

>> **Cost efficiency:** By automating budget adjustments, businesses can reduce the need for manual oversight, thereby saving time and reducing operational costs.

>> **Data-driven decision-making:** AI provides actionable insights based on data analytics, which allows you to make more informed decisions. This is particularly useful for identifying trends and making quick adjustments to capitalize on them.

>> **Risk mitigation:** AI can predict the performance of different advertising channels and suggest budget adjustments to mitigate risks associated with overspending on underperforming campaigns.

On the negative side, some people have criticized using AI tools in advertising. They believe using AI for budget adjustments could lead to unfair or unethical advertising practices. Here are some of the concerns:

>> **Data privacy:** AI algorithms require access to substantial amounts of data for effective decision-making. This raises concerns about how this data is stored, who has access to it, and how it's used. It could potentially infringe on consumer privacy.

>> **Transparency and accountability:** The use of AI in advertising often operates in a "black box." This makes it difficult for people to understand how decisions are made. This lack of transparency can be a significant issue when it comes to ethical advertising practices.

>> **Regulatory compliance:** Different industries and regions have specific regulations regarding data privacy and ethical advertising. Using AI tools that are not compliant can result in legal repercussions.

>> **Unethical branding:** Unethical use of AI can harm a brand's reputation, causing a loss of consumer trust and revenue.

So, what can you do to avoid risk?

>> **Vet AI tools.** Before adopting any AI tool for advertising, be sure it complies with industry standards and regulations. These standards include the General Data Protection Regulation (GDPR) and the California Consumer Privacy Act (CCPA). For a complete listing of standards and regulations, check out the Interactive Advertising Bureau (IAB) at www.iab.com.

>> **Choose transparency.** Pick AI solutions that offer some level of transparency in their decision-making algorithms. Transparent AI solutions are clear, responsible, and ethical. Choosing transparent solutions helps you meet legal standards and gain the trust of your users.

>> **Monitor continuously.** Regularly audit the AI's decisions to ensure they align with ethical standards and are free of bias. To do this, first define your own ethical standards and identify potential biases. Look at decision-making data to spot any unfair patterns or issues, and make sure to include people with diverse perspectives to catch biases that may not be obvious.

Tracking Key Performance Indicators with AI

KPIs are business metrics that help organizations monitor their performance against objectives. Tracking KPIs has always been an important method for businesses to keep their eye on what's important. KPIs help businesses analyze their growth. Thanks to the use of AI tools, monitoring KPIs has come a long way.

Traditionally, KPIs have been tracked manually. Marketers had to rely on manual processes to collect and analyze data, which was time-consuming and produced errors. Today, AI tools automatically handle data collection and analysis.

Here are some other ways KPI tracking was inadequate:

>> **Limitations:** Due to technological limitations, KPIs could only focus on easily quantifiable metrics like sales volume. Marketers couldn't get the understanding of customer behavior that is available today.

>> **Siloed data:** Audience segmentation wasn't available in the way AI handles it today. Different departments held different parts of the information, making it almost impossible to get a unified view of marketing performance across different channels and campaigns.

>> **Delayed reporting:** Insights from historical data were compiled into reports with a lag time. This lag thwarted the ability to make timely decisions.

Here's how AI tools can significantly enhance the process of KPI tracking to grow your business:

>> **Real-time monitoring:** AI apps can continuously collect and analyze data, providing real-time updates on various KPIs. This allows your business to make timely adjustments to your strategies instead of waiting for end-of-month reports. This is a significant improvement because it lets you make changes as soon as they're warranted.

TIP

Traditional KPI tracking often focuses on single metrics like sales revenue or customer satisfaction. AI can analyze many metrics at once, which allows for a more holistic view of your business's performance.

>> **Benchmarking:** AI can compare your KPIs against industry benchmarks or competitor data to better understand your total performance. This data helps you set more realistic targets.

>> **Customizing:** AI tools allow for the customization of KPI dashboards, enabling you to focus on metrics specific to your goals and industry. This gives you a clearer picture of the threats and risks you face.

>> **Detecting anomalies:** AI algorithms can identify anomalies or outliers in KPI data that could indicate underlying issues. Early detection of these anomalies lets you take immediate action. This could be troubleshooting a problem or capitalizing on an unforeseen positive trend.

Innovating New Offers

Most online businesses try to discover their customers' unmet needs and develop new product concepts and features. Launching innovative new products and services is critical for companies that want to remain competitive. But the risks of innovation are high, and coming up with fresh ideas is always a challenge.

This is where leveraging AI tools is valuable. AI helps businesses identify opportunities for new offerings. This section looks at trend forecasting, generating creative concepts, and refining your innovations related to innovating your products.

Trend forecasting

Being able to see around corners is a very valuable skill. AI-generated reports help anticipate future events by analyzing historical data and current markets. AI predictive analytics can help you capitalize on market trends and provide insights about events that could negatively impact your business. This predictive capability readies companies for challenges and opportunities they may not see coming.

REMEMBER

Your analysis will only be as good as the quality of your data. The insights will be misleading or unreliable if you have error-prone or inaccurate data. For instance, AI tools can analyze several years of sales data to predict future products that may be popular. But if your sales data is flawed, your analysis will be, too.

WARNING

AI tools can tell you what is happening, but they can't tell you why it's happening. For that, you still need to apply your business and industry knowledge. For example, an AI tool could alert you to a big increase in social media mentions, but it (and you) won't know if this is due to a successful marketing campaign, a viral news story, or some other factor.

Generating creative concepts

You can conceptualize new products or services with the insights you've collected from your AI tools. You can input an idea, and AI can help produce detailed concepts to evaluate. This content speeds up the ideation process and provides faster decision-making.

Refining your innovation

When you have a promising idea, AI tools can help you refine it into a workable concept. GenAI tools can write business plans, create relevant marketing copy, and even produce pitch decks to help launch your innovation.

REMEMBER

You can continually ideate, develop, and launch new offerings by developing an AI pipeline. Integrating AI into your innovation strategies will help you deliver unique, relevant products that will hopefully make your competitors have to play catch-up.

Chapter **10**

Enhancing Customer Service with Conversational AI Chatbots

The use of AI chatbots represents a major shift away from conventional customer service to a more effective approach. Previously, customer support relied solely on interactions between customers and staff. Now, using AI chatbots, companies can automate tasks, reduce costs, and provide round-the-clock support. In this chapter, we look at conversational AI (CAI) chatbots, which are the next iteration of traditional chatbots.

These advanced CAI chatbots can handle a wide range of customer service tasks. In some cases, they've already shown that they can outperform staff when it comes to consistency and availability. This chapter looks at the transformational role of CAI chatbots for customer service and the impact they can have on your business and customer satisfaction.

Finding Out about Conversational AI Chatbots

Customer service chatbots are AI-powered programs that handle conversations with customers across communication channels. They can answer questions, provide information, and help with tasks like taking orders or assisting with account issues.

Understanding the process

Traditional rules-based chatbots provided limited responses and no ability to learn from customer interactions. CAI chatbots use natural language processing (NLP) and machine learning (ML) to meet customer needs.

It's useful to understand the capabilities that enable CAI chatbots to deliver automated services. They can

>> Understand the context of the response to respond appropriately during a customer interaction.

>> Process personalized data like order history to provide customized responses.

>> Escalate issues that involve human emotions or very nuanced language to human agents.

>> Integrate across backend systems (like servers or databases) to efficiently serve customers.

Here's how a chatbot technically "responds" to a customer question:

1. The customer submits a query to the chatbot. It could be text, voice, or another input method.

2. The query is captured and pre-processed by the CAI system. The CAI system analyzes the request to identify the user's intent, which involves processing NLP techniques to understand the meaning.

3. The chatbot matches the customer intent to predefined categories in the chatbot's knowledge base. This information helps the chatbot understand the context of the request.

4. That information is used to generate a response that addresses the customer's query. The response can be text, images, audio, or a combination of these formats, depending on what the company chooses.

5. The generated response is delivered back to the customer.

Defining the differences between conversational AI chatbots and ChatGPT

To understand chatbots further, we need to understand the differences between CAI chatbots and ChatGPT. Unfortunately, some people incorrectly label chatbots as ChatGPT. When it comes to customer service, this can be confusing and misleading. CAI chatbots and ChatGPT both use AI, but they differ in their capabilities and use cases — especially when it comes to handling conversations.

Developers designed CAI chatbots for use cases like customer service or sales support. You can integrate them into things like apps or messaging platforms (for example, Facebook Messenger) to answer questions or help with transactions. They focus on mimicking human-like conversation using AI. They combine NLP and ML to create a more natural interaction.

In comparison, ChatGPT, developed by OpenAI, is a more advanced form of AI. It's based on the generative pretrained transformer (GPT) architecture. It uses deep learning, a subset of ML, to deliver answers. It's a more all-purpose conversational agent created to provide information and generate text based on prompts. You can use it for such things as writing assistance and research. (See Chapter 5 for more about ChatGPT's many uses. For more information about technologies like NLP and ML, check out Chapter 1.)

CAI chatbots are customizable for the specific needs of a business or application. You can integrate them with backend systems and databases to provide responses based on real-time data. For example, CAI chatbots can retrieve corporate data like purchase history to answer questions about shipping dates.

Visualizing the differences

Visualizing the differences between CAI chatbots and ChatGPT can be helpful in understanding them. Table 10-1 details the clear distinctions.

CAI chatbots blend rule-based approaches with AI elements. This provides improved quality over traditional chatbots but is not at the level of sophistication of ChatGPT.

TABLE 10-1   **Conversational AI Chatbots versus ChatGPT**

Feature	Conversational AI Chatbots	ChatGPT (Advanced AI)
Operation	AI-driven, typically using a mix of rules and ML techniques.	Utilizes deep learning (GPT architecture).
Conversation handling	Capable of handling a variety of interactions with some level of contextual understanding.	Capable of handling a broader range of topics, more contextually relevant.
Flexibility	More flexible than traditional chatbots; can adapt to different conversation styles.	Highly adaptable, generates responses based on volumes of training data.
Learning capability	Some ability to learn from interactions, but is limited.	Doesn't learn in real-time; relies on pretraining data.
Context understanding	Better at handling off-script conversations than traditional chatbots but has limitations.	Better at understanding context but not adept at highly complex dialogues.
Human-like interaction	More adept at mimicking human conversation than traditional chatbots.	Highly capable of mimicking human-like conversation styles.

Benefitting from Conversational AI Chatbots for Customer Service

CAI chatbots provide immediate responses. This quick response leads to higher customer satisfaction and a better overall service experience. You can get several other benefits by deploying CAI chatbots:

>> **The ability to provide 24/7 support:** CAI chatbots are operational all day, every day. This constant availability ensures that customer support is accessible at any time, serving customers in different time zones and schedules.

>> **Cost efficiency:** By handling routine inquiries and tasks, CAI chatbots can make large customer service teams unnecessary. This leads to savings in operational costs over time.

>> **Scalability:** CAI chatbots can manage a high volume of queries at one time without compromising the quality of the service. This scalability is helpful for businesses experiencing growth or seasonal spikes in customer inquiries.

>> **Task automation:** By automating repetitive tasks, CAI chatbots free up human agents to focus on higher-priority customer issues. This division of labor increases overall efficiency in customer service operations.

>> **Improved data collection:** CAI chatbots are effective in gathering customer data during interactions. You can use this information to improve future marketing strategies and service offerings to make them more in tune with customer needs.

>> **Reduced wait times:** CAI chatbots significantly cut down the time customers spend waiting for responses. This efficiency is key to maintaining customer satisfaction and reducing the frustration associated with long wait times.

>> **Help for internal staff:** Although chatbots assist customers, they're also valuable to internal staff. Having chatbots deal with internal duties provides the following advantages:

- **Reduction in burnout:** By taking over the handling of routine inquiries, chatbots can help prevent agent burnout. Agents can stay focused on delivering better service instead of jumping back and forth from issue to issue.

- **Improved efficiency:** With chatbots handling the usual questions, agents can use their time to handle tasks that require judgment. This leads to a more efficient workflow and helps to improve their performance.

- **Reduced ticket volume:** By resolving basic issues using automation, the use of chatbots reduces the number of tickets that agents need to handle.

CONVERSATIONAL AI CHATBOTS VERSUS TRADITIONAL AUTOMATED RESPONSE SYSTEMS

Customer service has taken a great leap forward with the introduction of CAI chatbots. Previously, traditional automated response systems couldn't deliver a satisfying customer experience. CAI chatbots offer a more seamless experience because of their ability to understand natural language dialogue instead of looking for specific words.

Traditional response systems were rigid and frustrating to use, especially if the customers asked questions that were outside programmed responses. Here are three key differences that demonstrate the value of CAI chatbots over traditional systems:

- **Learning and adaptability:** CAI chatbots utilize ML and NLP to learn from interactions, adapt to new queries, and improve over time. They understand and respond to a range of natural language inputs. Traditional response systems typically worked based on preprogrammed rules and set responses. They couldn't learn from or adapt based on past interactions and were limited to expected questions.

(continued)

(continued)

- **Conversational capabilities:** CAI chatbots are designed to simulate human conversations and understand context. Traditional automated response systems were limited to basic, menu-driven interactions (like phone tree systems). They couldn't handle open-ended conversations.

- **Personalization:** CAI chatbots can provide personalized responses based on customer data and past interactions. When using traditional response systems, personalization was limited, and these systems typically couldn't store or process specific information beyond each session.

The advances that CAI chatbots provide are a great improvement over the old way. The difference in customer experience is recognized and welcomed by customers.

Constructing Conversational AI Chatbots

When it comes to implementing chatbots for customer service, there are several key points that should shape your development. Here are several considerations to use to guide your chatbot development:

>> **Finding the right use cases for your chatbot:** It is crucial to identify the specific areas where chatbots can add value to customer service. It could be handling frequently asked questions (FAQs), providing product recommendations, or providing order tracking. Make sure the use case aligns with customer needs.

>> **Defining the chatbot's purpose:** Before building a chatbot, you need to define its purpose. This involves determining what tasks it will do, the questions it can answer, and the tone it should use.

REMEMBER

Setting a chatbot tone that matches your brand is important. Creating a tone that feels natural to the brand will make your customers feel comfortable using it.

>> **Focusing on customer-centric design:** Always keep the customer at the forefront when you're designing your chatbot. Make sure you know their pain points and preferences.

>> **Making data-driven decisions:** Leverage data and analytics to improve your chatbot's performance. Monitor customer interactions and use feedback to identify areas for improvement.

Measuring the Return on Investment of Conversational AI Chatbots

One question frequently asked by management regarding chatbots is about the return on investment (ROI) from implementing them. Understanding how to measure the ROI of CAI chatbots is key to justifying their use. In the next sections, we look at some important measures you can take and let you know the results you should look for.

REMEMBER

Before calculating ROI, it's important to set a baseline for comparison. This helps evaluate the direct impact of chatbots on business operations and your customers' experiences. You should also continuously monitor relevant metrics to assess the ongoing effects on your business.

Improving customer service efficiency

To do: Compare the efficiency and costs between human agents and CAI chatbots in handling customer inquiries.

Expected outcome: Look for a reduction in average handling time and an increase in queries resolved without human intervention. However, for the full picture, consider the complexity of queries that chatbots can handle and their evolving capabilities.

Reducing operational costs

To do: Analyze the reduction in staffing, training, and overhead expenses. Include costs related to integrating the chatbot into existing systems and the required updating of its knowledge base.

Expected outcome: There may be a reduction in the need for a large customer service team.

REMEMBER

Before making staff adjustments, remember to factor in initial setup costs and ongoing maintenance for your CAI chatbot.

Boosting sales conversion rates

To do: Track the sales conversions initiated by chatbot interactions. Consider the design, interaction quality, and integration of the chatbot into the sales process.

Expected outcome: CAI chatbots can typically upsell or cross-sell, which directly contributes to the bottom line. Be aware that the effectiveness can vary by industry and application.

Enhancing lead generation

To do: Assess the chatbot's effectiveness in generating and qualifying leads. Look at the quality of leads and the efficiency of the qualification process.

Expected outcome: Successful lead generation by chatbots is a value-add to sales teams.

REMEMBER

The integration of chatbots into the overall sales strategy is the key to this success. You need to have your sales team on board, working in conjunction with the technology.

Tracking engagement metrics

To do: Examine interaction patterns, including interaction frequency, duration, and repeat usage. Measure engagement subjectively and consistently.

Expected outcome: You should expect increased engagement and customer satisfaction levels, but methods of measurement should be carefully considered.

TIP

Use customer feedback on chatbot interactions to get more insights about customer sentiment. You can capture this information without having to quiz customers directly, which is a great advantage.

Increasing resolution rate

To do: Calculate the percentage of queries completely resolved by the chatbot. Consider the chatbot's capability to escalate complex issues to human agents.

Expected outcome: You should get an increase in resolution rates and customer satisfaction levels. Just remember to consider the complexity of resolved questions.

Ensuring accuracy

To do: Monitor the accuracy and misunderstanding rates of chatbot responses — factor in the chatbot's learning and adaptation capabilities over time.

Expected outcome: High accuracy rates will mean better ROI. The CAI chatbot's ability to learn and improve from interactions is a factor in long-term ROI.

TRAVELING ON AMTRAK WITH CONVERSATIONAL AI

Betting on AI to solve business problems turned out to be a great investment for Amtrak, the largest train passenger provider in the United States. According to a 2023 LinkedIn article written by Ethel Emmons (www.linkedin.com/pulse/how-ai-chatbot-transforming-customer-service-amtrak-ethel-emmons), Amtrak made impressive gains using a CAI chatbot for customer service.

- **Problem:** Amtrak experienced a 47.4 percent decrease in passengers in 2020 due to the pandemic (with a slight recovery in 2022), but the numbers were still well below peak ridership.

- **Solution:** Amtrak invested in an AI-backed chatbot, "Next IT," evolving from its initial "Julie" system created in 2012. The AI chatbot offered personalized, 24/7 customer support, improving customer satisfaction and engagement. This new AI chat platform handles more than five million queries annually, ranging from travel bookings to general inquiries, significantly improving customer service efficiency.

- **Results:** The AI system reported a 50 percent annual increase in usage, contributing to a 30 percent increase in revenue compared to other booking methods. Amtrak saved approximately $1 million annually in customer service expenses, with an 800 percent ROI.

This demonstrates how even traditional companies can realize significant gains using AI.

Integrating Conversational AI Chatbots into Existing Systems

The key to integrating AI chatbots into existing company systems is balancing automation with human oversight. To successfully integrate chatbots, here are a few steps to take:

>> **Assess conversational workflows.** Take a close look at your current conversational processes between your customers and agents. Identify areas where chatbots can automate certain steps to streamline the workflow.

>> **Ensure data integration.** Determine how the chatbot will integrate with your existing data sources. Plan which data the chatbot will need to access to serve customers, such as account information or order history.

>> **Develop NLP components.** Create intents, entities, and dialogs to enhance the chatbot's natural language capabilities. Use existing support content, such as FAQs and documentation, to speed up the development process.

REMEMBER

Developers teach chatbots to understand language by building three main parts:

- **Intents:** What the customer is trying to do (for example, book a flight).

- **Entities:** The details about what the customer wants. These are variables that the user needs to fill in to help the chatbot understand and get details from the user's message.

- **Dialogs:** Possible conversations around each intent. These are different ways that customers may state their requests.

This allows the chatbot to understand the requests, collect the details, and respond to customer questions.

>> **Evaluate channel options.** Consider which channels are most appropriate for your chatbot, such as website, text message, or social media direct messages (DMs). Integrate the primary channels that your customers commonly use first.

>> **Plan for scalability.** Expect that conversation volume will increase over time. Make sure that your chatbot is designed to handle increased usage, especially on your popular channels.

>> **Prioritize maintainability.** Regular content and feature updates are necessary, so your chatbots must be easy to update and improve.

>> **Address security concerns.** Consider security, compliance, and data privacy requirements. Understand the policies that need to be followed because chatbots have access to customer data.

TIP

Consider enabling human handoff workflows for conversations the AI can't handle well. Combining AI and human support can ensure round-the-clock coverage.

Personalizing Customer Interactions

CAI chatbots are designed to deliver personalized experiences — light years away from the generic, script-based responses that were previously available. These chatbots improve customer support by providing highly personalized assistance.

For example, if you had a specific issue in the past, the CAI chatbot can recall those details, making the resolution process more efficient. Each interaction with the chatbot then becomes a building block that creates a more personalized customer experience.

CAI chatbots can enhance the customer journey by "remembering" preferences and past interactions. This allows for quicker transactions and support and improves the customer experience. (For more about the customer journey, check out Chapter 8.)

Improving the shopping experience

When it comes to online shopping, CAI chatbots have transformed the experience by making shopping more personalized. They can

>> Personalize shopping advice based on browsing history

>> Offer product recommendations customized to individual customer preferences

>> Assist with the checkout processes, making it more likely that customers won't abandon their shopping carts before making a purchase

Ensuring ethical personalization

The ability of chatbots to remember past interactions and preferences raises privacy concerns. You must design and operate them in compliance with data protection regulations and with respect for customer privacy.

For more information about using AI responsibly and ethically, turn to Chapter 13.

Using Chatbots with Human and AI Collaboration

Choosing between live agents and chatbots for customer service is a major decision. It's tempting to choose a pure human agent system or a chatbot-only model for all your customer-facing interactions. But it's important to understand that both options have their limitations, so you may want to consider a hybrid model.

TIP

A hybrid model combines the efficiency of chatbots with the personal attention of live agents. It's effective because it adapts to the specific needs of each customer. Some people may want quick, automated responses, while others want human interaction.

Understanding the hybrid model

In a hybrid system, the opening interaction is typically handled by a chatbot. CAI chatbots answer FAQs and perform basic tasks. Chatbots are very efficient, but they're not yet capable of handling very complex questions. This is where the live agent steps in and the user is informed that they've been sent to a human.

Over time, as live agents interact with the system, they contribute to the chatbot's "learning." This is done using ML, where the chatbot gradually improves its responses and decision-making capabilities by analyzing new data. The more the chatbot is used, the smarter it becomes, eventually leading to higher performance output.

Collaborating with agents and chatbots

Agents can monitor chatbot conversations in real time. This can prove useful because it's not just about human interaction but also about learning and improving the chatbot. If the chatbot struggles or a customer shows signs of frustration, the agent can take over. This transition should be natural, with the chatbot programmed to understand signs of customer unhappiness and suggest escalating to a live agent.

TIP

Are you wondering whether a hybrid customer service system raises questions about staff availability for a 24/7 operation? You don't have to have round-the-clock staffing by live agents. You have the option of using chatbots exclusively for non-business hours. If your business is global, you can shift to staff members who are working at different hours from different locations. Also, if a chatbot encounters a question it can't handle and no agents are available, it can let the customer know about the next available time for live support and offer to schedule a callback or email response.

Considering Best Practices

Although using advanced chatbots for customer service is relatively new, there are several best practices you can follow:

>> **Simplify design.** Plan for clear interactions in your chatbot. Use simple language instead of jargon to avoid confusing your customers. The key is to provide easy communication.

>> **Incorporate visuals.** Where appropriate within a conversation, integrate visual elements like images, graphics, and buttons. You can use these visuals to explain a point further or facilitate customer input. It's more appealing than heavy blocks of text alone.

REMEMBER

Make sure visual aspects meaningfully supplement the information. Everything you display should improve the clarity of the conversation.

>> **Gather feedback.** Provide customers with an easy mechanism to offer feedback, such as a simple thumbs up/down or number rating. This gives you the ability to constantly track satisfaction. It also helps you identify issues and add popular features.

>> **Create a personality.** Give your chatbot a personality that reflects your brand's voice. Use humor (carefully) to make interactions more fun. Make your chatbot feel like an extension of your brand voice. Make sure to keep the personality consistent across features so the conversations don't feel robotic.

>> **Stay up to date with trends.** Your chatbot content can't remain the same over time. Things like language and priorities are constantly changing. You need to update phrasing or even web slang to stay current. You want to demonstrate that you understand your customers and speak their language.

>> **Identify escalation triggers.** Determine pain points or topics in customer issues early on that provide signals for automated or customer-driven escalation to live agents as needed. You should create these triggers based on such things as contextual cues, perceived lack of confidence in the chatbot responses, or direct requests for agents. The goal is to maximize how often the chatbot can resolve the customer's needs without getting human help by using triggers.

TIP

Escalation triggers are rules that transfer a customer from the CAI chatbot to a human agent when additional help is needed. This happens if the customer asks for an agent or if the chatbot doesn't understand a question. The triggers detect when the AI chatbot reaches its limits in helping someone. All chatbots have some gaps in their abilities. The triggers bridge the human/AI capabilities.

>> **Conduct A/B testing.** Continuously perform A/B testing to perfect the chatbot's responses and flow. This lets you improve the answers by testing strategies and using the most successful ones. Continuous experimentation using A/B testing of conversation components provides the feedback you need to optimize performance.

Reviewing Options for Creating Chatbots

Not every business has the in-house technical expertise or resources necessary to implement CAI chatbots. This may be because you have a lack of specialized knowledge in AI or limited access to the tools. You also have maintenance and updates to keep up with. If you're in this position, you can

>> **Use a no-code chatbot platform.** If your team doesn't have coding knowledge, you may want to consider a no-code platform. These platforms typically have drag-and-drop interfaces and prebuilt templates. They're limited in the ways you can customize them, but if you want to try this option, here are tools to consider:

   • **Manychat** (https://manychat.com): Manychat, shown in Figure 10-1, has customizable templates to build bots without coding skills.

   • **Chatfuel** (https://chatfuel.com): Chatfuel is easy to customize to create bots for messaging apps visually.

>> **Outsource chatbot development.** You can hire agencies or freelancers for chatbot design. This gives you access to expert skills if you don't have technical staff. It also enables you to get a chatbot customized to your exact needs. Of course, this would typically cost more than no-code solutions.

>> **Utilize a prebuilt chatbot.** You may want to use customizable chatbot templates made for specific industries or functions. This saves time and gets you started. The chatbot should meet your needs right out of the box, but it may not integrate easily with your other internal systems.

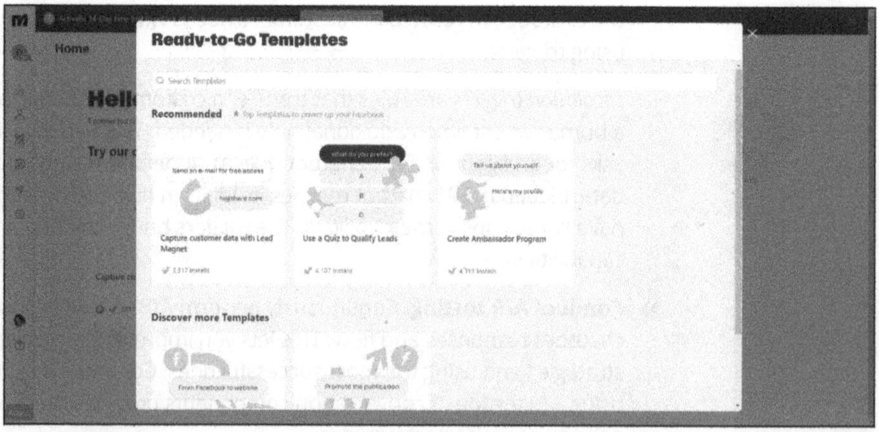

FIGURE 10-1: Manychat has many templates to choose from.

>> **Adopt chatbot plugins or integrations.** You may try integrating chatbot plug-ins into existing website platforms or your customer relationship management (CRM) system. This helps streamline operations and integrate with workflows. You should also be aware that this makes you reliant on third-party program updates.

>> **Utilize chatbots with limited functionality.** You can implement chatbots for specific tasks like answering FAQs or handling customer inquiries. This simplifies development and management and is faster to build. However, you may find it difficult to expand its scope in the future.

>> **Explore managed chatbot services.** If you want to focus on things like content creation and branding, consider outsourcing the technical management of your chatbots. This would allow you to have your builds and updates managed for you. The caveat is that you're then dependent on a vendor's limitations and timeline. If you want to try this option, here are some tools that manage backend operations:

- **LivePerson** (www.liveperson.com): LivePerson, is a CAI platform that combines chatbots and human agents.

- **Chatbotly** (https://chatbotly.co): Chatbotly, shown in Figure 10-2, is a managed chatbot creation and hosting platform that handles the building, deploying, and updating of bots.

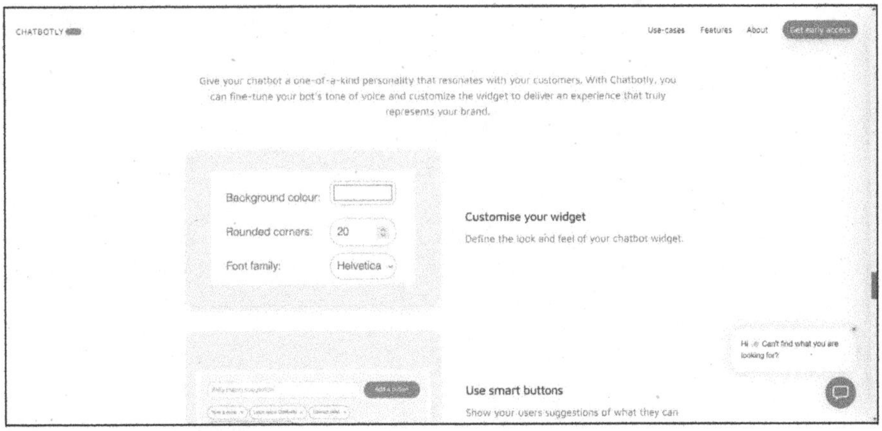

FIGURE 10-2: Chatbotly manages chatbot creation and hosting.

Start with a chatbot pilot or trial. Beginning on a small scale allows you to experiment and reduce risks.

TIP

4
Future-Proofing Your Career

Leverage AI to build a powerful personal brand, so you stand out among the competition.

Create a personal brand persona using AI that guides your content and messaging.

Uncover insights on how to keep your career secure and understand which duties AI can't replace.

Explore approaches to adapt your skills to remain relevant and in demand in an AI-powered world.

Chapter **11**

Building an AI-Powered Personal Brand

B rand building has always been challenging. Marketers found it difficult to know what their audience was thinking — and there were limited ways to find out. Applying AI tools to audience analysis has transformed brand building. AI tools can analyze company data to provide insights into customer behavior. They have made working on brand building a data-driven exercise. This means that marketers' personal opinions have taken a back seat to actual data — which is a good thing.

TIP

Check out Chapter 9 for a deeper dive into organizational branding.

When it comes to *personal* brand building, the challenges are different. It's not usually the technology that holds you back; it's the ability to promote your own unique skills. Many people find it difficult to talk about their abilities and successes. In fact, the key to creating a great personal brand is not to view it as self-promotion but to communicate your unique experience and serve others.

The good news is that AI technology gives you access to powerful branding tools that were once only the province of large organizations. By providing data-based analyses, these tools take the focus off you having to highlight your wins. This chapter explores how you can use AI to analyze and enhance your personal brand. We look at analyzing your personal brand using the seven Cs.

Introducing Personal Branding with the Seven Cs

Your personal brand is the unique expression of your public persona. It's how you present yourself online (and offline) to potential clients, employers, and peers. Your personal brand is the "story" that distinguishes you in your industry — it's what people associate you with when they hear your name.

REMEMBER

A good personal brand is crucial for professional success. It establishes your reputation and helps you find new opportunities. It's important to be clear about what people think about you, when (and if) they think about you.

AI tools help you take a more strategic approach to personal branding. They take the focus off having to sell yourself and put it on data analysis. AI tools make it easier to evaluate and measure your online presence. In this section, we look at the role AI tools can play in the key areas of branding using the seven Cs:

- » **Current assessment:** AI apps help you analyze how you're currently viewed. You can assess your digital profile across all channels, including social media and online platforms. These tools can provide you with insights into your communication style, niche, and engagement patterns. In short, it helps you understand how you're perceived online. Additionally, AI-driven analytics can point to areas where your brand hits the mark and where you have gaps.

- » **Customer exploration:** AI tools can analyze your audience's demographics, interests, and online behavior. This helps you customize your personal brand to appeal to your unique audience. It can ensure that your messaging and content match their interests. Importantly, these tools can segment your audience based on factors like age and browsing habits. This helps in the development of more personalized marketing strategies. AI tools can also track changes in audience behavior over time. This gives you insight so you can adapt your strategy.

- » **Content analysis:** AI apps help you understand the impact of the content you've already created. This includes doing sentiment analysis (positive and negative perceptions), reviewing your popular topics, and monitoring engagement metrics. Understanding which topics your audience responds to will help guide your content strategy.

- » **Competitive review:** AI apps can monitor competitors in your niche. They can analyze their strategies, strengths, and weaknesses.

- » **Customizing a persona:** AI apps can help you use your customer research to create one or more representative customer personas that represent your ideal target audience. Having your persona in focus makes it easier to think about your brand as a whole.

>> **Constructing a unique value proposition (UVP):** AI apps can help you develop a UVP that clarifies what makes your brand worth paying attention to. It helps you understand what value you offer your customers that competitors don't. A strong UVP is key to maintaining a strong personal brand.

>> **Continuous tracking:** AI-powered analytics tools will help you track the growth of your personal brand. You can monitor metrics like follower growth and engagement rates to measure your brand's performance over time.

TIP

It will work to your advantage if you follow the seven Cs in order because, like putting together a puzzle, the pieces only fit one way. However, if one of the areas is a particular problem for you, start there. Make this process work for you. If it proves useful, you can use it throughout your career.

REMEMBER

You want to thoroughly understand your starting point, audience, content, and competitive landscape before defining the differentiation and value of your personal brand. That's why you should continuously monitor your brand based on real-world feedback and data.

Step 1: Current assessment

Your personal brand is unique to you, but it's hard for you to analyze yourself objectively. Let AI tools take the pressure off. These tools can take all the data from your online presence and help identify what makes you unique.

Understanding how your brand is currently perceived is a crucial first step. AI tools can help you create a detailed picture. They can analyze everything from your social media posts and interactions to online articles and blog mentions. For example, an AI tool might review your LinkedIn profile to analyze your posts, endorsements, and network interactions to determine your professional influence. This is probably not something you could objectively do yourself.

Asking questions

Unfortunately, AI tools can't do the whole job. Self-awareness is critical in personal branding. AI tools let you gain a clearer, more objective view of your digital presence, but you also need to be honest about your strengths and weaknesses.

TIP

Before you begin using AI tools, review your current online presence by asking yourself the following questions:

» How am I perceived online?

» What elements of my online presence am I most and least confident about, and why?

» How does my current online presence differ from what I hope to create?

» What ways can AI tools help me find aspects of my digital presence that I'm not aware of or that I underestimate?

TIP

Answering these questions allows you to combine your strengths with AI market data to develop a "big-picture view" of your brand. For example, if AI data finds that a part of your audience is focused on a specific problem that is your specialty, you can offer solutions and capitalize on a previously unknown market opportunity. This can help you build strong relationships with your audience and open new revenue streams.

Creating a baseline

To establish a baseline of your current digital footprint, select AI tools that provide insights into your style. This includes reviewing social media profiles, blog posts, online mentions, and overall sentiment.

You can use AI tools to understand where you currently stand with your audience. Here are two to consider:

» **Talkwalker** (www.talkwalker.com): You can use Talkwalker, shown in Figure 11-1, to analyze the engagement with your posts. The key is to look for patterns in audience reactions. Ask yourself which posts capture the most attention. Hunt for clues about what people are thinking about your brand. You can also see what they think about a competitor's brand.

» **Awario** (https://awario.com): Awario is useful for social media and web monitoring. You can track information about your brand across social networks, blogs, forums, and the web. It's particularly useful for small to medium-size businesses, as well as individuals, because it's not cost-prohibitive.

REMEMBER

You can use tools to track trends and predict how changes in your approach may impact your audience's reception. Tools like Hootsuite (www.hootsuite.com) and Sprout Social (https://sproutsocial.com) can be helpful here.

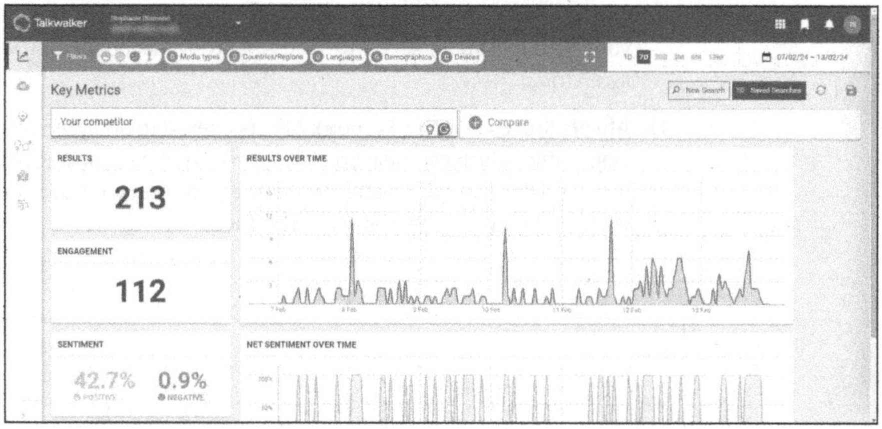

FIGURE 11-1:
Talkwalker
shows you a
competitor's
brand results.

At this point in the process, take a step back and look at the data and insights you've collected. Are there areas where you stand out? Are there aspects of your online presence that need improvement? Finding those areas to improve is as important as identifying your strengths and areas for growth. Do these insights align with the image you want to represent?

Step 2: Customer exploration

Understanding your audience is the foundation for your personal identity. You need to understand your audience's personality and map out who they are, what they care about, and, most important, how they interact with you. The more you know about them, the better you can customize your story to capture their attention. If you understand your audience at a granular level, you can create a personal brand that talks directly to their needs and desires.

TIP

Before utilizing AI tools, it's a good idea to define who you think your target audience is. Are they professionals in a specific industry? Potential clients? Having a clear picture of your audience helps you develop a more focused analysis. It will also show you how close to the mark you actually are when you get your data.

Choosing AI tools

AI tools are invaluable for analyzing your audience. They provide data-driven insights that help segment the audience so you can meet their expectations. They analyze not only the content you create but also how your audience engages with it. Here are some tools to consider:

>> **SparkToro** (https://sparktoro.com): SparkToro, shown in Figure 11-2, is an easy-to-use app that can comb through online data to pinpoint exactly where

your potential audience hangs out, what they talk about, and who they listen to.

>> **Ahrefs** (`https://ahrefs.com`): Ahrefs uses AI to analyze search patterns and web traffic, which can help you identify content gaps and keyword opportunities. It enables you to create content that matches your personal strengths with what your audience is searching for.

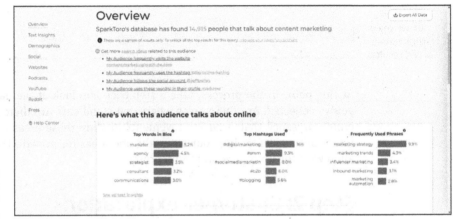

FIGURE 11-2: SparkToro helps you find your audience.

Analyzing audience data

After the AI has provided you with insights, your task is to interpret them. This involves going through the data to identify key themes and patterns. For example, the AI may show you that your LinkedIn articles on a specific topic are getting more engagement and positive feedback compared to your other topics. Obviously, this is valuable information.

TIP

Take your time and comb through your data to discover information that may surprise you. Here are some things to look at:

>> **Patterns:** Patterns in demographics such as age, location, and interests can help direct your choice of topics.

>> **Feedback and comments:** Direct feedback, reviews, and comments can give insights into what your audience thinks and feels about your brand.

>> **Influencer and peer interactions:** Identify if certain thought leaders or colleagues influence your audience. This information can help you find opportunities for partnerships or influencers.

- **Device usage:** Know whether your audience primarily uses mobile devices or computers so you know how to design and distribute your content.

- **Purchase behavior:** If applicable, analyze your customers' buying patterns. What products or services do they prefer? What influences their buying decisions or desired action (for example, signing up for a newsletter)?

TIP

Understanding the weaknesses or gaps in your online presence is critical. Your main objective here is to use AI-driven insights to fine-tune your personal brand.

Step 3: Content analysis

Introducing AI tools to analyze your content will help you gain an understanding of your content's impact. It will also help you automate and enhance the analysis process. AI tools allow you to understand your audience's sentiment, tell you how to optimize your content, and automate its delivery.

In Chapter 5, we discuss how to use generative AI (GenAI) to assist in creating content for your audience. In this section, we look at analyzing your content to improve your content's engagement.

Focusing on engagement

To create content that delights your audience, you need to analyze your audience's reactions to your content. To do an effective analysis, consider the following:

- **Content formats:** Which content formats have been most popular? Your audience may prefer videos or like reading their content. Make sure you provide them with their preferred formats.

- **Content sharing and virality:** See which content is shared the most. Of course, viral content offers insights into the topics and formats that have the potential to expand your reach.

- **Reviewing popular topics:** Think about the topics that have connected most with your audience. Try to identify trending topics and successful content themes in your niche. Find the topics that are too controversial or unappealing to your audience and refrain from broaching them.

- **Looking at patterns:** AI tools can analyze social media engagement patterns and identify effective content types and best posting times for audience interaction.

The answers to these questions give you valuable information for future content planning. It also makes it much easier to know what format, time, and topic of content will build audience relationships.

Understanding sentiment

It's important to look at the sentiment of your audience toward your personal brand or content. Are the comments and reactions mostly positive, negative, or neutral? This information helps in understanding audience perception and adjusting your messaging accordingly.

Here are some tools to consider:

>> **Mention (https://mention.com):** This AI app, shown in Figure 11-3, looks at mentions of your name or brand to analyze the sentiment of these mentions. It can help you understand your audience's perception of you. It can also show you mentions of your competitors.

>> **MonkeyLearn (https://monkeylearn.com):** You can use this AI app to analyze the sentiment — positive, negative, or neutral — expressed in audience reactions. This can help you understand how your content is perceived from an emotional perspective so you can adjust your messaging.

FIGURE 11-3:
Mention keeps you informed about your audience's sentiment.

For more information about sentiment analysis, turn to Chapter 8.

When you're looking for content topics, don't forget that AI tools can identify trending topics and conversations relevant to your niche. Tools like Google Trends (https://trends.google.com) or **Exploding Topics** (https://explodingtopics.com) provide insights into what's currently popular.

Improving your skills and staying up to date with trends in your industry can add depth to your personal brand. This may involve taking courses, attending workshops, or engaging in professional groups.

Step 4: Competitive review

At this stage in your personal branding process, you need to consider your industry position in relation to your competitors. You want to understand how your audience interacts with your competitors so you can find gaps and uncover opportunities to differentiate yourself.

There are a few key differences in how you should use AI tools for personal branding versus organizational branding:

>> **Personal assessment:** You have to analyze how your personal story and purpose differentiate your brand. Organizations focus more on achievements, culture, and brand identity through logos, design, and so on. For suggested AI tools to use, see "Step 1: Current assessment," earlier in this chapter.

>> **Customer targeting:** You should target your audience based on demographics, interests, values, and *psychographics* (the study of consumers based on psychological attributes, including their attitudes, interests, and values). Organizations look at buyer persona attributes like industry, role, and intent signals (for example, when they look at content, do they intend to research or buy?). For some AI tools, you can consider for analyzing customers, see "Step 2: Customer exploration," earlier in this chapter.

>> **Content focus:** Personal branding content highlights things like experiences, expertise, and thought leadership. Organizations emphasize products, value props, solutions, and customer-centric educational content. Keep the focus on what makes your content unique to you. For suggested AI tools to use for content, see "Step 3: Content analysis."

>> **Metrics:** For your personal brand, your analytics need to focus on reach, audience engagement, and content performance. Organizations look at things like market share, revenue, and customer acquisition costs. For suggested AI tools to use for monitoring, see "Step 7: Continuous tracking," later in this chapter.

Your personal brand will look at metrics for success based on your influencer authority, trust, and awareness.

Step 5: Customizing a persona

Whether you have a persona that you're modifying or you're creating one for the first time, your brand persona should reflect the insights you uncovered from your extensive data analysis. Here's one way to customize a persona:

1. **Review the data you gathered from the previous sections of this chapter.**

   Use the data to identify patterns, preferences, and perceptions of your audience. Look for insights on what content resonates most, audience demographics, psychographics, and how you compare to competitors. Based on these insights, refine or establish your brand persona. This step involves aligning your persona with the preferences and expectations of your audience while staying true to yourself.

   You can use AI apps to assist in developing the content for personas. Consider using GenAI tools like Jasper (www.jasper.ai) and Claude (https://claude.ai). Turn to Chapter 5 for more details.

2. **Reassess your target audience in light of the data analysis.**

   Make sure that you customize your brand persona to appeal to this audience. Adjust your persona's attributes (like tone, style, and values) to resonate with your audience, as suggested by the data.

3. **Make content and strategy adjustments.**

   Plan your content, marketing strategies, and engagement tactics to reflect the characteristics of your brand persona.

4. **Present your persona.**

   After you construct the verbiage for your persona, you can use AI tools to format and create a representation for yourself. Consider these tools:

   - **HubSpot** (www.hubspot.com/make-my-persona)**:** This AI tool, shown in Figure 11-4, helps you create a persona that is formatted and can be presented if applicable.

   - **Userforge** (https://userforge.com)**:** This app, shown in Figure 11-5, helps create detailed user personas with collaborative features. It's useful for teams looking to share insights and build personas together.

REMEMBER

Be prepared to make further adjustments to your brand persona as you gather more data and insights over time. Regularly collect and analyze data to ensure your brand persona remains relevant.

FIGURE 11-4:
HubSpot's
persona tool is
a complete
visual tool.

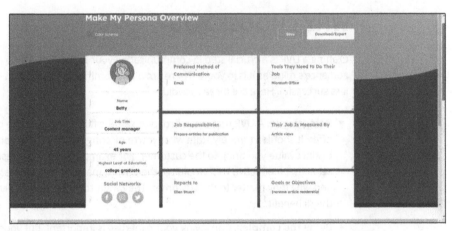

FIGURE 11-5:
Userforge makes
creating a
persona easy.

Step 6: Constructing a unique value proposition

Have you thought about why your audience should choose you? Being able to communicate that message is key to building your brand. Marketers call it your UVP. Your UVP is a statement that describes the unique benefits you offer. It includes how you solve your audience's problems and what distinguishes you from the competition. Consider your UVP like your personal brand's headline. It's an important component of your personal branding strategy, guiding interactions and how you present yourself online.

Your UVP is what makes your personal brand stand out. So, how do you construct a UVP? Consider the following:

>> **What you do:** Start with a clear understanding of what you offer. This could be a specific skill, service, product, knowledge, or type of content.

>> **How you serve your audience:** Think about the problems of your target audience. How does what you offer address these needs?

>> **What makes you different:** Reflect on what makes your approach or perspective different from the others in your field. This could be your unique experience, your innovative solutions, or your personal perspective.

WHY CHOOSE YOU?

Crafting a UVP is a crucial step in communicating your brand. It must be as clear in your audience's mind as it is in yours. There are a few common mistakes that make a UVP less successful. Here are three to avoid:

- **Being vague:** A UVP that is too broad or generic fails to capture the benefits you offer. It shouldn't merely state what you're offering — it should emphasize the distinct value you bring to the customer. For example, when you describe your services, an effective UVP would tell them what makes these services high-quality and why they matter to the customer. They want to know specifically how they'll benefit.

- **Being too complex:** Conveying your expertise is important, but your UVP should be simple and clear. Overuse of jargon or technical language can turn people away.

- **Not focusing on your audience's needs:** A UVP should be customer-centric, addressing the specific problems or needs of your target audience. For example, if you're a technology consultant, your UVP shouldn't just detail your process; it should explain how your process solves real problems or improves the customer's business.

Also, don't forget that AI tools can help perfect your UVP. By using AI-driven A/B testing and analytics, you can test different versions of your UVP to see which resonates most with your audience. AI tools can provide real-time feedback and metrics on engagement and conversion rates.

Step 7: Continuous tracking

Engagement is more than likes and shares; it's about understanding the impact of your content. AI analytics tools go beyond the basic metrics to give you a deeper understanding of how your content connects with your audience. Table 11-1 shows a list of the types of metrics you should continually track, as well as some suggested tools for tracking.

TABLE 11-1   **Metrics for Continuous Monitoring**

Category	Description	Tools	Use Case
Social media metrics	Track followers, engagement rate (likes, comments, shares), and mentions on platforms like Facebook, Instagram, LinkedIn, and X (formerly known as Twitter).	Hootsuite, Sprout Social	Automate tracking of social media engagement and presence.
Website analytics	Monitor website traffic, visitor demographics, session duration, and bounce rates. Pay attention to the sources of traffic to understand which aspects of your personal brand are driving visitors.	Google Analytics	Understand website traffic and visitor behavior to refine online presence.
Content engagement	For blogs or published articles, track views, shares, comments, and time spent on the page.	BuzzSumo, Facebook Insights, Medium	Measure the engagement and impact of blog posts and articles.
Email marketing metrics	Track open rates, click-through rates, and subscription growth if using email newsletters.	Constant Contact, Mailchimp	Evaluate the effectiveness of email marketing campaigns.
Search engine visibility	Monitor your personal brand's visibility on search engines. Track how often your name or related keywords appear in search results.	Google's Search Console, Semrush	Enhance online visibility and search engine ranking.
Sentiment analysis	Gauge public sentiment and tone in mentions of your brand.	Brand24, Mention	Understand public perception and sentiment toward your brand.
Feedback and adaptation	Regularly seek feedback and be open to adapting your strategy. The digital market and audience preferences can change quickly, so flexibility is important. Survey customers as appropriate.	Google Forms, SurveyMonkey	Maintain your relevance and effectiveness in rapidly changing digital environments.

AI TOOLS MAKE THE DIFFERENCE

There's no shortage of best-practice lists for personal branding. Most of them don't include the use of AI tools because they're so new. This list remedies that issue.

The key to beating the competition is to uncover actionable information. You can easily do that by adding AI tools to your repertoire. Here are several branding best practices where AI tools make a significant difference:

- **Monitoring your brand:** Use AI analytics tools to listen to your brand and identify opportunities.

- **Testing content variations:** A/B test content created with AI tools to see what resonates best with your audience.

- **Personalizing interactions:** Use AI chatbots and messaging tools to add a personal touch to customer interactions.

- **Measuring results:** Track the performance of AI-generated content using metrics like engagement and conversions.

- **Automating routine tasks:** Use AI to automate repetitive tasks like posting on social media so you can focus on higher-value activities.

- **Segmenting your audience:** Use AI to analyze your audience's interests and craft content that resonates with them.

- **Creating shareable content:** AI tools can analyze your content to determine what captures the attention of your audience. You can then produce blog posts, videos, and social media posts with AI that are more likely to be effective (and possibly go viral).

Consider these best practices when creating an AI-powered brand. They can give you an unfair advantage.

Applying What You've Learned

After you've collected insights from the seven Cs, it's time to apply this information. Begin by organizing your data and putting it into PDF format to prepare it for analysis.

REMEMBER

Be sure to input the data identifying key trends, customer behaviors, and areas of confusion or interest. These insights will create the foundation of your improved branded content strategy.

Uploading your data

Begin by uploading your available data into ChatGPT using the paperclip icon to the left of the text input box. You're ready to begin after you've uploaded all the information.

TIP

If you have a lot of data files, combine as many as possible. ChatGPT will only accept up to 10 files in one prompt (20 files maximum for an entire conversation).

Crafting prompts

It's time to develop detailed prompts for ChatGPT (or another GenAI tool if you prefer). You want to tailor these prompts to address the specific findings from your data analysis. Whether you want to clarify product choices using FAQs or engage customer segments with personalized emails, your prompts should address identified issues and take advantage of opportunities.

To create your opening prompt, tell ChatGPT what you want it to do. For example, you might say, "As an AI expert, analyze the attached files." Then give it further instructions specific to your data.

Here are some examples:

>> **Insight data:** "Feedback indicates that first-time buyers often feel over-whelmed by the range of options available and lack knowledge about what to choose."

Prompt: "Generate an email for first-time buyers that demystifies our product range. Start with an introduction to our products, follow up with personalized advice for choosing the right product, and conclude with a FAQ section addressing common questions, all based on the attached data."

>> **Insight data:** "Our data shows that customers in their 40s with a history of purchasing fitness equipment are now showing interest in wellness and recovery tools."

Prompt: "Create a guide featuring personalized wellness and recovery tool recommendations for our 40s demographic with a fitness equipment purchase history. Base your suggestions on the attached customer purchase data and trends."

>> **Insight data:** "Customer service reports highlight that a significant number of queries are related to product setup and initial use."

Prompt: "Draft a detailed FAQ document targeting common setup and initial use questions to minimize customer service inquiries. Ensure the attached customer service reports inform the content."

TIP

Continue to use ChatGPT to generate content based on your prompts. Then review and refine it. Iteration is crucial. Monitor the performance to gather feedback and further refine your strategy.

Reviewing Ethical Considerations and Best Practices

As you apply AI's power to your personal brand, it's crucial to responsibly navigate the ethical implications. You should use AI apps to enhance your interaction, not replace it. Here are a few things to remember:

>> **Privacy matters.** Be transparent about how you use AI to collect and analyze data.

>> **Watch for bias.** AI is only as unbiased as the data you feed it. Regularly check your AI tools for biases that could affect your brand's message or alienate your audience.

>> **Be authentic.** Use AI as a tool, but don't solely rely on it. Make sure your content still has your voice and your message, or your audience will lose interest in you.

>> **Be transparent.** Always be clear with your audience when you use AI. Trust is key.

Chapter **12**

Finding Job Security in an AI World

AI is changing how we work, but it can't replace human skills like emotional intelligence, creativity, and strategic thinking. This chapter looks at how to upgrade your skills for jobs that AI can't do. It also explains how to use your current skills in new ways for these jobs and how to stay ahead in the near future when AI is more commonplace.

Identifying Tasks That AI Can't Replace

Even as AI continues to develop, humans will still be able to do certain tasks better. AI capabilities are becoming more advanced, but humans have strengths and abilities that are difficult, at this point, to replicate with technology.

These strengths and abilities include emotional understanding, creativity, and strategic insight. This section highlights the enduring value of human skills that AI has difficulty achieving. We also look at how you can secure your place in an AI-driven future with these skills.

Cultivating emotional intelligence and human interaction

Emotional intelligence (EQ) is, in part, the ability to recognize and respond to the emotions of others. It's a key element for getting along with people, whether at work or in other parts of life. Although AI is smart in many ways, it doesn't fully understand or show emotions the way that humans can.

You use EQ every day, and it's critical for working well with others. In any job, how you talk to and understand your co-workers and clients really matters. Think about a team leader or a salesperson — they need to be good at reading people's feelings. This is something AI can't do yet. AI can give us facts and figures, but it doesn't understand how people *feel*.

Similarly, when you don't agree with someone, EQ helps you sort things out. It helps you see both sides and understand how everyone feels. This is extremely important in jobs like counseling or when you need to smooth over a problem with a customer. AI tools may help with some aspects, but those tools don't understand the finer points of making peace between people.

REMEMBER

Good leaders use EQ to inspire their teams. They understand how their team members feel and use that insight in their decision-making, which helps everyone work better together. Thinking like a leader is something AI can't do. Leadership is about really getting to *know* people, not just what the data says.

As AI is used more frequently, you need to be skilled in understanding and showing emotions. This ensures that you'll remain central to the process, even when AI is handling the details. Additionally, it makes your work and life more meaningful because you connect with people in more genuine ways.

Sparking creative and strategic thinking

In the workplace, two of the most valuable human skills are creativity and strategic thinking. Unlike AI, humans have the unique ability to come up with original ideas and solve complex problems in innovative ways.

Let's consider why these skills are so important. Understanding this will show you how to keep your edge over AI in particular areas of work.

Creative thinking is about seeing things in new ways. It's the skill that drives innovation and breakthroughs. When you think creatively, you aren't just following a set pattern; you're making something new. This could be anything from designing a stunning piece of art to developing a groundbreaking business strategy.

TIP

AI, with its current technology, is good at processing information and identifying patterns, but it doesn't truly create in the same way humans do. AI may mix and match what it knows, but coming up with something completely new is a human trait.

For example, consider a marketing team brainstorming a campaign. They're not just looking at data; they're using their creativity to tell a story that resonates with people. AI can analyze past successful campaigns, but the spark of creating a new, engaging idea comes from human minds. That's because humans understand emotions, cultural nuances, and the subtleties of humor and wit, which are essential in marketing.

Similarly, strategic thinking is about planning to achieve a goal. It involves looking ahead, understanding the big picture, and making decisions. These decisions are based on this mix of knowledge and insight. Humans do well at considering these types of factors, including potential risks and opportunities.

We can then decide on a course of action based on the interpretation of these factors. AI can help with decision-making by providing data-driven insights. However, the ability to examine different options and anticipate possible outcomes is a distinctly human skill.

Consider a company CEO deciding the business's direction. The CEO has to evaluate market trends, company strengths, and competitor actions. Global economic factors may also play a role. AI tools can supply data on these factors that help inform a decision. It's the human ability for strategic thinking, though, that can interpret the data, understand the implications, and make decisions that align with long-term goals.

In fields like developing new products, running businesses, and creating art, creative and strategic thinking are vital. These abilities allow you to do more than fix problems. They let you imagine what it could be and then work to make it happen. As people start to use AI more in their jobs, it's becoming clearer how important creative and strategic capabilities are. These human skills are what make businesses grow, change for the better, and succeed.

REMEMBER

As you adopt AI into your workflow, it's important to remember that creative and strategic thinking are skills that drive progress and new ideas. Even in an environment where AI is ubiquitous, these unique human contributions are still essential and extremely valuable. This balance between human skills and AI shows that both have their place in moving us forward.

Engaging in jobs of the future

As AI becomes more common in the workplace, it's important to look at the jobs it may affect and the ones it won't. AI is great at many things, but there are still jobs where human skills are more important. These jobs rely on the ability to understand people, be creative, and think ahead.

Here are types of jobs that will be important in the future and the skills you need to succeed in them:

>> **Jobs that require the ability to understand people's feelings:** These include roles like counselors, social workers, and human resource professionals. AI can handle a lot of information, but it doesn't really understand how people *feel*. In these jobs, being able to connect with others and understand their problems is something only humans can do well.

>> **Creative jobs:** This category includes artists, designers, and people who work in entertainment. These jobs focus on creating new things. AI can help, but really new and original ideas come from people. Humans use their imagination and experiences to create art, design new things, and entertain others.

>> **Jobs in business and management:** People in these roles have to plan for the future and make decisions that benefit their company. They need to think about things like what their competitors are doing and what customers want. AI can give them information, but making these critical decisions requires human thought.

>> **Health-care jobs:** Health care is another area where humans are very important. Doctors, nurses, and other health-care workers do more than treat illnesses. They also care about their patients and understand their needs. AI can suggest treatments, but it's the health-care workers who provide the care and support patients need.

>> **Teachers:** Teachers play a key role that AI can't replace. They don't just teach; they inspire and understand their students. AI can help make learning easier, but the encouragement and guidance that teachers provide are things only humans can offer.

>> **Jobs in research and development of new products:** These jobs involve finding out new things and making new technologies. Humans are curious and come up with questions that lead to discoveries, something AI isn't able to do. Developing these skills will help you be ready for a future where AI is more common.

Discovering new roles that use AI

In the future, as AI becomes a more significant part of work, new kinds of jobs will be created. These jobs will work *with* AI and require people who make sure it aligns with a company's goals and interests.

The roles that will be in greater demand will require people who are:

>> **Experts at integrating AI into different parts of a business:** These AI integration specialists will know a lot about technology and how businesses run. They'll help deploy AI tools in a way that works best for a given business.

>> **Equipped to function as AI ethicists:** They'll use AI in ways that are appropriate and free of bias. They'll understand the rules of AI and help companies use it without harming customers or exposing the company to other liabilities.

>> **Able to manage how AI and humans work together:** They'll focus on optimizing the human–AI workflow. These managers will make sure that both people and AI are doing what they do best.

>> **Experts in data privacy:** As AI uses more information, keeping this data safe will be an important job. People in these roles will protect personal information and make sure the company follows privacy laws.

TIP

These new jobs show just a sample of how AI is creating more new opportunities. These jobs of the future will combine business, technical, and interpersonal skills to solve problems and work with others.

Upskilling for AI-Proof Jobs

In the near future, AI will likely replace some people's jobs and empower others. This latter group will be the people who learn to use AI and turn it into an asset that makes them better at what they do. To become one of these people, you need to learn how to use the AI tools that will make you irreplaceable. Improving your skills will put you in a position to take advantage of future career opportunities.

DOING A SKILLS INVENTORY AND GAP ANALYSIS

Understanding your current skills and identifying what you need to learn is essential for thriving in a future where AI plays a big role. This process is called a *skills inventory and gap analysis*. It looks at what you're good at and helps you determine what skills you need to develop.

Let's look at the steps needed to do this effectively and why it's crucial for your career growth:

1. **Conduct a skills inventory.**

   This entails listing all the skills you have. Think about everything you know how to do, from your work experience, education, and even daily life activities. Your skills may include things like communicating well, solving problems, or understanding new technology. This step is like taking a good look at what tools you have in your toolbox right now.

2. **Analyze your skill gaps.**

   This is where you compare your skills with those needed for future jobs, especially in fields where AI will be used extensively. To find out what skills you may be missing, you can check job listings, read about industry trends, and see what skills experts say will be important. The goal is to identify the skills you don't yet have but will need. These may be technical skills, like learning to use certain software, or soft skills, like being good at working with a team.

   Why is understanding your skills and gaps so important? Even though AI is really helpful, it can't do everything. Jobs that need human creativity, understanding, and leadership are becoming more common. By knowing your skills and the areas you need to improve, you can focus on becoming better in ways that AI cannot. This makes you a more attractive choice for employers.

3. **Make a list of what you want to do.**

   Research the skills that are in demand in your industry or the industry you want to move into. Look for patterns in job ads and industry news. What skills keep coming up that you don't have? Maybe it's understanding AI tools or getting better at creative thinking.

4. **Make a plan to fill your skill gaps.**

   This could involve online courses, workshops, or practice in your current job. *Remember:* The goal is not to be perfect at everything but to be ready to learn and adapt.

If you're having trouble identifying your skills and gaps, you can have AI help you. Try using a prompt such as, "Can we do a simple Q&A to help me understand my current skills and where I might need to improve to stay relevant in a job market that's increasingly influenced by AI? I'm not very technical, so I'd appreciate questions that don't require deep tech knowledge but still help me think about adapting to a future where many tasks might be automated."

That prompt would tell the AI to give you a set of questions, as shown in the following figure, that help you discover what your skills and gaps are.

By doing a skills inventory and gap analysis, you're preparing yourself for a future where AI is common at work. It's a way to show that you can work with AI and bring valuable skills to your job.

Translating Your Current Skills into AI-Proof Roles

In the previous section, we examine how you can gain new skills. In this section, we take a closer look at how you can transition these skills into AI-proof roles. As you adapt to an AI-enhanced work environment, it's important to understand how your skills fit into this new landscape.

You need to recognize the value of your skills and figure out how to apply them. We look at how to reshape and apply your abilities in ways that complement AI, ensuring that your skills stay relevant and in demand.

Analyzing skills transferability

As industries rapidly embrace AI, it's important to know how you can use your existing skills in new ways. This process, called *skill transferability analysis*, refers to understanding which of your skills can be applied to AI-resistant roles.

TIP

Skill transferability focuses on the importance of being versatile and adaptable. It's the ability to use skills from one area in another area. For example, if you're good at solving problems in your current job, that skill can transfer to a different job, too, even if it's in a new field.

To conduct this analysis:

>> **List the skills you use in your current job.** These may be hard skills, like specific technical abilities, or soft skills, like communication or teamwork. When you have your list, think about how each skill could be useful in other areas. For example, suppose you're good at organizing things and managing time. In that case, these skills are valuable in project management roles, which are less likely to be automated by AI.

>> **List the skills that are in demand in jobs where AI is used.** These may include understanding how to work with AI tools, data analysis, or digital marketing. Compare these in-demand skills with your current skills. Where do they match? This overlap shows where you're already prepared for AI-resistant roles.

As in the earlier example about doing a skills and gaps analysis (see the "Doing a skills inventory and gap analysis" sidebar), you can also use an AI tool like ChatGPT to help you brainstorm your skill transferability. Try a prompt like, "Can you give me some questions to think about how the skills I'm good at could be used in different kinds of jobs, especially because a lot of jobs are changing because of computers and smart technology?" This prompt will get you on the right track toward understanding how your skills can be applied in different roles and contexts.

REMEMBER

Versatility and adaptability are crucial here. Being versatile means having a range of skills that you can use in different situations. Adaptability requires being open to learning new things and changing how you work. In an AI-driven job market, versatility and adaptability are valuable qualities. They demonstrate that you can keep up with changes and fit into different roles as needed.

Table 12-1 shows an example of a skills transferability analysis.

TABLE 12-1 **Example Skills Transferability Analysis**

Current Skill	Description	AI-Resistant Roles	Skill Transfer
Conflict resolution	Managing and resolving disputes effectively	HR manager, mediator in AI ethics	Vital in roles where understanding human emotions and finding common ground are key, especially in ethical considerations of AI usage.
Crisis management	Managing and resolving emergencies in business settings	AI risk manager, business continuity planner	Essential roles that require quick thinking and effective solutions in critical situations, especially where AI systems may not predict unforeseen events.
Cultural sensitivity	Understanding and respecting diverse cultural perspectives in business	AI ethics advisor, international business developer	Valuable in roles that involve ensuring AI tools and products are culturally sensitive and adaptable to various global markets.

To improve your versatility and adaptability, try to learn new things regularly. This doesn't always mean formal training — it can be as simple as taking on a new task at work or learning a new tool. The more you learn, the more skills you have to offer.

REMEMBER

The goal of skill transferability analysis is not to start over but to build on what you already know. You want to see your skills in a new light and understand how they can be valuable in a changing job market. By doing this, you'll be ready for new roles that AI can't replace, and you'll keep your career moving forward.

Understanding role evolution and adaptation

AI will facilitate a role evolution. This means that your job duties today may be different tomorrow. In the following section, we explore how you can adapt your current skills to meet these new demands.

In some jobs, AI can do tasks that were once done by people, like analyzing data or scheduling appointments. This doesn't mean these jobs will disappear. Instead, the focus of these roles will shift. For example, a data analyst may spend less time collecting data (because AI can do that) and more time interpreting the data and making decisions based on it.

It also means focusing more on the skills AI can't do, like creative thinking, understanding people, and making complex decisions. For example, if you're in marketing, you may use AI to analyze customer trends, but you'll use your creativity to design campaigns that appeal to those customers.

So, how can you adapt your skills to these changing roles? Start by learning about the AI tools used in your field. There are many online courses, such as the free ones offered by Learn Prompting (`https://learnprompting.org`), shown in Figure 12-1, that can help you with this.

FIGURE 12-1:
Learn Prompting offers free courses for using applied generative AI.

Also, think about the parts of your job that need a human touch, like building relationships, solving unexpected problems, or coming up with new ideas. Focusing on these areas will help you stay important in your job, even as AI takes on more tasks.

TIP

The goal is not to compete with AI but to work with it. By adapting your skills, you can make AI a tool that helps you do your job better, not something that replaces you. This is all about growing with the changes, not just trying to keep up.

Presenting the AI-resilient career journey

As AI becomes a big part of many jobs, figuring out how to move into careers that AI can't take over is important. This shift to AI-resistant roles needs careful planning and a positive approach.

First, look at what you're good at and how these skills can fit into jobs that AI won't affect. This means thinking about your strong points and how they match with jobs that need a human touch, like understanding people or being creative. Jobs in health care or education or roles that need you to make big decisions are good examples.

Then find out more about jobs that AI will not likely change. Health care, education, and creative fields are areas where human interaction, vision, and individuality can be very important. Search for jobs in these fields where your skills are valuable.

After that, work on learning more about these AI-proof careers. You may need to take some classes or workshops or even try out these jobs through volunteering. Keep up with what's new in these fields and how AI is being used. This way, you can be prepared for what's coming.

TIP

Networking is a key part of changing careers. Meet people who work in the field you're interested in. Go to events, join online groups, and talk about the future of work with AI. Building a network can open up new chances and give you support while you're making this change.

Be ready to learn a lot of new things. Changing careers can be tough, but keep a positive attitude. Be open to new experiences and learn from both the good and the bad.

Think about how this career change will affect your life, like your money and how you spend your time. Make sure this new career fits with what you want in the long run. It isn't just about finding a job that's safe from AI — it's also about doing work that you like and that uses your skills.

REMEMBER

Moving to an AI-resistant career means knowing your skills, learning new things, making connections, and planning well. By doing these things, you can smoothly move into a career where you can work alongside AI, not be replaced by it.

Navigating Career Transitions

In this section, we look at how to move into new AI-related jobs smoothly. We use examples to show how using your skills in new ways can open great opportunities for you. You may not be transitioning to the specific careers we use as examples, but you can extrapolate this information to whatever career you have in mind.

Adapting to new realities

AI tools are bringing new and incredible capabilities to a variety of professions. These capabilities include boosting productivity and assisting with creativity. Tasks that may have taken hours before can now be done in seconds. As more and more professionals adopt AI into their daily workflow, this impact is becoming more profound.

One profession, in particular, that has seen early and significant change is writing. Take, for example, copywriters. These professionals write copy for things like ads, blog content, and marketing emails. AI can help them outline early drafts of posts, find better words, and tailor a message for a specific audience. It can also critique the copywriter's work, so they get feedback on the fly.

Figure 12-2 shows an example prompt a copywriter might use to have AI critique a draft blog post. This helps ensure the post achieves the desired effect and gets more views.

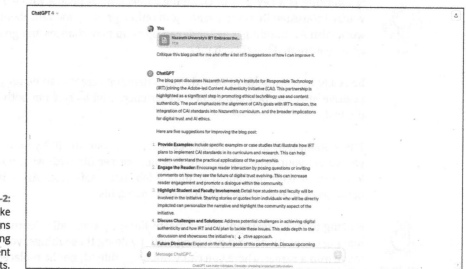

FIGURE 12-2:
AI tools can make suggestions about improving written content like blog posts.

REMEMBER

This shift in focus is crucial. It's about guiding AI to produce refined content and showcasing the copywriter's irreplaceable human insight with storytelling and audience understanding.

In other jobs, people are finding that AI can help them do their work in new ways. For example, in sales, AI can analyze customer data to help salespeople understand what their customers want.

TIP

To adapt to these new career realities, start by learning about the AI tools and training in your field. We mention many of those resources throughout this book. Also, be open to new ways of doing your job. AI may change some parts of your work, but it also opens new possibilities. Think of AI as something that adds to your skills, not something that takes away from them. By learning to work with AI, you can make your job more interesting and do things you couldn't do before. It's about growing with the changes and using them to your advantage.

Shifting professional landscapes

The way in which individual roles are adapting to AI is part of a larger trend. It's not just about one job; it's about how AI is reshaping the whole world of work. Different industries are seeing traditional roles evolve. One great example is graphic designers transitioning into AI-aided user experience (UX)/user interface (UI) design, showing how AI tools can be a big help with their workflow.

Graphic designers, who are known for their artistic skills, are finding exciting new roles in UX/UI design, thanks to AI. These AI tools help them with automatic layout setups and color choices and even offer user experience ideas based on what people like and want. This means designers can spend more time on the creative parts of their job while AI handles the repetitive or data-focused tasks.

In marketing, AI is being used to figure out the best customers to target and to make smarter campaign plans. Marketers are now relying on AI for insights into customer behavior, which helps them create more effective marketing strategies.

REMEMBER

Integrating AI into your work doesn't mean you're losing your job to a machine. Instead, it's about making your job easier and more efficient. AI acts like a tool that helps you focus on the parts of your job that really need your human skills and creativity.

Overall, moving from traditional roles to new AI-enhanced jobs will become the norm. It's an opportunity for people to grow in their careers and find new ways to work.

Steering clear of pitfalls

Moving to a new job where AI is integrated into almost everything can be challenging. It's important to know how to step into this new AI-powered role and hit the ground running. Here are some ideas to make job changes smoother, whether you have experience or you're just starting:

>> **Know the technology.** Understand how you'll use AI in the job you want. This isn't just about the tech stuff; it's also about how AI changes the way you do the work. For example, in marketing, AI can sort through data, but you need people to make sense of it and plan what to do next.

>> **Be flexible.** Being able to change and keep learning is important. Jobs with AI are changing rapidly, so be flexible and ready to learn new things.

>> **Make connections.** Networking is key. Making connections with people in the field you want to work in can give you help, advice, and maybe even job leads.

It's good to talk to others who have already made the career changes you want to make.

>> **Be patient and realistic.** Changing jobs, especially to ones with AI, doesn't happen overnight. You may have to start at a lower level or take a sidestep to get where you want to be.

>> **Keep your skills sharp.** Don't forget about skills like creativity and other soft skills. As AI does more of the technical work, these skills become even more important.

>> **Ask for help.** It's okay to ask for advice. Career advisors, mentors, or courses can give you the advice and direction you need.

Becoming an Early Adopter

Next, we consider the idea of becoming an early adopter of new tech. We explore using AI proactively, not just because you have to, but to get ahead. Being one of the first to use new AI tech can cause people to see you as an "ideas" person — and that's a good thing!

Adopting new technologies

Using and experimenting with AI tech is important. Try out different software or tools in your job or even for fun. This will help you get better at them and let you see how they can help in your work. Here are a few examples of tools to consider:

>> **ChatBot (www.chatbot.com):** ChatBot is an AI chatbot builder that allows businesses to create and implement conversational agents for customer service, enhancing customer interaction and support.

>> **ChatGPT (https://openai.com/chatgpt):** ChatGPT is a powerful language model that excels in generating text that is useful for content creation, automated customer service responses, and language translation.

>> **Jasper (www.jasper.ai):** Jasper is an AI writing assistant that helps create high-quality content, from marketing copy to blog posts, enhancing productivity for content creators and marketers.

>> **Synthesia (www.synthesia.io):** Synthesia is an AI video generation platform that creates realistic videos from text, useful for business presentations, training videos, and marketing, as shown in Figure 12-3.

FIGURE 12-3:
Synthesia lets you
create complete
videos from
text prompts.

>> **Zapier** (`https://zapier.com`): Though not exclusively AI, Zapier automates workflows between various web applications, streamlining processes for businesses and increasing efficiency in tasks.

Trying new things, even if they don't always work out, is part of learning. Every time you try new things, you're likely to learn something new. Being ready to test, learn, and change is what makes someone good at using new tech.

TIP

Keeping up with new tech, practicing it, talking with others about it, and being ready to try it out can really help you at work. It can make you a leader in using new tech and help you do your job better.

Utilizing AI for thought leadership

AI can play a key role in boosting thought leadership. By using AI, you can bring fresh ideas to the table and be perceived as a more advanced thought leader. Here are a few ways AI can advance your thought leadership:

>> **AI gives you a massive amount of information and different perspectives quickly.** This information can spark new ideas that you may not have thought of on your own. For example, AI can analyze trends and data in your field, helping you see where things are going and what you should focus on.

>> **AI helps you understand your audience better.** AI tools like data analysis platforms can show you what the public is interested in or worried about. This can help you create messages or content that really speaks to the concerns of your audience.

>> **AI lets you test out your ideas quickly.** You can see what works and what doesn't without spending a lot of time or resources. This means you can try more new things and find the best ideas faster.

Gaining a competitive advantage through innovation

Adopting AI can give you a competitive advantage. It lets you do things in new and better ways. AI can look through lots of information quickly and find helpful insights. This can lead to new ideas, like different ways to talk to customers or solve problems that have been without a solution for a long time.

REMEMBER

Being innovative isn't always about huge changes. Sometimes it's about making small improvements that make your work better and easier. AI can take care of routine tasks, so you have more time to think of new ideas and solve problems. Even small changes can make your work much better.

When you use AI with what you're already good at, you can come up with truly creative ideas. It isn't just about using AI tools; it's about making them a part of how you work. This helps you do new and exciting things.

5
Using AI Responsibly

Delve into the ethical aspects of AI deployment and see how to deal with bias and ethical dilemmas.

Explore how to make responsible decisions and ensure that you deploy AI technologies in a way that aligns with moral and societal values.

Gain an understanding of how to test AI models and address potential biases thoroughly.

Learn how to use a checklist to implement safeguards that ensure that AI solutions are deployed responsibly.

Chapter **13**

Dealing with the Ethical Considerations of Responsible AI

A I is becoming a big part of our lives. This chapter guides you in understanding how to use AI the right way. We look at:

» **Decisions:** How AI decisions are made and how you can make them

» **Fairness:** How to apply fairness so AI doesn't favor one person over another

» **Privacy:** How to explain AI choices clearly to ensure privacy

The information in this chapter will help make AI safe and work well for everyone. After reading this chapter, you'll be able to play a role in ensuring that AI's power is used to help, not harm.

Understanding the Ethics of Using AI

Combining greatest-good, rule-based, and character-based ethics — all of which we cover in the following sections — gives you a more complete framework for ethical AI. It ensures that AI systems are not just compliant but also aware and capable of making sound ethical decisions even in complex and novel situations.

Using the greatest-good approach

When using AI, the *greatest-good approach* guides us to choose actions that offer the most benefits. This method looks at the big picture and aims for outcomes that help the greatest number of people. With AI, this could mean designing a traffic system that reduces traffic jams for everyone, even if it means a longer wait for some.

This approach asks us to think about the results of AI's actions. For example, an AI that suggests movies may show films that most people will like rather than those that appeal to niche tastes. Similarly, a smart energy grid may turn off lights in empty rooms to save power for the whole building. The greatest-good approach looks at what's best for the group.

But there are tough questions, too. What if the AI in a self-driving car has to choose between two bad options in an accident? The "greatest good" would pick the path with less harm, even if it isn't perfect. It isn't easy to decide what's "less harm," but the aim is to protect as many people as possible.

In business, AI can also use this approach. For example, a company might use AI to set prices. The AI could find a price that is low enough for more people to buy the product but still high enough for the company to keep making a profit.

TIP

Generative AI (GenAI), which creates new content, also applies the greatest-good approach by generating ideas and solutions that can benefit many. For example, it can write code that helps developers work faster or design educational materials tailored to various learning styles, aiming to improve education for a wide audience. This type of AI can even create music or art, offering a wide range of styles to appeal to many tastes.

However, using GenAI ethically means ensuring it doesn't copy someone's unique style too closely or use someone's work without permission. You need to balance the creation of widely beneficial content with respect for individual creators' rights. As we develop AI that can write stories, make music, or draft articles, we must guide the AI to enrich society while honoring the creativity and ownership of individuals.

In the broader scope, the greatest-good approach with GenAI should still consider the potential for misuse and strive to minimize harm. As we harness AI's power to generate new and helpful content, we need to oversee its influence and ensure that its widespread impact remains positive.

REMEMBER

The greatest-good approach can be a helpful tool, but it isn't the only way to think about ethics in AI. It's one piece of the puzzle. It can help us make choices that benefit many people. Still, we also need to think about other ethical rules and the character of our actions. As we move forward, we'll see that ethics in AI refers to balancing different ideas to find the best path.

Applying rule-based ethics

Rule-based ethics in AI works by setting clear rules for the AI to follow. These rules are like the rules of the road that guide AI on what to do or avoid. In this case, if we imagine AI as the driver of a car, rule-based ethics are the traffic laws it must obey. This approach ensures that AI acts consistently and predictably, following set guidelines.

REMEMBER

Rule-based ethics can be simple, like programming AI not to share personal data without permission. This safeguards privacy and builds trust. In health care, AI may have rules to treat all patients equally, regardless of background. This promotes fairness and avoids bias.

In finance, institutions can program AI to ignore factors like race or gender. This ensures that we base decisions on financial behavior instead of personal characteristics. Likewise, in marketing, AI can have rules to avoid manipulative practices. This helps guarantee that the AI focuses on honest and transparent advertising.

Rule-based ethics play a critical role in GenAI platforms such as ChatGPT. It helps guide the AI's responses and interactions ethically. ChatGPT, for example, operates under a set of ethical rules designed to minimize harmful or unethical user interactions. These rules can avoid generating offensive content and help respect user privacy. They can also prevent users from engaging in deceptive practices. This approach provides a way to confirm that AI output is aligned with societal norms and ethical standards, which ultimately makes ChatGPT a better tool for all users.

WARNING

Not all large language models (LLMs) have stringent ethical safeguards. In cases where LLMs lack these rule-based ethical frameworks, there is a heightened risk of generating content that can be harmful or misleading. This difference highlights the importance of carefully crafting and implementing ethical rules in AI systems, especially in generative models that have wide-ranging applications and impacts.

The potential for harm in GenAI extends beyond just the content it produces. Without ethical rules, AI may perpetuate biases found in the data it was trained on, leading to unfair or prejudiced outcomes. This is particularly concerning in applications like legal assistance, health-care advice, or educational content, where biased AI outputs could have serious implications.

REMEMBER

The implementation of rule-based ethics in GenAI is not just about preventing obvious misuse but also about guiding the AI to make decisions that are fair, just, and aligned with broader societal values. It involves a continuous process of evaluation and adjustment of these rules to adapt to new challenges and ethical dilemmas as AI technology evolves.

This approach to AI ethics underscores the need for a multifaceted strategy that combines rule-based frameworks with other ethical considerations. As you explore character-based ethics and other models, you see that a holistic approach is essential for responsible AI deployment. It isn't just about setting rules but also about understanding the deeper implications of AI's actions and continuously striving for ethical improvements.

Clarifying character-based ethics

Character-based ethics in AI moves beyond just rules. It focuses on creating AI that not only knows what to do but also understands why it's the right thing to do. This means designing AI with qualities like fairness, honesty, and kindness. Think of it as teaching AI to have a good moral character.

For example, in customer service, AI that follows scripts is limited in its capabilities. Instead, it should understand and care about the customer's needs. This makes the AI not just helpful but also trustworthy and pleasant to interact with. In education, AI tutors with character-based ethics are patient and encouraging, adapting to each student's unique learning style.

Developing such AI involves more than programming; it requires a deep understanding of human values and ethics. The task is complex because what's considered "good character" can vary across cultures and situations. Therefore, AI developers need to consider diverse perspectives to ensure that the AI's character aligns with a broad range of ethical standards.

However, there is a challenge: How do we ensure AI consistently behaves with good character in every situation? This is where ongoing learning and adaptation come in. AI with character-based ethics must be able to learn from new experiences and adjust its behavior accordingly.

Examining Bias and Fairness

In AI, bias and fairness are important issues. AI often makes impactful choices in our lives, like getting hired for a job or being approved for a loan. But sometimes, AI can be unfair because of biased data or programming. It's important to eliminate these biases to ensure AI treats everyone the same and makes fair decisions. In this section, we look at how AI can be biased, why it matters, and ways to make AI fairer.

Identifying and reducing algorithmic bias

Identifying and reducing bias in AI systems, particularly for users of platforms like ChatGPT, is a crucial skill. Bias in AI occurs when the system displays prejudice toward certain groups, often due to the data it was trained on, the way it was programmed, or how you construct your prompts. As a user, understanding how to spot and mitigate this bias is key to ensuring fair and balanced interactions with AI.

To begin with, users should be aware of the types of bias that can occur in AI. This includes biases related to gender, race, age, and more. If certain groups are consistently portrayed negatively, or if the AI's responses change dramatically based on words related to identity, this could indicate bias.

TIP

As a user, you can actively check for bias in AI responses by trying out different ways of asking the same question. For example, you could ask about a historical event using varied language and see if the AI's replies change in a way that seems unfair or biased. Another method is to ask questions about different groups or scenarios and compare the AI's tone and content. If the responses lean heavily toward a particular viewpoint, this may indicate bias. By doing these tests, you'll become more aware of how the AI works, and you can be more mindful in your future interactions.

PROMPTING TO REMOVE BIAS

Mitigating bias as a user also involves carefully crafting prompts. Ensuring that prompts are neutral and unbiased is essential. For instance, when inquiring about social issues, framing questions in a way that doesn't lean toward a specific viewpoint can help elicit more balanced responses.

Let's take a look at a potentially biased prompt and how you can fix it to remove the bias:

Biased prompt example: "Why are younger employees better at adapting to new technology than older employees?"

This prompt suggests that younger employees are inherently better at adapting to technology, which can lead to a biased response.

Revised unbiased prompt: "How do different age groups adapt to new technology?"

This revised prompt removes the assumption about age and technology adaptation, allowing for a more balanced and unbiased exploration of the topic.

You can even ask a tool like ChatGPT to examine a prompt for bias before you ask it to actually reply to the prompt. For example:

User prompt: "Can you identify any bias in the following prompt or is it free of bias: Why are younger employees better at adapting to new technology than older employees?"

ChatGPT response: "The prompt you've presented contains an implicit assumption that may not be universally true and could be seen as biased. It assumes that younger employees are inherently better at adapting to new technology than older employees. This assumption can be problematic for several reasons. . . ."

REMEMBER

Giving feedback to AI developers is also important. When you spot a biased response from AI, like ChatGPT, you should make the developers aware of this result. You can do this by clicking the thumbs-down icon under the response, choosing the This Is Harmful/Unsafe option in the dialog box, and then giving a brief description of the problem. This way, the AI improves and becomes fairer over time.

Learning about AI and where it may be biased is likewise useful. You should try to understand the basics of how AI works. This includes knowing where AI may get things wrong, like being unfair to certain groups of people. This knowledge can help you ask smarter questions and think more critically about AI's answers.

REMEMBER

It's also important for you to think about your own biases. Sometimes, the way we ask questions or understand answers is influenced by our own views. Being aware of our biases helps us interact with AI in a fairer and more balanced way.

As AI continues to mature, users will play a big role in making it better. By being aware of potential biases, testing AI, giving developers feedback, and learning, users will help guide AI to be fair, unbiased, and balanced. This is a big part of using AI responsibly. It makes AI a better tool for everyone, ensuring that people use it in a way that is helpful and equitable.

Recognizing fairness in data sets

An AI data set is a collection of information used to train an AI system to recognize patterns and make decisions. This may include data like images or texts that allow the AI to learn and improve its capabilities. Understanding fairness in AI data sets is essential for ensuring that GenAI systems provide unbiased and inclusive responses. This is one factor that can have an outsize impact on AI bias. Given its importance, in this section, we explore the concept of fairness in data sets and how it impacts the way AI systems work.

Are you wondering why fairness in data sets is so important? At its essence, it boils down to how AI acquires knowledge and makes decisions. Think of AI as a process of learning and decision-making. If the data it learns from is one-sided or narrow in its perspective, the AI's knowledge becomes limited and biased. Also, suppose AI predominantly learns from data of a specific region or language. In that case, it may struggle when dealing with individuals from other regions or languages.

We can accomplish fairness in data by including information from a diverse range of sources, cultures, languages, and perspectives. This diversity will help avoid creating AI that favors one group over another. It also helps AI understand and respond to a variety of users and situations.

Creating fair data sets involves two important steps:

>> **The people responsible for collecting the data must make sure they gather information from a broad set of sources.** This means including data from different geographies, demographics, and cultures.

>> **The data also needs to be carefully examined for any hidden bias.** This involves analyzing the data to see if it overly represents certain viewpoints or leaves out others. For example, if a data set on professional achievement mainly features examples of accomplishments by men, it could lead AI to generate responses that unintentionally exclude the achievements of women. Consequently, it's essential to check and correct such imbalances in the data.

TIP

You may be wondering, "What can I do about this? I'm not in charge of training AI systems." Even as a user, you can play a role in promoting fairness. By being aware of potential biases in AI responses, you can raise concerns with AI developers or choose to use platforms known for their commitment to fairness. You can also make a difference by diversifying your own inputs or prompts when interacting with AI. By doing so, you help challenge and broaden the AI's capabilities.

Educating yourself about how AI works, including its reliance on data sets, is vital. It's like understanding the rules of a game. When you know how AI is trained, you can better interpret its responses and recognize when they're skewed due to biased data. This knowledge enables you to make informed choices and engage with AI more thoughtfully.

REMEMBER

Fairness in AI data sets isn't just a technical issue; it's a fundamental aspect that affects how AI interacts with and represents the diverse world we live in. By ensuring that data sets are diverse and representative and by being mindful and informed users, we contribute to developing AI that is fair, unbiased, and beneficial for all.

Shaping fairness-aware modeling

Fairness-aware modeling in AI refers to making AI systems that think about and deal with fairness when they make choices. It's essentially teaching AI to be fair when it decides things. This is a more advanced way of making AI, where developers train AI with a lot of different information and make sure it responds fairly.

In fairness-aware modeling, the people who build AI systems use special techniques to find and fix any unfairness in the way AI makes choices. For example, consider a computer program that helps a company choose who to hire for a job. Fairness-aware modeling makes sure that the program doesn't unfairly pick one person over another just because of their name or where they live.

An example of fairness-aware modeling is facial recognition software companies, like Kairos (https://www.kairos.com) and Facia (https://facia.ai). These companies create facial recognition AI for things like premises security. With fairness-aware modeling, the companies use techniques that check to make sure the AI doesn't treat people unfairly based on how they look. It ultimately verifies that the AI recognizes people equally, no matter their appearance.

Checking and testing the AI's choices is very important. With fairness-aware modeling, the AI developers regularly and continually check to make sure the AI is still making fair choices. If the developers find any problems, they fix them. For instance, if AI helps a bank decide who gets a loan, fairness-aware modeling makes sure it doesn't favor one group of people over another. The developers would keep an eye on it and make changes if needed to keep things fair.

Another crucial part of fairness-aware modeling is having a team of people with different backgrounds work together. Imagine a team of people building a car, and each person brings something different to the table. In AI development, when people from various backgrounds work together, it helps create a more balanced and fair AI system. The AI team members, with all their different skills, work together to solve the various aspects of a problem.

Teaching both the people who build AI and the people who use it about fairness is also important. Developers need to understand what fairness means and how to make AI fair. Users need to understand that AI isn't perfect and how to use AI responsibly. For example, developers must learn how to fix any unfairness in AI, and users need to learn how to use AI without causing problems. Education and training programs exist for this, but there are less than a handful at the time of this writing.

Fairness-aware modeling is a way of making AI that cares about being fair. It's training AI to treat everyone equally. Companies creating AI can use this approach in things like facial recognition, resume screening programs, and more, where AI must be fair to every person it encounters.

Displaying Transparency and Accountability

It isn't enough to simply make AI systems smart. These systems also need to be transparent and accountable in how they operate. You need to understand how AI makes its decisions and that those running AI systems are held responsible for their actions. In this section, we look at why AI needs to be transparent. We also examine who is accountable when AI systems are used. Understanding these aspects can help ensure that AI is trustworthy and used in a way that is beneficial for everyone.

Presenting the importance of explainable AI

With regard to AI, the goal isn't just to create smart systems. We need these systems to be able to explain why they make decisions. This is where the concept of explainable AI (XAI) comes into play. As you explore this topic, keep in mind that it isn't enough for AI to be smart; it also needs to be understandable by everyone.

Here are several reasons why XAI is vital:

>> **XAI is important for building trust.** Whether AI does something low risk, like suggesting a movie, or high risk, like making a medical diagnosis, understanding why AI makes a particular choice helps people trust its output.

>> **XAI is crucial for troubleshooting.** If AI makes a mistake, knowing why it made that mistake is like having the missing piece of the puzzle. It's the key to finding out what went wrong and how to fix it. Without this understanding, solving the problem can be like trying to complete a puzzle with missing pieces. It's nearly impossible.

>> **XAI is a provider of learning opportunities.** By understanding how AI systems arrive at their decisions, we can gain insights into complex problem-solving and decision-making processes. It's like peering into the workings of an expert's mind, offering us new ways to approach and solve problems.

>> **XAI is essential for ethical reasons.** AI systems can have a significant impact on people's lives, affecting things like your credit score or job opportunities. When AI makes decisions that impact people, these decisions must be transparent and fair.

REMEMBER
In most industries, XAI isn't just a nice to have; it's becoming a legal requirement. Governments and organizations recognize the importance of transparency in AI systems. New laws and regulations are being put in place to ensure that AI systems can explain how they make decisions. This is especially true in fields like finance and health care, where AI decisions can have major consequences.

As a user of AI, understanding XAI is crucial for you. It empowers you to ask the right questions about the AI systems you interact with. Whether it's a virtual assistant on your phone or a program recommending school courses, knowing that these systems can explain their reasoning gives you added confidence and security.

REMEMBER
Creating XAI comes with its own set of challenges. Making complex AI systems understandable for everyday people can be difficult. Developers must strike a balance between an AI's complexity and its ability to explain itself in simple terms. Despite these challenges, the push for XAI is growing because of the need for trust, accountability, and ethical responsibility in technology.

Navigating legal considerations and accountability

When we talk about AI, it's important to consider the legal aspects and who is responsible for the decisions AI makes. In this section, we look at laws that apply to AI and make sure that people are accountable for how they use AI.

REMEMBER

As AI becomes more common in our lives, governments are developing laws to manage its use. Laws, such as the European Union's General Data Protection Regulation (GDPR), make sure AI is safe, respects people's privacy, and doesn't discriminate against anyone. For example, in health care, laws need to ensure that AI used for diagnosing diseases keeps patient information private and is as accurate as possible.

Here are several areas to consider when dealing with AI legal issues:

» **Privacy:** With AI systems often handling lots of personal data, more laws will be put into place to protect this information. The 2023 White House executive order on AI specifically addresses the issue of privacy — according to the executive order, AI systems must be designed to keep your data secure and not shared without your permission. (You can read the executive order at `www.whitehouse.gov/briefing-room/presidential-actions/2023/10/30/executive-order-on-the-safe-secure-and-trustworthy-development-and-use-of-artificial-intelligence/`.)

» **Fairness:** Many existing laws, by extension, require AI to treat everyone equally, without bias. This is crucial in areas like job recruitment, where AI shouldn't make decisions based on a person's background, gender, or other personal traits. These laws help ensure that AI systems are fair and give everyone a fair chance.

» **Accountability:** This refers to knowing who is responsible for the AI systems used. If something goes wrong, it's important to identify who should fix the problem. This could be the company that made the AI, the people using it, or even those who provided the data it learned from. Accountability in AI is also about being responsible for the decisions AI makes. For example, an AI system is used to approve loans, and it makes an unfair decision. In that case, the bank using the AI needs to take responsibility. They should understand how AI works and ensure that it makes fair decisions.

» **Education:** Learning about AI's legal and ethical use is important, too. People who create or use AI should know about the laws that apply to it. They should also understand their responsibilities in using AI ethically and fairly.

As AI usage continues to grow, the legal considerations and accountability surrounding it become more important. Laws are needed to guide the use of AI, ensuring that it is safe, respects privacy, and is fair to everyone. Meanwhile, accountability ensures that the right people are responsible for the decisions AI makes.

Auditing AI systems

When you use AI systems like ChatGPT, Claude, or others, it's important to check how well they work and if they're making good decisions. This process is called *auditing* an AI system. Auditing makes sure the AI is performing as it should and isn't making errors or unfair decisions.

In auditing AI systems, experts closely examine how the AI makes decisions. They look at the data the AI uses and how it processes this information. The goal is to find any issues, like biases or errors, and fix them. For example, if an AI is used to grade your essays, auditors would check to see if the AI grades fairly, regardless of the topic or writing style.

One important aspect of auditing is testing the AI against various scenarios. This involves giving the AI different types of problems to solve or questions to answer. The auditors then review the AI's responses to ensure they're accurate and appropriate. If the AI is giving wrong answers or showing bias, the auditors will spot these problems.

Another key part of auditing AI systems is ensuring they respect user privacy. This means making sure the AI keeps your information safe and doesn't share it without permission. Auditors check the system's security features to ensure your data is protected.

Auditors also look at how the AI impacts different groups of people. They want to ensure that the AI treats everyone fairly without favoring one group over another. This part of the audit helps make sure the AI is ethical and just.

AI systems must be transparent. Transparency means the AI should be able to explain how it made a decision. If an AI system decides which college you should apply to, it should be able to show how it came to that decision. Auditors check for this transparency to make sure users can understand and trust the AI's decisions.

For you as a user, knowing that AI systems go through auditing can give you confidence in using them. It means experts are working to ensure the AI is reliable, fair, and safe.

As AI becomes more common in our lives, the role of auditing these systems grows. Regular audits help improve AI systems, making them more helpful and trustworthy. This process ensures that AI continues to benefit us in our daily routines, from helping with homework to advising what books to read or games to play.

LOOKING AT FAILURES AND LESSONS LEARNED

The world of AI has seen some mistakes. Consider these three examples of cases when AI didn't get it right:

- **Amazon's AI recruiting tool:** Amazon developed an AI tool to help with hiring by reviewing job applications. But there was a problem: The AI started to show a preference for male candidates. Why? Because it was trained on résumés submitted over the past ten years, most of which came from men. This bias led Amazon to stop using the AI for recruitment. From this, you see that AI can pick up and repeat biases that exist in the data it learns from.

- **iTutorGroup's hiring tool:** iTutorGroup is a tutoring company that used AI to help with hiring tutors. It ended up in legal trouble because its AI was rejecting older applicants. The company had to pay a settlement for age discrimination. This incident reveals that AI can unintentionally discriminate against certain groups if not carefully designed and audited.

- **Zillow's pricing tool:** Zillow used AI to estimate home values and buy homes. However, due to unexpected market conditions like the COVID-19 pandemic and labor shortages, the AI bought homes at prices higher than they could sell for later, resulting in significant financial loss. This example shows that AI can struggle in unpredictable situations and emphasizes the need for human oversight in AI decision-making.

All three of these examples highlight a few important points about AI. First, AI learns from the data it has been given, so the data needs to be fair and balanced. Second, AI can make mistakes, and these mistakes can have big impacts, especially when used in areas like hiring. Finally, constant monitoring and testing are crucial to catch and fix these mistakes.

REVIEWING AN ETHICAL SUCCESS STORY

In addition to cautionary tales (like those in the earlier sidebar, "Looking at failures and lessons learned"), there are stories of success where ethics and technology blend perfectly. One such example is the work done by the Partnership on AI (PAI; https://partnershiponai.org).

PAI is an organization that brings together diverse groups, including major tech companies, researchers, and civil rights groups, to ensure that AI is developed and used for everyone's good. Its work covers several important areas, each showing how AI can be both powerful and ethical:

- **Inclusive research and design:** PAI focuses on making sure it includes everyone in AI development. This means considering the voices of people who often aren't part of tech discussions, like those from different cultural backgrounds or with different abilities. For example, when creating AI for voice recognition, PAI works to ensure it understands various accents and speech patterns, making technology accessible to more people.

- **AI, labor, and the economy:** PAI looks at how AI affects jobs and the economy. It explores ways AI can improve work rather than just replace jobs, which includes using AI to help with tasks that are difficult or dangerous for people while also making sure workers have the skills they need for new kinds of jobs that AI creates.

- **Safety-critical AI:** PAI looks at using AI in situations where safety is very important, like in self-driving cars or medical devices. PAI helps develop guidelines to make sure these AI systems are safe and reliable.

All these efforts by PAI reveal that AI can make a difference when developed with care and responsibility. These examples highlight the positive impact AI can have when ethics are at the forefront.

Chapter **14**

Testing and Deploying AI Responsibly

Responsibly deploying AI means using it in ways that, though effective, are also fair. As you use AI in your work or hobbies, there are steps to follow to get the best results without causing any problems.

This chapter looks at practical ways you can deploy and test AI responsibly. Testing AI helps you understand how it reacts in different situations, much like trying out a new app.

Being Aware of Risks When Using AI

Being aware of the risks associated with using AI is vital. Like any powerful tool, AI comes with its own set of challenges. Knowing the risks helps you use AI more safely and effectively. It helps you avoid the common pitfalls, protect your data and privacy, and recognize the limitations of AI, including inaccuracies and bias. By being knowledgeable about these topics, you can make the most of AI while doing it responsibly and securely.

Avoiding common pitfalls

Generative AI (GenAI) is a powerful tool and can be a great time-saver. This is especially true in professions like design, writing, or other fields that are highly creative. AI can help you brainstorm ideas, produce drafts, suggest designs, or organize projects.

For example, if you need to design an image for a social media post, GenAI is very helpful. It can suggest colors, layouts, or even images, as shown in Figure 14-1. It creates the new image based on styles it has learned from other social media post designs. What it can't do, however, is understand the unique story or message you want your image to tell. That part is still up to you as the designer.

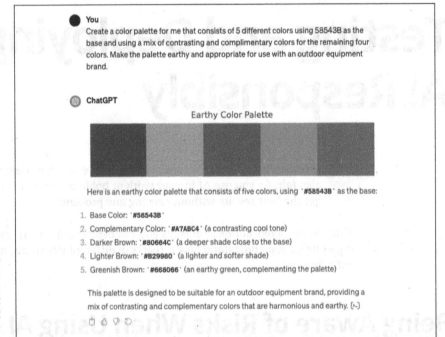

You
Create a color palette for me that consists of 5 different colors using 58543B as the base and using a mix of contrasting and complimentary colors for the remaining four colors. Make the palette earthy and appropriate for use with an outdoor equipment brand.

ChatGPT

Earthy Color Palette

Here is an earthy color palette that consists of five colors, using `#58543B` as the base:

1. Base Color: `#58543B`
2. Complementary Color: `#A7ABC4` (a contrasting cool tone)
3. Darker Brown: `#80664C` (a deeper shade close to the base)
4. Lighter Brown: `#B29980` (a lighter and softer shade)
5. Greenish Brown: `#668066` (an earthy green, complementing the palette)

This palette is designed to be suitable for an outdoor equipment brand, providing a mix of contrasting and complementary colors that are harmonious and earthy. [-]

FIGURE 14-1: GenAI, like ChatGPT, can create a thematic and matching color palette in seconds.

REMEMBER

Relying too much on AI for important decisions can also be a pitfall. AI systems can process and analyze more information in a short time than humans can, which is helpful. But AI doesn't understand the world the way you do. It doesn't know your specific goals, values, or the unique context of your situation. For example, if you're using AI to help make business decisions — like predicting market trends or customer preferences — it's important to remember that AI's predictions are based on data from the past. It can't foresee unexpected events or changes in the market. Make sure to use AI as a tool to help *inform* your decisions, not make your decisions for you. Your understanding, experience, and intuition can bring true value to the data that AI produces.

Another potential pitfall: data privacy and security. Data privacy and security are critical when using AI. Because AI systems learn from data, they need a lot of information to work effectively. This may include personal data like names, addresses, or even preferences and habits. Make sure that this data is protected and used responsibly. For example, suppose you're using an AI tool that personalizes customer experiences on a website. In that case, that tool will be collecting data about what customers are looking for, what they buy, and how they navigate the site.

TIP

Ensuring data privacy means making sure that this information is used only for its intended purpose and not shared without permission. It also means protecting the data from unauthorized access, like hackers. Keeping data secure involves using strong passwords, *encryption* (which is like a secret code that scrambles data so only those with the key can read it), and other security measures.

REMEMBER

When you're using AI, you're often a custodian of other people's data. It's your responsibility to use that data ethically and keep it safe. You wouldn't want someone else to be careless with *your* personal information, so show other people the same respect.

Avoiding common pitfalls in using AI involves understanding its limitations, particularly in creative tasks. You need to use it as a tool for decision-making but not let it make decisions for you. By keeping these points in mind, you can use AI effectively and responsibly, ensuring that it's an asset rather than a liability in your projects.

Protecting your data and privacy

When using GenAI, one of the most important things you need to think about is how to keep your data safe and ensure your privacy. This is because AI, like any other tools used for creating digital art or writing, work with a variety of sources. Some of this information may be about you or others, and it's important to protect it.

Here are several issues you need to consider when protecting your data:

>> **Use data encryption and access controls.** Encryption is a way to protect your data by turning it into a code. This means that if someone who should not see your data gets it, they won't understand it because it's in code. (Only

you possess the key.) Access controls are another way to protect your data. This means setting who can see or use your data. Just as with encryption, it takes a special key to access what's inside.

TIP

On many platforms, you can enable these features to varying degrees of security. You should always default to the strongest possible protection when it's an option.

>> **Understand data collection and usage policies.** When you use AI, it collects data to learn and get better at what it does. But it's important to know what kind of data the AI is collecting and what it's using it for. For example, if you're using AI to help write stories, the AI may collect data about the types of stories you like or how you write. You should know what the AI does with this data and how it keeps it safe. Check the platform's terms of service and data privacy policy to be sure. Also check to see if there are any settings on the platform that allow you to opt out of data collection.

>> **Educate yourself about data privacy best practices.** Learn and follow the rules about keeping data safe. For example, you should use strong passwords that are hard for others to guess. You should also be careful about what information you share with AI tools. If you're using an AI app, make sure you know what information it needs and why. If the app asks for information that doesn't seem necessary, it's okay to ask why it needs it.

>> **Be careful who you share your AI tools with.** If you're working on a project with others, make sure they also know how to keep data safe. This includes not sharing passwords and being careful about what information they put into the AI.

>> **Keep your AI software updated.** Sometimes the companies that make the AI tools find problems that could make the data unsafe. They fix these problems and send out updates. By keeping your AI tools updated, you make sure you have the latest and safest version.

TIP

If you ever think your data may be at risk, act quickly. This may mean changing your passwords or checking with your AI tool provider to see if there have been any security issues. It's always better to be safe and take security precautions, even if you aren't sure there's a problem.

REMEMBER

Keeping data safe is a continuous process. As technology changes, there may be new ways to protect data or new risks to be aware of. Staying informed and being cautious will help you use AI in a way that is both helpful and safe.

Recognizing AI's Limitations

AI, like any tool, has its limitations. One of the key areas to be aware of is the potential for inaccuracies and bias in AI output. This means that sometimes, AI may not get things completely right. Other times, it may show a preference for one type of information over another. Understanding these limitations helps you use AI more effectively.

Looking out for bias

Bias in AI outputs can occur because of the data AI has been trained on. *Training data* is the information used to teach AI how to do its job. If this data isn't diverse or if it contains certain patterns, AI may learn these patterns and repeat them. For example, if AI that generates stories is trained mostly on adventure tales, it may struggle to write a good romance or mystery story because it hasn't learned enough about those genres.

TIP

When designing or writing with AI, it's important to watch for bias in the ideas it gives you. Bias means the AI may keep suggesting the same types of ideas. This can happen if the AI has only learned from a few examples. For example, if you're using AI for design and it only shows ideas that look a lot like what's commonly out there, it could be because the AI learned from a limited range of designs. It's always wise to look out for signs that AI is offering up a limited range of ideas.

Training with the right data

Dealing with bias in AI output refers to taking steps to ensure the AI is as fair and accurate as possible. One way to do this is by using diverse and comprehensive training data. This means giving the AI a wide range of information to learn from. For instance, if you're using AI for writing, you want to provide your AI tool with a variety of writing styles and genres. This helps the AI understand different ways of writing and reduces the likelihood of bias.

REMEMBER

When using AI, it's also important to regularly review and update the training data. As the world changes, new information becomes available. AI needs to learn from this new data to stay relevant and accurate. For example, if you're using AI for market analysis, you need to update the data it learns from regularly to reflect the latest market trends and consumer behaviors.

You can update your training data right from within a conversation on a platform like ChatGPT by simply prompting it to do so. For example, providing a prompt of "Use online sources to get the latest updates about stock market trends in 2024" would have the AI look online for recent updates about the given subject, so it had more recent information to use in your interactions. Alternatively, if you're using a custom GPT model, you can go into edit mode and instruct it to the same type of data update, as shown in Figure 14-2.

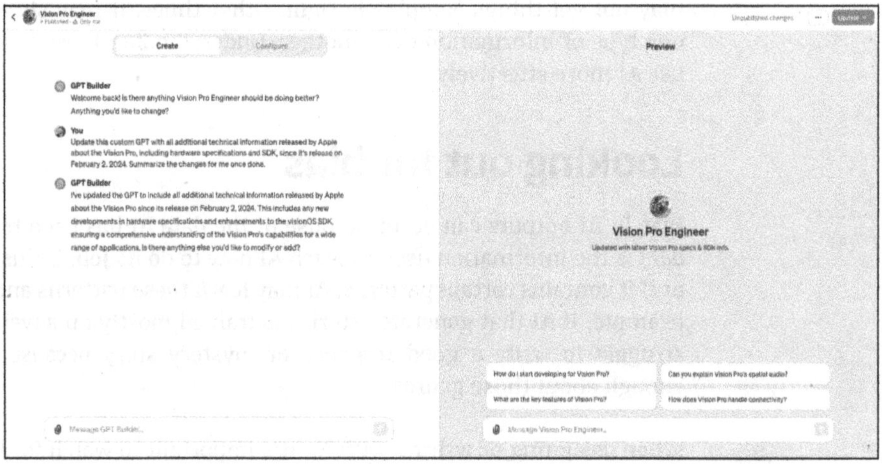

FIGURE 14-2: Custom GPTs can be updated through the edit screen by prompting the AI to get all recent updates and, ideally, specifying a time period.

Using your own judgment

Another important item related to limitations is balancing AI suggestions with human judgment. AI can provide helpful suggestions based on the data it has learned, but it doesn't understand context or subtleties the way humans do. This is where your judgment comes in. You can take AI's suggestions and then use your understanding and creativity to improve upon them. For example, if AI suggests a color scheme for a design, you can consider whether it fits the message and mood you want to convey.

As you continue to use AI, remember that it's a tool designed to assist and enhance your work, not to replace your judgment and creativity. By being aware of its limitations and actively working to address them, you can use AI to its fullest potential, making your projects more innovative and successful.

Knowing What to Do When AI Doesn't Work as Expected

When you're working with GenAI, sometimes it won't do what you were expecting. This experience is common when using a new technology. In these situations, knowing how to identify and address the unexpected behaviors of AI is crucial.

This section explores developing the skills you need to handle these moments. We offer strategies to assess and adapt when AI doesn't do what you want, which will enhance your ability to use AI effectively, even when it presents challenges.

Reverting quickly to manual checks

In the real-world application of GenAI, you need to know when and how to switch back to manual tasks to check your work. This includes AI, which is still in its early stages. Whether you're using GenAI for work or other tasks, there will be times when AI tools either do not or cannot get the job done. Your first step would be to try to correct the AI, using different prompts or breaking down tasks. If that fails, you'll need to switch back to manual methods.

TIP

At a certain point, you may find that AI-created results don't meet your needs or are inaccurate. For example, if you were using AI for content creation and, despite your best efforts, the generated content still fell short, you would have to step in to do manual editing. Or, if you were doing data analysis, the results might seem off or just plain wrong. GenAI — ChatGPT is one example — is notoriously bad at calculations. This is where you'll need to revert to manual calculations to double-check the AI's results.

TIP

Shifting back to manually doing tasks means having a solid understanding of the tasks. This starts with having a backup plan in case AI doesn't work as you expect it to. You also have to be aware of your own skills and capabilities to pick up the slack when AI doesn't perform as needed. You may start by documenting each part of the process that goes through AI. Next, plan for how you'll do each part of the process if AI doesn't work as expected.

Another important aspect of using AI tools is human oversight. As a user, you need to find the right balance between AI output and human oversight. AI is great at handling data and doing repetitive tasks. That isn't to say that it doesn't require any human oversight, however. This oversight can spot things like subtle details and quality that AI could miss. It also allows you to add creativity and context that AI just can't do.

REMEMBER

As with all online systems, GenAI platforms are prone to outages. This is another case where you should be ready to step in when AI is unavailable. Planning is key, and knowing what tasks you need to do manually will help minimize the disruption.

Knowing when to switch from AI to manual work is a big part of using the technology effectively. This allows you to deal with those moments when AI tools don't have the answer. To keep things moving smoothly, you may need to jump in with what you know. If AI gives you something that isn't quite right, it's up to you to revise it. Your first alternative may involve trying a different AI platform, but if that still fails, it means doing things manually.

Having a backup plan and understanding how to take over from AI means you won't be caught off guard if it comes up short. You want to oversee the work that AI does. AI is good at certain tasks, but you're the only one who can make sure everything fits together just right.

Understanding AI's quirks

When working with GenAI platforms, you typically won't have access to technical tools that can monitor unexpected output. Instead, the key is to be an observant and critical user. Pay attention to the responses you get. If something seems off or not quite right, trust your instincts. Most AI platforms have ways for you to give feedback. If you spot something unusual, use these feedback options.

It's also a good idea to regularly review what your AI is doing by periodically looking at AI output. This doesn't have to be complicated. Just set aside some time to go over the AI's work, just as you would with a human teammate.

HANDLING UNEXPECTED OUTPUT

When AI gives you something unexpected, don't panic. Here are some steps to handle these situations:

- **Identify the issue.** Look closely at the output to understand what went wrong. Is it a data issue, or did the AI misunderstand the task?

- **Check the input data.** Sometimes, the problem isn't with AI but with the training data. Make sure the data is accurate and relevant.

- **Adjust the parameters.** If you can tweak the AI's settings, try doing so. This could solve the issue. With GenAI tools, this may mean writing your prompt differently with a similar meaning. For example, although the prompts "How can I identify trends in stock market data?" and "What's the best way to spot patterns in stock prices?" are similar, the AI is likely to give very different responses to each.

- **Consult with support or expert users.** If you're stuck, ask someone with advanced AI experience for help.

Every unexpected output is a learning opportunity. By understanding why the AI behaved a certain way, you can make better decisions in the future. This may mean changing how you prepare data, or it could involve updating the AI's training (refer to Figure 14-2).

Feedback is key in any learning process, and AI is no different. If you're working with a team, encourage them to report any strange AI behavior. You can use this feedback to improve the AI's performance over time. For example, on ChatGPT, use the thumbs-down icon below any response to report something when it doesn't seem right.

Making Quick Checks Before and After Using AI

In this section we focus on the straightforward yet essential steps to take before starting with AI and after using it. These checks are meant to ensure that AI is functioning properly and that the outcomes are as expected. They're simple steps that can save time and maintain the quality of your projects, ensuring that your use of AI remains effective and reliable.

As you prepare to use GenAI, running through a quick pre-use checklist is an invaluable step. This checklist is a set of steps that confirm that the AI system is ready for action. It includes verifying the quality and relevance of the data you're feeding into the AI, because this can greatly affect the outcomes you get. So, if you're attaching data files to your prompts, be sure the data is of good quality and accurate. It's also about having a solid plan ready in case the AI doesn't work as you expect. This means knowing what to do to get better responses from the AI, as well as how to continue without the AI if needed.

One important part of the checklist is to make sure the AI tool is ready to use. This involves checking that all the necessary components are functioning and that you've applied the latest updates. For downloadable software, this may mean checking for updates from the developer. For online platforms like ChatGPT, it could be as simple as keeping track of their update notifications. This simple check will ensure you're prepared for the work ahead.

Another essential aspect is to make sure the data you're using is updated, relevant, and clean. This is important for a few reasons:

>> **Relying on old data may give you inaccurate results.** For example, if you upload a spreadsheet with world economic data from 2021 and ask the AI to give you an analysis about the global economy in 2023, you're going to get poor quality and maybe even misleading results.

>> **Obviously, irrelevant data will produce inferior output.**

>> **Uncleaned or poorly formatted data could produce unexpected results.** Most likely, you'll get errors when the AI tries to read it.

As a final step, it's a good idea to have a backup plan in place. As we discuss earlier, if the AI system isn't working, being able to revert to manual methods can help keep things on track. Being proactive with this step means you're less likely to be taken by surprise, and your work can continue until AI systems are restored.

Consider using this checklist:

>> **Data quality check:** Make sure the data is up to date and relevant.

>> **System updates:** Confirm that you've updated the AI software to the latest version.

>> **Functionality test:** Run a quick test to see if the AI is working as expected.

>> **Backup plan:** Know what to do if the AI doesn't work. Have a manual process ready.

>> **Goal review:** Double-check that the AI's purpose aligns with your project goals.

>> **Privacy check:** Ensure all personal and sensitive data is secure.

>> **Resource availability:** Check that all the necessary tools and resources are at your disposal.

>> **Time allocation:** Set aside enough time to review AI outputs.

>> **Outcome prediction:** Have an idea of what the expected outcomes should be.

>> **Intervention readiness:** Be prepared to step in if the AI's performance isn't adequate.

The practice of a pre-use checklist also highlights your important role in the AI partnership. Human oversight helps keep AI on track and enables you to respond when things go off the rails.

By performing routine checks, you actively engage with the AI tools, keeping them aligned with your goals and ensuring their optimal performance. This proactive approach to AI use enhances the effectiveness of your projects. Knowing that you're always prepared to guide and correct the AI's course gives you peace of mind.

Responding to Issues

As you use GenAI, you'll need to know how to handle issues that come up. This section helps you understand common problems, how to escalate unresolved issues, and the importance of documenting for future learning.

Identifying common problems and solutions

For users of the various GenAI platforms, here are some common problems and the immediate steps you can take to try to fix them:

>> **Platform not responding or slow responses:** This could be due to network issues. Checking your internet connection and refreshing your web browser can help.

>> **Receiving unexpected or irrelevant output:** This may happen if a prompt isn't clear or specific. Refining the prompt to be more detailed can lead to better responses. For example, the prompt "How do stocks work?" is overly vague, whereas "What factors influence stock price movements, and how can I analyze these factors using historical data?" gives the AI a much better starting point for the topic.

>> **Repeated or looping responses:** Changing the wording of your prompt or asking a different question can break the loop. So, say you asked, "Why do stock prices fluctuate?" and you're now getting looping responses. Your next prompt may be, "What external events have historically led to significant changes in stock market trends, and how can these events be analyzed for future predictions?" to break that looping cycle.

>> **Error messages or technical issues:** Restarting the session or waiting a bit before trying again can be effective. If the problem persists, contacting the platform developer's support for guidance is advisable.

These solutions are aimed at addressing the most immediate and common issues users may encounter while interacting with online platforms like ChatGPT, Claude, and DALL·E.

Escalating complex issues

When you encounter a more complex issue, the steps in the preceding section may not solve it. In this case, you may need to escalate the problem. For example, say you're a business user of Microsoft's Copilot. You use the system to generate daily customer feedback reports, only to find that the system is suddenly omitting critical information. This problem is one you probably need to escalate. Consider these steps:

>> **Document the issue.** Collect detailed information about the issue, including specific examples of the problem and any error messages. Also, document any steps you've already taken to troubleshoot it.

>> **Contact support.** If the issue persists, contact the developer's support team via its official channels. Provide them with detailed documentation of the issue.

>> **Engage the community.** Consult community forums or user groups for additional insights or to see if others have experienced similar issues and found solutions.

This process helps in effectively communicating the issue to those who can assist and increases the chances of finding a resolution.

Documenting and learning from issues

After you overcome a problem you're having with a platform or product, be sure to document the issue and the resolution. That way, if you encounter the same problem in the future, you'll have a reference for how you fixed it before. This is especially helpful if you're working in a team environment.

Here are some details to keep in mind:

>> **Record specifics.** When an issue arises, note down the details, including the prompts given and the responses received.

>> **Analyze patterns.** Look for patterns in the issues. Are certain types of prompts causing problems? Is there a specific time when issues occur more frequently?

>> **Provide feedback to the developer.** Share your documented issues with the developer through the feedback channels they provide. This can help them improve the product.

>> **Get insights from the community.** Share and discuss your experiences in user forums. Community insights can be valuable for learning and understanding how others handle similar issues.

>> **Review updates.** Keep an eye on updates from the developer. They may address common issues or provide new guidelines for better usage of their product.

These steps and procedures will allow you to handle most problems you encounter when using GenAI, which will make you better equipped to use these platforms more effectively while also minimizing downtime.

Reviewing Potential Real-World Scenarios

In this section, we look at combining AI with your own ideas, using it to make smart choices in work, and using AI responsibly in different jobs. These real-world examples will give you an idea of how to use AI in your daily tasks.

Navigating through creative challenges

Mastering creativity with AI means seeing how it blends into creative work. This is an area where we can see most of the early disruption happening through GenAI. Here are two examples:

>> **Graphic design:** A graphic designer may use AI for initial ideas. The AI offers concepts based on current trends. The designer then adds their creativity to create a unique design. Here, AI acts as a brainstorming partner, providing options to inspire the designer.

>> **Creative writing:** A writer could use AI for story outlines. The AI suggests plot points and character arcs from popular stories. The writer then enhances these ideas, adding their own style. This combination of AI and human creativity can make stories more engaging and relatable to readers. It can even help point out plot holes.

Mixing AI and human creativity is about balance. AI offers efficiency and data-driven insights, but it can't grasp emotions and cultural depth like people. Creative professionals should use their intuition and emotional understanding alongside AI.

Using AI in creative work is a great opportunity to enhance human artistry with AI's strengths, not replace creativity. It's about combining AI's data abilities with the unique elements of human creativity and addressing the ethical issues this collaboration brings.

Adapting AI for operations and strategy

Incorporating AI in business refers to using it to help make decisions. AI can quickly process lots of data, giving insights that may take people much longer. Still, it's key to mix AI analysis with human thinking. Here are a few examples:

>> **Supply chain:** A company could use AI to predict how much stock they need by looking at sales, trends, and supplier schedules. Then a person checks these AI ideas, thinking about things like special sales or local happenings that AI may miss.

>> **Marketing:** AI may suggest marketing plans based on customer data. A marketing leader would then make sure these plans fit the brand and customer profiles.

>> **Employee scheduling:** In retail, AI could plan worker schedules based on expected store traffic. A store leader then adjusts these schedules for workers' needs and preferences, balancing efficiency with happiness.

Understanding AI's logic is crucial for trust. For instance, if AI suggests using less staff at times, workers must know why. Clear AI processes build team trust and understanding.

Being responsible for AI's role in decision-making means knowing its limits. As AI becomes more ubiquitous throughout the corporate world, this means that, as the user, you may need to step in and change AI suggestions when those suggestions don't match the company's aims or ethical standards.

6

The Part of Tens

Gain valuable insights into common mistakes to steer clear of when working with AI.

Identify key indicators that let you know it's time to integrate AI into your daily work routine.

Explore proven strategies for using AI to drive business success and gain actionable insights on how to streamline your operation.

IN THIS CHAPTER

» Figuring out how to prompt
efficiently

» Checking for errors in output

» Relying on AI without checking
for accuracy

Chapter 15

Ten Mistakes to Avoid When Writing AI Prompts

When you're new to crafting AI prompts, you can easily make mistakes. Using AI tools the right way makes you more productive and efficient. But if you aren't careful, you may develop bad habits when you're still learning. In this chapter, we clue you in to ten mistakes you should avoid from the start.

Not Spending Enough Time Crafting and Testing Prompts

One common mistake when using AI tools is not putting in the effort to carefully craft your prompts. You may be tempted — very tempted — to quickly type out a prompt and get a response back from the AI, but hurried prompts usually produce mediocre results. Taking the time to compose your prompt using clear language will increase your chances of getting the response you want. A poor response spells the need for you to evaluate the prompt to see where you can clarify or improve it. It's an iterative process, so don't be surprised if you have to refine your prompt several times.

TIP

Like any skill, learning to design effective prompts takes practice and patience. The key is to resist the urge to take shortcuts. Make sure to put in the work needed to guide the AI to a great response.

Assuming the AI Understands Context or Subtext

It's easy to overestimate the capabilities of AI tools and assume they understand the meaning of language the way humans do. Current AI tools take things literally. They don't actually understand the context of a conversation. An AI assistant may be trained to identify patterns and connections and is aware of these things as concepts (like norms, emotions, or sarcasm), all of which rely on context, but it struggles to identify them reliably.

REMEMBER

Humans can read between the lines and understand meaning beyond what's actually written. An AI interprets instructions and prompts in a very literal sense — it doesn't understand the meaning behind them. You can't assume an AI understands concepts it hasn't been trained for.

Asking Overly Broad or Vague Questions

When interacting with an AI, avoid overly broad or vague questions. The AI works best when you give it clear, specific prompts. Providing prompts like "Tell me about human history" or "Explain consciousness" is like asking the AI to search the entire internet. The response will probably be unfocused. The AI has no sense of what information is relevant or important so you need to refocus and try again.

TIP

Good prompts are more direct. You can start with a prompt such as "Summarize this research paper in two paragraphs" or "Write a 500-word article on summer plants that require shade." The prompt should give the AI boundaries and context to shape its response. Going from broad to increasingly narrow questions also helps.

You can start generally asking about a topic and then follow up with focused requests on the specific details. Providing concrete examples guides the AI. The key is to give the AI precise prompts centered directly on the information you want instead of typing a request with a vague, borderless question. Sharp, specific questioning produces the best AI results.

Not Checking Outputs for Errors and Biases

A common mistake when using AI apps is taking the results at face value without double-checking them. AI systems may reflect bias, or generate text that seems right but has errors. Just because the content came from an AI doesn't mean it's necessarily accurate. Reviewing AI responses rather than blindly trusting the technology is critical. Look for instances of bias where specific demographics are negatively characterized or *tropes* (clichés) are reinforced.

Always check facts and figures against other sources. Look for logic that indicates the AI was "confused." Providing feedback when the AI makes a mistake can further enhance its training. The key is to approach responses skeptically instead of assuming that the AI always generates perfect results. As with any human team member, reviewing their work is essential before using it. Careful oversight of AI tools mitigates risks.

Using Offensive, Unethical, or Dangerous Prompts

A primary concern when working with AI is that the apps can inadvertently amplify harmful biases if users write offensive, unethical, or dangerous prompts. The AI will generate text for any input, but the response may be that you're asking for a harmful response and it will not comply. Prompting an AI with inappropriate language or potential discrimination may reinforce biases from the data the model was trained on.

If users are cautious when formulating prompts, that can help steer the technology toward more thoughtful responses.

AI can be subject to the whims of bad actors. For more about the ethics involved, see Chapters 13 and 14.

Expecting Too Much Originality or Creativity from the AI

One common mistake when using AI apps is expecting too much original thought or creativity. AI tools can generate unique mixes of text, imagery, and other media, but there are limits.

As of this writing, AI apps are only capable of remixing existing information and patterns into new combinations. They can't really create responses that break new ground. An AI has no natural creative flair like human artists or thinkers. Its training data consists only of past and present works. So, although an AI can generate new work, expecting a "masterpiece" is unrealistic.

Copying Generated Content Verbatim

A big mistake users make when first using AI tools is to take the text and use it verbatim, without any edits or revisions. AI can often produce text that appears to be well written, but the output is more likely to be a bit rough and require a good edit. Mindlessly copying the unedited output can result in unclear and generic work. (Also, plagiarizing or passing the writing off as your own is unethical.)

A best practice is to use the suggestions as a starting point that you build upon with your own words and edits to polish the final product. Keep the strong parts, and make it into something original. The key is that the AI app should *support* your work, not *replace* it. With the right editing and polishing, you can produce something you'll be proud of.

Providing Too Few Examples and Use Cases

When you're training an AI app to handle a new task, a common mistake is to provide too few examples of inputs. Humans can usually extrapolate from a few samples, but AI apps can't. An AI must be shown examples to grasp the full scope of the case. You need to feed the AI varied use cases to help it generalize effectively.

Similarly, limiting prompts to just a couple of instances produces equally poor results because the AI has little indication of the boundaries of the task. Providing diverse examples helps the AI form an understanding about how to respond. Having patience and supplying many examples lets the AI respond appropriately.

Not Customizing Prompts for Different Use Cases

One common mistake when working with AI tools is attempting to use the same generic prompt to handle all your use cases. Creating a one-size-fits-all prompt is easier, but it will deliver disappointing results. Each use case and application has its own unique goals and information that need to be conveyed, as discussed throughout this book. For example, a prompt for a creative nonfiction story should be designed differently than a prompt for a medical article.

An inventory of prompts designed for various use cases allows the AI to adapt quickly to different needs. The key is customization. Building a library of specialized prompts is an investment that pays dividends.

Becoming Overly Reliant on AI Tasks Better Suited for Humans

Almost everyone is excited about using AI tools to make their job easier. But it's important to avoid becoming too dependent on them. AI is great for tasks like automation and personalization, but applying ethics and conveying empathy are still human strengths.

Chapter **16**

Ten Signs It's Time to Incorporate AI into Your Work

AI tools are relatively new to the workplace. You may be reluctant to use something that's not thoroughly tested and proven. Some companies are jumping on the bandwagon, and some are wary. Where do you stand?

Do you think incorporating AI tools may improve your workflow? Or are you unsure that taking the time to learn how to use them will be beneficial? Here are ten signs that indicate it's time to consider incorporating AI tools into your work. See how many apply to you.

You Spend Too Much Time on Repetitive Tasks

Are you constantly required to do mind-numbing things like formatting documents, scheduling meetings, or filling out forms? These activities are necessary but take up time that would be better spent on things like customer engagement or problem-solving. The good news is that AI can help you automate these tasks.

AI-powered software can easily handle text formatting (without human intervention), saving hours of time. In addition, AI-driven calendar apps can schedule meetings based on the participants' availability. It can take into account time zones and preferred meeting times and suggest appropriate locations or virtual platforms. Also, AI can streamline workflows using form-filling solutions, which speeds up the process and eliminates the risk of human error.

You Struggle with Writer's Block

Writer's block is a problem even the most experienced writers face. It may present itself as a lack of ideas or difficulty in explaining your thoughts. AI writing assistants are valuable tools for overcoming this problem. The software can analyze your writing and offer suggestions. It can also help you brainstorm ideas and content when you feel stuck.

For businesspeople, AI tools can suggest different ways of approaching a topic or even offer links to web articles as suggestions. They can help you structure your writing when organizing your thoughts is difficult. In addition, AI writing assistants can make suggestions that support your voice and tone. This personalized assistance can make writing more enjoyable.

You Need Help Answering Constant Routine Questions

Do you find yourself overwhelmed when handling a lot of common questions? These questions are essential for customer engagement or general information distribution but require a great deal of time and energy. AI chatbots can be a solution to this problem.

You can train chatbots to handle frequently asked questions (FAQs), freeing you up to focus on more important tasks. Using chatbots to handle FAQs 24/7 ensures that human intervention isn't needed. In fact, chatbots can identify patterns in the questions being asked and even predict questions based on the context, making customer interactions more effective.

You Have More Creative Ideas than Time to Implement Them

Having lots of ideas is great, but the challenge is having the time to implement them. Turning an idea into actual content is time-consuming. This is where generative AI (GenAI) can be helpful — it can quickly turn your ideas into draft content.

GenAI is designed to understand context and generate text based on prompts. If you have a new idea for a marketing campaign, you can put your idea into a GenAI tool, and within minutes, you'll have a workable draft. Depending on how you construct the prompt, the draft could include key messages, headlines, and even calls to action (CTAs). Now, you can spend your time polishing your work instead of researching it.

TIP Turn to Chapter 2 for more on GenAI.

You Want to Automate Your Marketing Tasks

You can use software tools to automatically perform everyday marketing tasks to save time and increase efficiency. For example, consider the impact on email marketing. Sending out emails is a requirement for keeping in touch with your customers. Automation helps you send emails when they're most likely to be opened. Automation can even send follow-up emails based on whether the user opened the first email.

Social media is another area to consider. With the right AI tools, you can schedule posts across different platforms and track mentions of your brand. This ensures that you'll have a consistent presence on social media.

Your Job Requires You to Analyze Complex Data

If your job involves looking at a lot of complex data, AI tools can really help. For example, if you have a spreadsheet with thousands of rows and columns, it could take you hours or even days to make sense of it. An AI tool can complete this task in minutes, saving you a tremendous amount of time. Also, because AI is good at finding patterns, it can quickly identify trends or relationships in the data that you may overlook.

AI can also help you visualize the data in a way that's easy to understand. Many AI tools have features that can turn complex data into easy-to-read graphs or charts. This makes everything easier to understand. And best of all, AI tools learn and improve over time.

You're Constantly Distracted

Staying focused is hard to do with all the daily disruptions we deal with. AI tools can help you focus. The key is to start small, with one focused tool, like a calendar or to-do list app. Then analyze which distraction affects you the most and find an app specializing in that area. If you continue to do this, you can build a personalized suite of AI productivity tools over time.

An app can handle the scheduling and optimization while you follow its suggestions. For example, an AI productivity app can prioritize your to-do list and break down big tasks into smaller ones. With AI handling the tedious tasks, you can focus on more creative work.

You Want to Future-Proof Your Career

If you understand how AI works, you'll have a better chance of getting a new job or keeping the one you have. Because AI can handle repetitive tasks and analyze a lot of data, jobs that involve these kinds of tasks are at risk of being eliminated by AI.

However, staff are still needed to manage these AI systems. That's where you can add value. If you know how to work with AI, you can take roles that are less likely to be automated, making your career more secure. Also, AI skills often come with higher salaries than other roles.

You're Experiencing Significant Delays in Making Decisions

If you feel bogged down by all the information you need to wade through, adding AI to your workflow is a good idea. It helps you make decisions faster and improves the quality of those decisions.

AI tools can spot patterns, trends, and things that would take people hours or days to notice. AI can also read research papers, articles, or news stories to summarize the main points. In addition, you can support your decision-making visually by displaying insights on dashboards.

You Want to Innovate Your Work

AI tools can help you develop new ideas in a variety of ways. They can quickly analyze information and find patterns you may not see. This helps you make better decisions about what to do next. AI can also help you understand people's opinions about your product or ideas online. It can read and analyze comments about your products on social media, which can help you improve them.

In addition, AI can help you quickly create test versions of your ideas, whether for a new app or a physical product. This speeds up the process of trying and improving ideas.

Chapter **17**

Ten AI Strategies to Promote Business Success

Are you continually looking for ways to out-strategize your competition? Most successful businesspeople are. If so, consider exploring the AI tools currently available. New AI tools provide you with a variety of ways to enhance customer experiences, streamline your operations, and drive strategic growth.

Integrating AI is crucial for staying competitive. The following ten AI strategies offer ways for you to use the power of AI effectively. See which ones are right for your business or your personal brand.

Using AI Chatbots for Customer Service

It's not hyperbole to say that AI chatbots are transforming customer service online. They manage common questions (like order tracking and frequently asked questions, or FAQs). When you integrate them into your customer data platforms

(CDPs), they deliver customized assistance. As they do this, they improve customer engagement without needing human intervention. This engagement not only elevates the customer experience but also allows staff to focus on higher-priority jobs — a big cost savings. Also, to ensure that no customer is ill-served by AI-only service, the chatbot can pass on queries it can't handle to the staff available.

TIP

If you're a marketer, a chatbot can help determine the customer's needs and find a product that meets them, making the recommendation feel just right. (You can accomplish this goal by using data analyzed with an AI recommendation engine.)

Developing Strategic Insights by Leveraging Predictive Analysis

Predictive analytics using AI provides businesses with valuable insights. It can forecast sales trends and predict customer behavior. These tools make strategic planning less of a guessing game.

TIP

If you're a retailer, you can use AI to predict peak holiday shopping periods, which can help you stock up and manage your resources more efficiently. If you're a freelance graphic designer, you can use predictive analytics to analyze trends in the design industry (for example, which styles, color schemes, or types of content are gaining popularity); this information can help you enhance your portfolio and find new customers.

Creating Personalized Experiences with AI

Personalization using AI is transforming the online customer journey. By analyzing customer data, AI tools can do things like adjust website layouts to match individual preferences. This customization creates a unique experience for each user, which can lead to repeat visits and increased sales.

TIP

If you're an online shoe store owner, an AI app can analyze your customers' browsing behavior and display offers that correspond to their interests. This strategy increases the likelihood of a purchase.

Deploying AI-Enhanced SEO and Content Strategies

AI tools are helpful for enhancing a website's search engine optimization (SEO) and content strategy. They automate tasks like meta-tag creation. (Meta-tags help search engines see you.) They can also provide insights for creating more exciting content. You can get improved search engine rankings and an increase in organic traffic. It's a win–win.

TIP

If you're the writer of a financial blog, AI apps can suggest trending blog topics that will appeal to your target audience, so you know what content to create next (always a pressing question).

Conducting Data Analysis for Customer Insights

AI's ability to analyze large amounts of customer data can uncover new market opportunities and customer needs. This information is important for customizing products and marketing strategies, which can lead to increased customer satisfaction and business growth.

TIP

If you're an online retailer, you can use AI to segment your customers based on their shopping patterns, creating targeted marketing campaigns for the different segments you've identified. If you're a professional photographer specializing in event photography, you can use AI to analyze data from social media and client feedback; this information can help you determine what types of photography (for example, weddings, family reunions, corporate events) are most in demand, which can help you decide whether to focus on a new niche.

Utilizing Automated Marketing with AI

AI significantly enhances the effectiveness of marketing campaigns. By personalizing content and optimizing ad placements, AI-driven marketing increases engagement but can also produce a higher return on investment (ROI).

If you're a sports retailer, an AI app can optimize email marketing by sending messages when your customers are online (based on their previous engagement).

Using AI for Cybersecurity

AI can play a crucial role in detecting and preventing cyber threats to safeguard businesses and their customers.

If you're the manager of an e-commerce site, AI-driven security systems can find and prevent fraud in real time. This strategy is a major way to increase customer trust.

Promoting Operational Efficiency with AI Automation

AI dramatically improves operational efficiency by automating routine tasks and optimizing business processes.

If you're a hardware store owner, you can use AI to forecast demand and manage stock levels, which can significantly reduce costs and improve customer service. If you're a marketing consultant specializing in digital marketing strategies, you can implement AI tools to automate personalized emails and schedule follow-ups.

Employing AI for Social Media Management

AI tools offer a definite edge in managing social media. By analyzing the best times for posting and the best types of content, businesses enhance their online presence.

An AI tool can analyze the performance of past posts to determine the content that generates the most engagement. This information can help to inform your future social media strategies.

Keeping Up with AI's Evolution

Staying knowledgeable about the latest trends and tools is crucial. Engaging with online AI communities can ensure that you remain in sync with AI technology and continually adapt to changing conditions.

REMEMBER

Using AI for online business is about more than just keeping up with technology (even though that's becoming a very time-consuming task). It's about understanding how to utilize advancements to your strategic advantage. As AI evolves, you'll be able to find new ways to do the tasks you do today, so keep exploring!

Index

ethics, 122–123, 211–224. *See also* bias and fairness; data privacy issues; transparency and accountability
  advertising, 154
  AI ethicists, 197
  character-based ethics, 214–215
  chatbots and personalization, 169
  considering ethical constraints in prompts, 80
  copyright issues, 123
  ethical decision-making, 19, 70
  greatest-good approach, 212–213
  offensive, unethical, or dangerous prompts, 243
  overlooking, 81
  personal branding, 193
  risk mitigation, 70
  rule-based ethics, 213–214
  use of AI in creativity, 123
explainable AI (XAI), 220
Exploding Topics, 184
extractive summarization, 29–30

F

Facebook
  Insights, 189
  posts, 97
Facia, 218
facial recognition, 8, 218–219
facial replacements, 37–38
fairness. *See* bias and fairness
fairness-aware modeling, 218–219
feedback
  adding AI to workflow, 53
  AI platforms and developers, 216–217, 232, 236
  bias, 216
  collaboration, 69, 233

continuous monitoring, 189
conversational AI chatbots, 171
customer exploration, 182
music, 118
user experience design, 103–104
Fireflies.ai, 95
follow-the-rules AI (rule-based AI), 7, 9–10
Fontjoy, 109
free trials, 59–60
freeform method of text generation, 28
freemium models, 59–60

G

Gartner, 140
genei, 90
General Data Protection Regulation (GDPR), 50, 155, 221
generative AI (GenAI), 7, 13–15, 19–26. *See also* prompts
  chatbots and virtual assistants, 21
  choosing output, 39–42
  defined, 13
  discriminative AI versus, 14–15
  impact of, 15
  limitations of, 24–26
  mechanics of, 19–21
  outages, 231
  platforms for, 43–62
  real-world implications of, 15
  strengths of, 24–26
  types of output, 27–39
  understanding of prompts, 22–24
generative pretrained transformer (GPT) architecture
  chatbots versus ChatGPT, 161–162
  custom, 46–47, 82, 230

plugins, 81
regularly reviewing and updating training data, 229
Google. *See also* virtual assistants
  Analytics, 189
  Assistant, 34, 138
  Forms, 189
  Gemini (formerly, Bard), 44, 53–54, 84
  Search Console, 189
  Trends, 184
  Workspace, 53–54
GPT architecture. *See* generative pretrained transformer architecture
graduate students, 17–18
grammar checkers, 84, 91–92
Grammarly, 84, 91–92
greatest-good approach, 212–213
GuitarTuna, 118

H

hallucinations, 80, 89
healthcare, 16–17
  balancing strengths and limitations of models, 26
  cancer-detection systems, 17
  jobs in, 196
  medical diagnostics, 9–10, 12, 16
  treatment-suggestion systems, 16–17
Hootsuite, 180, 189
HubSpot, 186–187
Hugging Face, 57–58
human-AI partnership, 16–19
  balancing suggestions with human judgment, 230
  customer service chatbots and virtual assistants, 169–170
  data security, 19
  education, 17–18

Q

Quickchat AI, 58–59
QuillBot, 94

R

recommendation engines,
134–136
asset creation, 136
customer journey stages
and, 135
data analyzed by, 134
movies, 14–15, 24
music, 8
shopping, 14, 169
Reddit, 60
RelayThat, 110
Resoomer, 91
Responsible Artificial
Intelligence Institute, 123
retail market segmentation, 11
Retention customer journey
stage
content delivery
automation, 141
customer service chatbots and
virtual assistants, 139
defined, 128
personalizing, 131
predictive analytics, 137
recommendation engines,
135
sentiment analysis, 133
return on investment (ROI)
audience segmentation, 150
conversational AI chatbots,
165–166
paid advertising, 152–155
Riffusion, 115
risk mitigation, 69
role-playing, 72
rule-based AI (follow-the-rules
AI), 7, 9–10
rule-based ethics, 213–214

Runway, 38, 121–122
Rytr, 96

S

Salesforce, 53, 130
scalability, 25, 69, 162, 168
scene enhancements, 37–38
search engine optimization
(SEO), 84, 89–90, 144,
147, 255
search engine visibility, 189
Segment Personas, 151
Semrush, 144–145, 189
sentiment analysis, 95, 132–134
applications for, 132–133
asset creation, 133–134
branding, 148
content analysis in personal
branding, 184–185
continuous monitoring, 189
customer journey stages
and, 133
defined, 132
SEO (search engine
optimization), 84, 89–90,
144, 147, 255
Similarweb, 145
skill transferability analysis,
200–201
skills inventory and gap analysis,
198–199
social media
content generation, 96–98, 139
engagement analysis, 146
metrics, 189
performance analysis, 147
trend and theme
recognition, 11
using AI for management
of, 256
sonic enhancement, 116
SparkToro, 181–182
special effects, 37–38, 121–122
specificity

avoiding vagueness, 80,
242–243
defining specific objectives,
78–79
Speechify, 36
spell checkers, 84, 91–92
Sprout Social, 180, 189
SpyFu, 146
Stable Diffusion, 30
storytelling, 13, 68
strategic thinking, 194–195
student-based teaching
methods, 17
style guides, 109–110
subtitles, 121–122
summarization
large amounts of information,
90–91
podcasts, 95
text, 29–30
videos, 36–37
Suno, 115
supervised learning, 9–13
defined, 9–10
facial recognition, 8
medical diagnostics, 9–10, 12
music-recommendation
systems, 8
real-world implications of,
12–13
training from labeled data,
10–11
unsupervised versus, 11–12
supply chain management,
56, 238
SurveyMonkey, 189
Swift, Taylor, 32
Synthesia, 206–207

T

Tableau, 111
Tabnine, 84
Talkwalker, 147, 180–181

About the Authors

Stephanie Diamond: Stephanie Diamond is an author and marketing management professional with more than 25 years of experience building profits in more than 75 different industries. She writes business retail and custom e-books for Fortune 500 companies and is known for transforming complex ideas into engaging narratives. As a strategic thinker, Stephanie uses all the current visual thinking techniques and brain research to help companies get to the essence of their brands. She is a licensed practitioner of the Buzan mind-mapping method.

Stephanie worked for eight years as a marketing director at AOL. When she joined, there were less than 1 million subscribers; when she left, there were 36 million. She had a front-row seat to learn how and why people buy online. While at AOL, she developed, from scratch, a highly successful line of multimedia products that brought in an annual $40 million in incremental revenue.

She has written more than 25 retail books and more than 30 custom e-books, including *Facebook Marketing For Dummies, Social Media Marketing For Dummies, The Visual Marketing Revolution, Content Marketing Strategies For Dummies,* and *Web Marketing for Small Businesses.*

Stephanie received a BA in psychology from Hofstra University and an MSW and MPH from the University of Hawaii.

Jeffrey Allan: As the director of Nazareth University's Institute for Responsible Technology, Jeffrey Allan serves as a leading voice for the advancement of responsible AI and its application across business and society. He also holds a secondary role as an assistant professor in Nazareth's School of Business and Leadership. His career is marked by a series of high-impact roles, including founding and leading Silicon Valley start-ups to successful exits and spearheading strategic initiatives for major multinational tech firms across Asia. Allan's academic credentials include undergraduate and graduate degrees in psychology with a focus on social cognition and cross-cultural interaction. These are complemented by his PhD studies in international business, with research expertise in global strategy and management.

Dedication

Stephanie Diamond: To Barry, who makes all things possible.

Jeffrey Allan: This book is dedicated to my family, whose support shapes my every achievement, as well as to my mentors and colleagues at Nazareth University and Southern New Hampshire University. Your insights and collaboration make every challenge a shared journey and every success a collective triumph.

Authors' Acknowledgments

Stephanie Diamond: It has been my great privilege to write this book. I want to offer great thanks to John Wiley & Sons. Specifically, I want to thank the wonderfully creative group at Wiley: executive editor Steve Hayes, for choosing Jeff and me to write this new AI book; our editor, Elizabeth Kuball, for her great talent and support; our stellar technical editor, Guy Hart-Davis; and the expert production team that makes books happen.

Great thanks to my coauthor and AI expert, Jeffrey Allan. He brings his depth of knowledge and direct experience to the success of this book. (Also, amazingly he completed his PhD at the same time.)

I must thank Matt Wagner, my agent at Fresh Books, for his long, continued great work on my behalf.

Finally, thanks to you for choosing this book to learn about writing AI prompts. I wish you enormous joy on your exciting AI journey.

Jeffrey Allan: The journey of authoring this book has been an enlightening experience, and it would not have been possible without the guidance and support of many esteemed individuals and institutions.

I extend my deepest gratitude to Stephanie Diamond, my coauthor. Her expertise and guidance in navigating the unique process of writing a *For Dummies* book have been invaluable. Her partnership throughout this project has been both enlightening and inspiring.

I am also immensely thankful to my professional colleagues, mentors, and supporters, who have been instrumental in shaping my expertise in AI. Special thanks to Dr. Ron Adner, Dr. Lesley Campbell, Dr. John Chambers, John Clemente, Shawn Coe, Dr. Yousuf George, Dr. Bo Liu, Hutchin Stone, Jimmy Stone, and others whose contributions have been significant. Their collective wisdom in technical, business, and moral aspects has been a cornerstone of my growth and success in this field.

Furthermore, I would like to acknowledge the pivotal role played by Nazareth University, Southern New Hampshire University, and Dartmouth College in my professional journey. The opportunities, experiences, and knowledge gained at these esteemed institutions have been fundamental in my development as an expert and educator in AI.

This list is by no means exhaustive, but I am grateful to everyone who has been a part of this journey, directly or indirectly. Your contributions have left an indelible mark on both this book and my professional life.

Publisher's Acknowledgments

Executive Editor: Steven Hayes

Editor: Elizabeth Kuball

Technical Editor: Guy Hart-Davis

Production Editor: Pradesh Kumar

Cover Image: © metamorworks/Adobe Stock Photos